Getting A Job

Getting A Job

A Study of Contacts and Careers

Second Edition

Mark Granovetter

The University of Chicago Press
Chicago and London

To my parents

The University of Chicago Press, Chicago 60637
The University of Chicago Press, Ltd., London
© 1974, 1995 by Mark Granovetter
Appendix D © 1985 by The University of Chicago
All rights reserved. First edition originally published 1974.
Second edition 1995
Printed in the United States of America

21 20 19 18 17 16 15 14 13 12   6 7 8 9 10

ISBN-13: 978-0-226-30581-3 (paper)
ISBN-10: 0-226-30581-3 (paper)

Library of Congress Cataloging-in-Publication Data

Granovetter, Mark S.
    Getting a job : a study of contacts and careers / Mark
Granovetter.—2nd ed.
        p.   cm.
    Includes bibliographical references (p.   ).
    1. Applications for positions—Case studies.   2. Employees—
Recruiting—Case studies.   3. Vocational guidance.   I. Title.
HF5383.G68   1995
650.14—dc20

                                                94-34203
                                                    CIP

Contents

Preface to the Second Edition

When *Getting a Job* (hereafter *GAJ*) was published in 1974, interest in the sociological study of the economy, especially in the U.S., was in decline. Mid-century economic sociology, sometimes known as the "economy and society" perspective, had culminated in the ambitious attempt of Talcott Parsons and Neil Smelser (1956) to integrate the economy into a general theory of social systems. But perhaps because this highly abstract argument did not offer clear guidelines for empirical research, little research followed it. And, as Parsons himself noted, the work did not find the audience among economists that he had hoped for (Parsons 1968: vii n). Meanwhile, the earlier lively interest in industrial sociology that flourished from the 1940's through the 1960's (for example, Homans 1950; Whyte 1955; Dalton 1959) had run out of steam, in part for the opposite reason—the *lack* of any clear-cut theoretical framework—and was absorbed into the more general subject of organization theory.[1]

In retrospect, *GAJ* was one of the first exemplars of what I have called the "new economic sociology," which differed from older work in its attention to a core rather than a peripheral aspect of the economy, and in its willingness to challenge the adequacy of neoclassical economic theory in one of those core domains.[2] It thus was one of the early works in what proved to be a vigorous revival of interest in the economy that continues unabated among sociologists. The decision by the University of Chicago Press to undertake a twentieth-anniversary edition of *GAJ* reflects this continuing vigor and also the centrality of labor market outcomes to several different areas of sociology, including stratification and organizations.

To "update" *GAJ* might have involved rewriting the text, but we decided instead to reprint the original in its entirety. Although there are certainly parts I would write and analyze differently with twenty years of hindsight, and with the explosion of new statistical methods, the original

[1] For a more detailed account of the ups and downs of economic sociology in the twentieth century, see my 1990 paper on "The Old and the New Economic Sociology."

[2] In the Introduction to our reader, *The Sociology of Economic Life* (1992), Swedberg and I analyze in more detail the variety of styles of work in current economic sociology, and the particular characteristics of the "new economic sociology."

version seems still to serve its purpose as an exploratory study that stimulates new research, and it is accessible to readers with a variety of backgrounds—including undergraduates, who have generally received the book well. The theoretical and empirical supplementation that a new edition requires has been achieved with two additions. On the theoretical side, I think it is fair to say that I did not fully appreciate the framework in which I was operating until some years after publication, especially when I wrote my 1985 article "Economic Action and Social Structure: The Problem of Embeddedness." That article provides a theoretical backdrop and justification for much of the argument in the book, and puts it in the broad context of a tradition of economic sociology tracing back to Max Weber. For this reason, several members of the editorial board at the University of Chicago Press urged that the article be reprinted as an appendix to the new edition, which we have done. Having this article available here will be especially useful for readers whose interest lies not only in labor markets but also in the more general issues of economic sociology.

The other quite obvious needs are for: 1) an assessment of whether the world has changed so much that the findings of *GAJ* are quaint relics of an earlier time, or are still pertinent to modern labor markets, and 2) a critical review of recent work in economics and sociology on the recruitment of labor. These needs I have addressed with an Afterword, summarizing and commenting upon recent work. That it took me far longer than I had imagined to research and write this essay indicates what a rich and growing field of study *GAJ* explores. My review suggests that the original findings lie well within the boundaries of what a current investigation might find, and that whatever dramatic technological, political, and economic changes may have occurred in the interim, contact networks still occupy in many labor markets a central role that cries out to be better understood, for theoretical and practical reasons alike. It is my hope that this new edition will make a serious contribution to that understanding, and will influence other scholars to see the value of a sociological approach to labor.

Evanston, Illinois
July 1994

REFERENCES

Dalton, Melville. 1959. *Men Who Manage*. New York: Wiley.
Granovetter, Mark. 1985. "Economic Action and Social Structure: The Problem of Embeddedness." *American Journal of Sociology* 81(3): 489–515.
Granovetter, Mark. 1990. "The Old and the New Economic Sociology: A History and

an Agenda." Pp. 89–112 in *Beyond the Marketplace,* edited by Roger Friedland and A. F. Robertson. New York: Aldine de Gruyter.

Granovetter, Mark, and Richard Swedberg, eds. 1992. *The Sociology of Economic Life.* Boulder, Colo.: Westview Press.

Homans, George. 1950. *The Human Group.* New York: Harcourt, Brace & World.

Parsons, Talcott, and Neil Smelser. 1956. *Economy and Society.* New York: Free Press.

Parsons, Talcott. 1968. Introduction to the paperback edition of *The Structure of Social Action.* New York: Free Press.

Whyte, William F. 1955. *Money and Motivation.* New York: Harper and Brothers.

Preface

Because the subject matter of this book cuts across several academic and practical fields—especially sociology, economics, and manpower allocation—it can be read from several different viewpoints. In the text I try to make these various routes into the subject explicit. After finishing the manuscript, however, I had a chance to read *Inequality*, by Christopher Jencks and his associates (New York: Basic Books, 1972), which brought into sharp focus, for me, a theme that I ought to have treated in more detail. At this stage, the best I can do is to alert the reader that there is a reading of my material somewhat different from the ones I have suggested within.

I was very much struck by the way the argument of *Inequality* dovetails with mine, despite the differences in assumptions and methods. Jencks and his colleagues argue—supported by an impressive array of analysis and data—that factors usually supposed to be at the root of inequality do not even seem to be very closely correlated with it statistically. Knowing a man's family background, intelligence (by standard measures such as I.Q.), educational attainment and even occupation—gives us remarkably little leverage in the prediction of his income level. The question then arises of what *is* at the root of the enormous observed variations in income. They speculate that an important factor is "luck: chance acquaintances who steer you to one line of work rather than another, the range of jobs that happen to be available in a particular community when you are job hunting, the amount of overtime work in your particular plant, whether bad weather destroys your strawberry crop, whether the new superhighway has an exit near your restaurant, and a hundred other unpredictable accidents. . . . In general, we think luck has far more influence on income than successful people admit (p. 227)."

These comments are really an afterthought, rather than part of their analysis. This may explain the pessimistic attitude toward the possibility of subjecting "luck" to systematic study. By contrast, the central theme of *Getting a Job* involves the explication of one element of what is usually considered "luck" in job-finding: having the right contact in the right place at the right time. The Jencks group found almost as much inequality of income *within* as between occupations. This is consistent with the considerable variations of income in my professional, technical, and managerial sample. Also consistent with the Jencks argument, I find this variation strongly related to whether or not personal contacts were the source of job-information—the higher the income, the more likely the presence of contacts. My basic argument is that one can pursue a systematic analysis of this variety of "luck" by developing and applying ideas about social structure. The point is not to deny the significance of chance in social life—in this I agree wholeheartedly with the argument of *Inequality*—but to bring the operation of chance into its social context, where it can be more properly understood.

Mark S. Granovetter
Cambridge, Massachusetts
January 1974

Acknowledgments

The project reported here took shape in the course of discussions with Harrison White who advised the dissertation of which the present study is a substantial revision. I owe him a great intellectual and personal debt; his influence appears in some form in every chapter.

The manuscript has been read in whole or part by the following individuals who have contributed greatly to whatever clarity I have been able to achieve: Scott Boorman, Ellen Granovetter, Ann Orlov, Peter Rossi and Charles Tilly. Conversations and communications with Robert Cole, Ivan Chase, Peter Doeringer, John Dunlop, Mitchell Polinsky, Philip Stone, Michael Useem, and Donald Warwick have been most valuable to me in clarifying ideas and methods.

My greatest debt is, naturally, to the hundred people who allowed me into their homes and gave freely of their time to answer questions that sometimes seemed pointless to them. Their insight into their own situations formed the necessary basis for any further insight I may have supplied here. I am also indebted to the additional hundred eighty-two individuals who returned my mail questionnaire, frequently with illuminating and unanticipated extra information or comments.

Special thanks are due to Pamela Skalski, Nellie Miller, Janis Litrenta, and Cally Abdulrazak for their expert typing of the manuscript.

Getting A Job

Introduction

How people find jobs is a prosaic problem—but exactly for this reason, it relates closely to important issues in sociology and economics. Under the rubric "labor mobility" in economics, and "social mobility" in sociology, how people move between jobs and between occupations has received much study; but surprisingly little detailed attention has been given to the question of how individuals become *aware* of the opportunities they take. Most studies are either highly aggregated or highly individualized. At the macro level, excellent monographs detail the statistics of men flowing between categories (Blau and Duncan, 1967; Blumen et al., 1955; Carlsson, 1958); at the micro level, other studies offer plausible psychological and economic motives for particular individuals to *want* to change jobs (Kahl, 1953; Reynolds, 1951; Morse, 1953). Important as these concerns are, they are not those of the present study. Rather, I have chosen to concentrate on the issue of how the information that facilitates mobility is secured and disseminated. This question lies somewhere between the micro- and macro-level concerns described above, and is a potentially crucial link in their integration; it is an important part of the study of the *immediate* causes of mobility, and, as in other social science problems, failure to specify immediate causes leads to inability to link micro and macro levels of analysis.

How mobility information travels bears on general social theory as well. The scarcity of information available to those engaging in mobility is striking. Complete and systematic data on job opportunities is extremely hard to collect; even trained investigators with government grants encounter difficult obstacles (Dunlop, 1966; Ferber and Ford, 1965). Thus, a single individual operating with

heavy constraints on his or her time and resources is likely to un-
cover only a small proportion of those openings he might plausibly
fill at a given time. The use of mass media advertising and employment agencies does not substantially alter this situation.

Some have assumed that the advent of "modernization" leads to
widespread use of formal and "universalistic" procedures, liberating
individuals from the limitations once imposed by particular social
milieus (for example, Sjoberg, 1960:192). But empirical sociological
studies continually demonstrate the crucial importance of informal
interaction in systems that are formally rationalized (Selznick, 1949;
Dalton, 1959; Crozier, 1964). The present study offers another
example of this kind: the heavy dependence of individuals on their
existing set of personal contacts for information about job-change
opportunities. (If everyone found his or her job "through the *New
York Times*," the subject would have little sociological interest!)

We can view this as an instance of the enormous, though often
unnoticed, constraint placed on individuals by the social network in
which they find themselves. A primary focus of my analysis will
thus be the dynamics of information flow through such networks. In
this regard, I will be pursuing the findings of earlier studies which
indicated that information which leads to action is more likely to
move through chains of personal contact than through mass media,
or more impersonal routes (Katz, 1957; Coleman et al., 1966; Lee,
1969).

Connections with economic theory will also be probed. I must
consider to what extent my findings can be explained by the usual
tools of supply and demand and marginal principles of optimization.
In neoclassical economics, employment is a central variable at both
the micro and macro levels. But, as in the sociological analysis of
mobility, the levels are not convincingly integrated. A given amount
of aggregate demand is said to result in a certain level of employment; that is, when there is work to be done, it is assumed that
people will be employed to do it (barring already full employment).
How to make the connection between work that needs to be done
and people who are willing to do it is not specified. When the mechanisms of a theory—the immediate causes—are neglected in this way,

we are at a loss to understand what happens when predicted results fail to occur, as when blacks are unemployed in periods of high aggregate demand. Where possible, therefore, I will comment on the relevance of my findings for the economic theory of labor markets.

Most of the literature in this area has been created by American labor economists motivated primarily, in many cases, by concern with either unemployment or labor shortages. They have focused on blue-collar workers. The common practice has been to divide methods of finding jobs into "formal" and "informal" ones. The "formal" category includes commercial and public employment agencies and advertisements. "Informal" methods include the use of personal contacts of any kind, and also direct application to an employer (or his personnel agent) not previously known personally to the job-seeker.

The blue-collar studies, carried out from the 1930's to the present, in American cities of widely varying size, economic base, and market conditions, have been remarkably similar in their conclusions. All showed that formal mechanisms of job allocation rarely accounted for more than 20 percent of placements. By contrast, 60–90 percent of jobs were found informally, principally through friends and relatives but also by direct application. (See De Schweinetz, 1932; Edelman et al., 1952; Lester, 1954; Lurie and Rayack, 1968; Myers and Shultz, 1951; Myers and Maclaurin, 1943; Parnes, 1954; Reynolds, 1951; Sheppard and Belitsky, 1966; Ullman and Taylor, 1965; Wilcock and Franke, 1963; Wilcock and Sobel, 1958.)

Only a few studies have investigated white-collar workers. Female clerical workers have been shown to use agencies and ads more often than blue-collar workers (of either sex), but still to rely more on informal methods than on any other kind (Shultz, 1962). Two studies of professionals, one of aerospace engineers and one of college professors, show little difference from the blue-collar studies in incidence of job-finding methods. In the engineering study (Shapero et al., 1965:50), 68 percent found their jobs by informal means: 51 percent by personal acquaintances and 17 percent by

direct application.[1] In Brown's massive study of college professors
(1965b; 1967), 84 percent used informal methods: 65 percent
personal contacts, 19 percent direct application. Brown's conclusions are consistent with those of Caplow and McGee (1958); but
exact comparison is not possible since they do not supply figures on
proportions finding jobs by various methods.

Nearly all of the above studies have been done from the point of
view of economists whose underlying theoretical framework has thus
been that of economic theory, with its emphasis on the concept of
"labor markets," and the relation of wages to mobility.

The present study is conducted from a quite different point of
view. Because, in the majority of cases, individuals hear about a new
job via personal contacts, and not through general announcements of
vacancies, an important sociological dimension can be introduced.
The actual transmission of information about job opportunities
becomes a more immediate condition of mobility than any characteristic of jobs themselves. No matter how great the "net advantage"
to an individual in changing from his present position to some
particular new one, he cannot move unless he secures the proper
information. Should social conditions arise which block this flow of
information between personal acquaintances, economic theory
would be of little help in understanding the problem.

No study has gone much beyond the statement that information
is secured from "friends and relatives." I will be concerned to
specify more exactly the origin, nature, and maintenance of the
interpersonal tie mediating the passage of information. This involves
asking how and when the job-changer first came to know the
person who ultimately supplied the necessary information, whether
the tie was weak or strong, forged in work or in social situations, and
in what ways the relationship was maintained between the time it
began and the time that information was passed. I will also be
interested in the circumstances under which information came to

---

1. Unlike most authors, Brown classifies direct application as a "formal"
method. I discuss the ambiguity of the "formal-informal" distinction on
page 9.

be passed, and how these "friends and relatives" happened to be in possession of the relevant information. Whether these aspects of job-changing depend systematically on characteristics of the job-changer or on general labor-market conditions will also be probed.

For a number of reasons, at the beginning of this study I decided to concentrate on professional, technical, and managerial workers. (For convenience, I shall refer to them hereafter as PTM workers.) It was, first of all, desirable to rule out social class as a confounding variable, while nevertheless choosing a fairly general sample. This stratum has been studied less than any other—I know of no other study offering information on a general random sample of such workers; moreover, I wanted to be able to see intensive and sophisticated attempts at job search. In view of the importance attached to their jobs by these people, I suspected that they would be the ones most likely to conduct such a search. (This assumption proved faulty; see Chapter 1.) Ruling out the effects of still another crucial variable, I limited my attention to males. Female career patterns are sufficiently different from those of males that a separate study would be necessary to do justice to them.

Having selected a stratum, I then needed a sampling location. I looked for a city or town which 1) was large enough to provide a reasonable-sized sample; 2) contained a high proportion of employed males in the specified category, so as to facilitate sampling; 3) was covered by a comprehensive (commercial) city directory listing job and place of work each year for each resident and 4) was close enough to Cambridge that I could do a substantial number of interviews myself. Newton, Massachusetts, a Boston suburb of some 98,000 inhabitants seemed the best choice.

I chose a sampling method in which I compared two consecutive city directories and took a random sample of those whose employer in the later edition was different from the one listed in the earlier. In addition, every person appearing in the new directory for the first time was included in the sample, and later dropped from consideration if he turned out not to have changed his job within the last five years. (The advantage of a sample with recent mobility experience was that of more accurate recall; this was especially important since I was to ask questions in great detail about not particularly memorable events.) Those who were taking their first job were included; those changing from one to another branch of the same company were excluded.

My goal was to interview 100 such individuals personally, and to collect a mail survey from 200 others. To this end, letters were sent to 457 potential respondents; this was a 45 percent random sample of all apparently eligible persons in Newton. The final yield was 100 personal interviews and 182 mail surveys. This represented response rates of 85.5 percent in the interview, and 79.1 percent in the mail survey, of all those who were ultimately found to be eligible.[2]

Every method, of course, introduces systematic distortions and it is best to be aware of what these are before evaluating results. Perhaps the most serious such distortion in the present work is that it was not practicable to interview respondents' employers. The value of conducting those interviews would lie not so much in checking the accuracy of the accounts given to me by respondents; while corroboration would be of some value, most of my questions could have been answered only by the job changer rather than the new employer. More important would be the account of what steps an employer had taken to fill the position in question, and how many prospects were considered. Comparison of how the employer was put in touch with unsuccessful candidates, to how he became linked with my respondent would be revealing. An economist would say that this study lays heavy emphasis on the supply side of the labor market, leaving out the demand process. While this shortcoming detracts from some ideal study, I do not think that it need vitiate the usefulness of the results presented here, which are more or less self-contained. Emphasis is on the sociological forces which make mobility opportunity available to individuals, rather than on how employers manage to fill vacant positions.

2. My sampling method is basically adapted from that of Reynolds (1951). A detailed account of sampling, consistency comparisons between interview and mail sample, and representativeness of the Newton population can be found in Appendix A.

A second important bias is introduced by taking only individuals who have changed jobs within five years, rather than a general random sample of PTM workers. I adopted this strategy to facilitate memory of mobility experience, as mentioned above, and also to rule out variations caused by secular trends over the longer period that a general sample would have involved. One would expect that a general sample, as compared to the present one, would be older, since younger men are more mobile, and therefore likely to be over-represented among recent movers. It may also be that recent movers are more adventurous than the general population of PTM workers. Arguments come to mind for their being either less competent or more competent, depending on the cause of their mobility. As a consequence of these or other differences, members of a general sample might show a somewhat different picture of the job-changing process. I, myself, doubt that the bias is a serious one, but in the absence of baseline comparative data, the reader must be warned to keep it in mind.

A third bias results from studying, here, only how the respondents secured information about the jobs that they *took*; this is clearly not the only information they receive about job vacancies, and it would be of particular interest to know more about whether there are systematic differences between how information that does and does not lead to a job change is secured. This is related to the second bias, in that men searching intensively for a new job, but not finding one to their liking during the specified five years, had no chance to be included in my sample. Some exploratory probing of my respondents convinced me, however, that I did not have the time or resources to carefully explore the problem of jobs not taken. Not the least of the problems involved was definition of what it means to say that a respondent has heard about a job that he might fill. While it is fairly clear what constitutes a hard job offer, there is a vast grey area consisting of opportunities that might or might not become hard offers depending on the actions of respondent, employer, and other interested parties. If the reader tries to write down a list of the jobs that might have been available to him during the past year, he will quickly see the difficulties involved.

A last bias is introduced by confining the study to change of *employer*: I have excluded job changes in the labor market internal to firms. Economists have made widely varying estimates of the significance of such markets. In a recent article, Dunlop remarks that for the "typical enterprise, hiring-in jobs are only a small fraction of the total number of job classifications" (1966:32; also see Lester, 1954:32–34.) Palmer, however, offers data suggesting that the proportion of job changes occurring *without* change of employer is less than 10 percent of all job changes (1954:51, 124). Her data is from the 1940's, and is thus especially interesting in view of Reynolds' idea that internal promotions are more likely in tight labor markets,[3] as in the 1940's (Reynolds, 1951:144.)

In compiling my sample, the number of cases I had to exclude because they involved mobility internal to a firm was much less than 10 percent. Changes of employer are far easier to detect than changes of "job" within a firm; no one's job is quite the same one day as the next, particularly in the case of PTM workers. This measurement difficulty may account for much of the apparent discrepancy between expected and observed mobility *within* firms. It would have been beyond my scope to resolve these difficulties in this study; moreover, job change in internal markets presents a somewhat different set of substantive issues than in external ones. Thus, in what follows, "job change" or "mobility" may be taken to be synonymous with "change of employer." *Nothing else is implied.* As personal interviews were more detailed than mail surveys, some tables in the text will be based only on the 100 interviews, others on the entire sample of 282. Data from a pilot study are not included in tables, but some anecdotal material is drawn from this source; these cases are clearly indicated. Levels of significance indicated in the tables are based on the chi-square statistic.

Finding Work: Some Basic Results

PTM workers use three basic ways of finding out about jobs: formal means, personal contacts, and direct application. Included

3. In this study, I follow the usual convention in designating as "tight" labor markets those in which more vacancies exist than men to fill them; the opposite situation (surplus of men) is called a "loose market."

under "formal means" are advertisements, public and private employment agencies (including those calling themselves "management consultants" or "executive search services"), interviews and placements sponsored by universities or professional associations, and placement committees in certain professions, notably in various ministries. The defining characteristic of formal means is that the job-seeker uses the services of an impersonal intermediary, between himself and prospective employers. By "impersonal" is meant either the lack of any personal contact (as in newspaper advertising), or use of an individual, who is specifically designated by himself or others, as an employment intermediary. "Personal contacts," by contrast, implies that there is some individual known personally to the respondent, with whom he *originally* became acquainted in some context *unrelated* to a search for job information, from whom he has found out about his new job, or, who recommended him to someone who then contacted him. "Direct application" means that one goes or writes directly to a firm, does not use a formal or personal intermediary, and has not heard about a *specific* opening from a personal contact.[4] Although the three methods are distinct, in principle, and pure cases outnumber others, the differences may become blurred in specific instances. Further discussion of the coding problem involved may be found in Appendix B.

In the present PTM sample, personal contact is the predominant method of finding out about jobs. Almost fifty-six percent of the respondents used this method; 18.8 percent used formal means (9.9 percent advertisements, 8.9 percent other formal means) and 18.8 percent used direct application; 6.7 percent fell into miscellaneous categories (including "not ascertained.") If one takes into account the usual over-estimation of the use of "direct application" (see Appendix B for further discussion), these figures are remarkably similar to those generally found for blue-collar workers.

4. Direct application has, in other studies, sometimes been included, with personal contacts, in the category "informal" methods; since the use of the expression "informal" has no particular logic to it, and has served only as a negative, residual category, I have dropped it here. Direct application could just as easily be called a "formal" method, as in Brown (1967). In fact, it is different from both formal methods and from the use of personal contacts; hence the three-way classification.

We must now ask, in some detail, why a given individual uses one method rather than another to find a job. Other methods may have been used, of course, besides the one that ultimately resulted in a job change. Hence, we have, to some extent, not only a question of propensity to use a method, but also one of why the respondent was able to do so successfully.

Most respondents prefer the use of personal contacts to other means. Other labor market studies indicate that employers express a similar preference for hiring methods. It follows that external economic conditions have less influence than might be supposed on the methods that connect people to jobs. In tight labor markets, employers are forced to use less preferred methods; but this is largely cancelled by the lower motivation of job-seekers or job-changers to do so. The opposite may be said of loose labor markets. Thus, studies done under various economic conditions have shown similar distributions of job-finding methods. (The statement about "cancelling" is crude, however, and ought to be subjected to more systematic investigation.)

As a first approximation, we may suppose that preferences for different methods are determined by some sort of cost-benefit analysis of job-search procedures by prospective job-changers. This is only an approximation because, as discussed in detail in Chapter 1, the image of the job-changer as conducting a search according to rational, utility-maximizing principles needs considerable modification.

Nevertheless, the preference described above *is* roughly justified by respondents on a cost-benefit basis; findings from various other studies support their judgment. Sheppard and Belitsky, for instance, for a mostly blue-collar sample, computed the proportion of those using a given method who obtained jobs through it. They found that "friends and relatives" received by far the highest rating (1966: 94). Brown, for each method used by his respondents, college professors, computed the number of jobs accepted as a proportion of the number of jobs found by that method; this is presumably a measure of the desirability of jobs found in various ways. The top five methods on this measure were different types of personal contact (1967:141). In addition, he reported more use of personal contacts in the finding of jobs of higher rank, smaller teaching loads, higher salaries, and greater prestige of college (1965b:227; 1967: 118). Next in quality of job produced was direct application ("blind letters" in most cases), followed by the various formal methods (1965b:241).

The PTM workers to whom I spoke believed that information secured through personal contacts is of higher quality than that available by other means; a friend gives more than a simple job-description—he may also indicate if prospective workmates are congenial, if the boss is neurotic, and if the company is moving forward or is stagnant. (Similarly, on the demand side, evaluations of prospective employees will be trusted better when the employer knows the evaluator personally.)

Various measures of the quality of jobs held by my respondents substantiate their idea that better jobs are found via personal contacts. Table 1 shows that those using personal contacts are most likely to say that they are "very satisfied" with their current job,

Table 1. Level of job satisfaction attained by job-finding method of respondent.

Level of satisfaction	Method used				
	Formal means	Personal contacts	Direct application	Other	Total[d]
Very satisfied	30.0%	54.2%	52.8%	47.1%	49.1%
Fairly satisfied	46.0%	36.8%	32.1%	47.1%	38.2%
Lower[a]	24.0%	9.0%	15.1%	5.9%	12.7%
N[b]	50	155	53	17	275
		$p = 0.03$[c]			

[a]Includes "neither satisfied nor dissatisfied," "fairly dissatisfied," and "very dissatisfied."

[b]Two-variable tables add to 100 percent in the columns. Rather than printing "100 percent" in each case, the number of cases on which column percentages are based is given.

[c]All significance levels are by chi-square test.

[d]Omitted from this and subsequent tables are respondents from whom a usable response was not obtained on any variable in the table.

Table 2. Level of income of respondent in present job, by job-finding method used.

	Method used				
Income	Formal means	Personal contacts	Direct application	Other	Total
Less than					
$10,000	28.0%	22.7%	50.0%	5.3%	27.6%
$10,000–14,999	42.0%	31.8%	30.8%	26.3%	33.1%
$15,000–24,999	24.0%	31.2%	15.4%	52.6%	28.4%
$25,000 or more	6.0%	14.3%	3.8%	15.8%	10.9%
N	50	154	52	19	275
		$p = 0.001$			

and least likely not to express satisfaction; direct application and formal means follow, in that order. Table 2 shows the strong association of income level with job-finding method. Nearly half (45.5 percent) of those using personal contacts report incomes over $15,000, whereas the corresponding figure for formal means is under one-third; for direct application, under one-fifth.

Jobs can also be classified by the nature of their creation. In some cases one directly replaces someone who has vacated a position; or an individual may be added on to do work similar to that which others are already doing. New positions may also be created: work may be done that has not been done before, or previously scattered tasks can be put together into one job. It seems likely that the most desirable positions would be found in the category of "newly created" jobs, since these would be most apt to have been tailored to the needs, preferences, and abilities of an incumbent. Table 3 shows that those finding a job through contacts are much more likely than those using formal means or direct application, to have had jobs newly created for them.

By taking the percentages on these tables in the opposite direction, we may view the same findings from the point of view of the system of jobs. Results are parallel: The more satisfied individuals are in their jobs, the more likely they are to have found them

Table 3. Origin of job, by job-finding method of respondent.

Origin of job	Method used				
	Formal means	Personal contacts	Direct application	Other	Total
Direct replacement	47.1%	40.5%	58.0%	38.9%	44.9%
Added on	31.4%	15.7%	18.0%	27.8%	19.9%
Newly created	21.6%	43.8%	24.0%	33.3%	35.3%
N	51	153	50	18	272

$$p = 0.02$$

through contacts. Jobs offering the highest salary are much more prone to be found through contacts than others: whereas less than half of jobs yielding less than $10,000 per year were found by contacts, the figure is more than three-quarters for those paying more than $25,000. The use of direct application falls steadily as the salary of a job rises; the use of formal methods is somewhat less regular in pattern, though least likely at the highest salary. Finally, newly created jobs are much more likely to be filled via personal contacts than are other types, and are least likely to be filled by direct application or formal means.

A related finding is that 57.9 percent of those who say they have recently thought about looking for another job found their present job through contacts, compared to 72.1 percent of those who have not considered changing ($p = 0.09$). This is parallel to the finding of Shapero et al. for aerospace engineers, that those recently leaving their company were considerably less likely to have entered via contacts than those who remained (1965:50). Discussions of labor force "attachment" would do well to consider method of recruitment. The fact that "stayers" are more likely to have been recruited through contacts than "movers" may result only from the fact that better jobs are found in this way. It may also be true, however, that the man who is thus recruited is more likely to become quickly integrated into the social circles of his workplace, having an entree in the person of his contact. The data of the present study are too limited to allow a choice between the two hypotheses.

To sum up, evidence is strong that the use of personal contacts by my respondents results in better jobs than other methods. A number of respondents even had the odd experience of being refused a job for which they applied directly, only to be accepted later for the same job through personal contacts. One postdoctoral student in biology received a letter from an institution to which he had applied for a job, saying that there were "no openings for an individual with your qualifications." But when his thesis adviser took a position there, the younger man went along as a research associate; he subsequently received an effusive letter expressing the college's delight at his appointment. An assistant professor of psychology tells a similar story; his inquiry about the position he now holds was never answered. But several months later, he received a call from someone he had once worked with, asking him if he would be interested in the position. The friend was unaware of his previous inquiry.

Since respondents prefer to find jobs through personal contacts, and this preference appears well-grounded, we must then ask why everyone did not do so. Here the influence of social structure must be probed. Some individuals have the right contacts, while others do not. If one lacks the appropriate contact, there is little he can do about it. While this is obvious enough, it is a difficult question, and a major focus of this study, to determine under what circumstances a given individual *will* have such contacts.

We may begin by asking whether groups with particular demographic characteristics are more or less prone to the use of certain methods. In this context, the standard sociological variables of religion, ethnicity, and educational background come to mind. Several studies have compared the behavior of black and white (usually blue-collar) workers; some found that blacks used formal means more than whites, others that they used them less often. (Crain, 1970; Lurie and Rayack, 1966:369; Sheppard and Belitsky, 1966: 174, 178; Ullman and Taylor, 1965: 283; Wilcock and Franke, 1963:130). A recent national survey of 14–24-year-old males found no racial differences in search behavior (Parnes et al., 1970:102–

Table 4. Job-finding method, by religious background of respondent.

Method used	Religious background				
	Protestant	Catholic	Jewish	None[b]	Total
Formal means	15.4%	16.9%	19.2%	16.7%	17.3%
Personal contact	55.1%	56.6%	57.6%	66.7%	56.8%
Direct application	23.1%	20.5%	16.2%	0.0%	19.2%
Other	6.4%	6.0%	7.1%	16.7%	6.8%
N	78	83	99	6	266
		p = n.s.[a]			

[a]Significance levels of 0.20 or less are reported; otherwise n.s. (= not significant) is indicated.

[b]Those responding "none" to religious preference were assigned to the religious preference of their parents, if any; where both respondents' and parents' preference are reported as none, the respondents' religious background is coded none.

104). In the present PTM sample, Table 4 shows that religious background had no particular impact on likelihood of using a given method. Similarly uninteresting tables could be produced showing that ethnic background and educational level attained has no relation to incidence of these methods. (As the present sample is over 99 percent white, no data on racial differences are produced.)

This finding may be surprising insofar as one expects differences in cultural background and personality traits to have an impact on behavior. Sheppard and Belitsky (1966) explicitly tested, for example, the notion that one's degree of "achievement motivation" would affect job-seeking behavior. While they did find some effects in predicted directions, these were rather weak. I will argue, in general, that a much more important type of determinant of one's behavior is one's position in a social network. By this is meant not only the identity of the set of people one knows and his relations to them but also the set known by that set, and so on, as well as the structure of connections among one's friends, friends' friends, and so on. The structure and dynamics of this network, though elusive and difficult to analyze, largely determine what information will

Table 5. Job-finding method, by age of respondent.

Method used	Age		Total
	Under 34	Over 34	
Formal means	25.3%	11.9%	18.9%
Personal contacts	47.9%	64.2%	55.7%
Direct application	22.6%	14.9%	18.9%
Other	4.1%	9.0%	6.4%
N	146	134	280
	$p = 0.002$		

reach a given person, and, to that extent, what possibilities will be open to him.

This is not to argue that culture and personality have no impact on one's position in this structure; only that the impact is not systematic or predictable. Nor is it my argument that people make no choices. Individuals clearly do not seize every job offer that reaches them; cultural and personality factors no doubt have their impact on which job one chooses to accept. A separate study would be required to do justice to this issue. The point is that if we confine ourselves to looking at jobs that people *do* accept, however the choice is made, structural factors have the largest influence on the method of uncovering those jobs. By "structural factors" I mean the properties of one's social situation that shape his contact network; one typically has little control over these factors.

An example is the effect of age. Blue-collar studies have uniformly shown that personal contacts are particularly important to individuals in the early stages of their career—especially in finding one's first job (De Schweinetz, 1933:87, 93; Reynolds, 1951:127). In the Newton sample, the finding is reversed: Table 5 shows that those in the younger half of the sample are considerably more likely to use formal means and direct application, while nearly two-thirds of the older PTM workers find their jobs through personal contacts.[5]

5. At this point, the reader might properly wonder if the earlier finding, that those using contacts find higher-paying jobs, is merely an artifact of the over-

Table 6. Job-finding method, by occupational category
of respondent.

| | Occupation | | | |
	Professional	Technical[a]	Managerial	Total
Method used				
Formal means	15.9%	30.4%	13.6%	18.8%
Personal contacts	56.1%	43.5%	65.4%	55.7%
Direct application	18.2%	24.6%	14.8%	18.8%
Other	9.8%	1.4%	6.2%	6.7%
N	132	69	81	282
		$p = 0.01$		

[a]Includes all technical, engineering, and scientific workers except college
professors or high school teachers of science.

This appears to be due to the greater specialization inherent in
PTM occupations; not yet having worked long in the specialized
field he has been trained for, the young PTM worker will have
acquired few useful contacts. He must thus fall back on formal
means and direct application. In the blue-collar case, however, less
specialization combined with less geographic mobility make it more
likely that some older friend or relative can help the young worker.
In their national sample of white, out-of-school youth, aged 14–24,
Parnes et al. (1970:104) similarly found that the proportion using
"friends and relatives" to find their job is smallest for professional
and technical work, increasing steadily to a maximum for semi- and
unskilled workers.

Still another structural factor appears if we break the PTM group
into its three constituent types of occupation; the results are shown
in Table 6. Technical workers are least likely to use personal contacts, and most likely to use formal means and direct application.
There are a particularly large number of agencies specializing in

representation of older PTM workers among those using contacts. This is
not the case. Controlling for age, the relationship persists within each age
group. Similarly, within each age group, the higher the salary, the more likely
one was to have used contacts. Among those in the older half of the sample,
over 80 percent of those earning $25,000 or more per year found the job
through contacts.

technical personnel, which makes it possible to use this route more often than for either professionals or managers; direct application may also be enhanced by the size and consequent wide reputations of many firms which hire technical personnel. Another factor is more subtle, and more structural; whereas scientists and technicians may work alone or in small groups, managers, by definition, must spend a great deal of time in personal interaction. In the course of a manager's career, many more personal contacts may be established than in that of a scientist; such contacts may later be useful.[6]

Individual cases also illustrate the impact of structural factors. One respondent was an engineer, blinded about seven years ago. Unable to maintain as many contacts as formerly, he found it necessary to seek work by formal means. A recent immigrant, though an experienced scientist in Japan, knew very few people in his field in this country, and so, from the point of view of contacts, was just "starting out."

In general, then, Brown's statement about the job-seeking behavior of college professors applies to the present overall PTM sample: "Formal methods [including direct application] are used only after informal contacts have failed to yield a good job" (1967: 117). Those who resort to these methods tend to be those who, for more or less structural reasons, lack the right personal contacts. There are, however, some positive reasons to use formal means:

Case #1: Albert W. was working for a large engineering firm, but was dissatisfied. He had personal contacts who could have been useful

6. The figure for professionals must be treated with caution since 58 of the 132 professionals (43.8 percent) are college professors, an atypical situation related to the large number of colleges in the Boston area. College professors are much more likely than other professionals to find jobs through contacts: 77.6 percent do so, as compared to 54.5 percent of high school teachers and 32.7 percent of other professionals. Although older respondents and those with higher incomes are over-represented among professors, this does not explain the strong disposition to use of contacts, as the older and higher-income respondents *among* professors are not more likely than the younger and lower-income ones to use contacts—they are, actually, a little *less* likely, though one cannot take relationships seriously based on such small numbers. Note that this implies that if professors were less prominent in the sample, the general tendency for older and higher income respondents to be more likely to use contacts would be even stronger.

but did not trust them enough to tell them he was looking for a new job; he therefore went to an agency specializing in technical personnel.[7]

Mr. W. was rather bitter about his experience, however. He reports that the agency scheduled him for interviews in the same room as personnel managers from his company, who would have recognized him and realized why he was there; he covered his face and hurried from the room. He cites this obvious blunder as an example of the utter impersonality of such agencies, which makes them distasteful to deal with. Many of those who had used agencies had similar attitudes. A ghoulish set of terms reflects their evaluation of such services and those who run them: "head-hunters"; "body-snatchers"; "flesh-peddlers"; "warm-body shops."

The appointment of Jewish Conservative rabbis, brought to my attention by one respondent, is an interesting case; formal means were instituted by centralized control for ideological reasons. Before 1947, congregations seeking a rabbi, and rabbis seeking congregations operated by the three methods described above. The situation came to be viewed as intolerable, as congregations considered most desirable found themselves with thirty or forty applicants; those thought less attractive had few or none. (The market was a tight one at the time.) Rabbis found themselves in "lineups" of applicants for interviews; a congregation that had an advantageous bargaining position could bid down the salary asked. Personal connections with members of the boards of trustees were of considerable importance.

All this was considered undignified for clergymen. In 1947–48, the Rabbinical Assembly, central administrative body of the Conservative Jewish movement, asserted control over placement of all Conservative rabbis. This was possible since all such rabbis were members. A placement committee now sends each congregation looking for a rabbi a list of three names, a "panel," from whom they may either choose one, after interviews, or ask for another panel. The committee chooses these names from among those rabbis who,

7. Anecdotal material in this study has been modified as necessary to protect the anonymity of respondents. Besides the use of fictitious names, this sometimes involves changing industry names and job titles.

upon receiving the list of vacancies circulated periodically, express
interest. The process continues until a rabbi is chosen. Rabbis or
congregations attempting to circumvent this system are subject to
effective sanctions. There appear now to be few or no exceptions to
this method of placement.[8] Its success recently stimulated the
Reform Jewish movement to adopt a similar system.

In effect, this action approximated the creation of an internal
labor market; individuals transfer from one congregation to another
as if from once branch to another of the same firm. It is unlikely
that the degree of central control necessary to implement such
a system could be duplicated in larger, nonreligious groups. There
are, at present, less than 1000 Conservative rabbis.

In this introduction, then, the basic theme has been set: personal
contacts are of paramount importance in connecting people with jobs.
Better jobs are found through contacts, and the best jobs, the ones
with the highest pay and prestige and affording the greatest satisfaction to those in them, are most apt to be filled in this way. With a
few interesting exceptions, those who do not find their jobs through
personal contacts, would have liked to do so, but were prevented
by "structural" factors. A few such factors were briefly sketched in
this chapter, but for a deeper understanding it is necessary to ask
more detailed questions about how people "use" personal contacts.
Who are these "contacts" that play such a crucial role in filling
the most coveted positions in our economic and social structure—
what relation do they hold to respondents, and what relation to
the jobs they channel respondents into? Under what circumstances
does information about these jobs come to be passed? On whose
initiative? These are the questions to which Part One is devoted.

8. Information on this placement procedure was secured through the
courtesy of a personal interview with Rabbi Gilbert Epstein, Director of
Placement, Jewish Theological Seminary, New York City.

Part
One
Toward Causal Models

In this section of the book I will attempt to develop and explore causal explanations. The event to be explained is the acquisition of job-information by my respondents and my focus is heavily on cases where personal contacts are used. What it might mean to "explain" such an event is ambiguous. Causal investigations may be undertaken at many different levels. The first distinction of level to be made here is that of time frame. We may distinguish between immediate causes and those that operate over long time periods, comparable at least to that of a man's average job tenure, in some cases to his entire career. Crosscutting the dimension of time is that of scale; some causes are immediate in the sense that they involve only the respondent and his personal contacts, whereas others involve individuals and jobs unknown to the respondent, possibly at considerable social distance, in a sense to be defined later. We may abbreviate these two dimensions to long-term/short-term, and micro/macro, although the dichotomies are crude. "Long-term" is really a residual category for causes that are not immediate, and "macro" has a similar relation to "micro." Hence, both "long-term" and "macro" causes may be less long-term and less macro than many aspects of society which we are accustomed to discuss under those rubrics.

Four sequences of short-term causal questions provide the substance of Chapters 1–4. These are: 1) in what types of interpersonal situations was job information passed? The answer to this leads also to a discussion of economic theory, which labels all such situations "job search"; 2) how were personal contacts connected to respondents and to the job information which they offered?; 3) What motivated contacts to offer job information? What characteristics of inter-

personal relations and networks facilitated the movement of such
information from its source to its ultimate destination? 4) How did
there come to be, in the first place, an opening in the job about
which information was passed? These four series of questions progress from micro to macro concerns, within the short-term time
frame.

Chapters 5 and 6 take up long-term causal questions. 1) How did
the respondent originally become connected to the person who
ultimately gave him job information? What characteristics of the
individual or of his life history contributed to this connection and
its maintenance? 2) What characteristics of a person's career, of his
movement through a system of jobs, affected his likelihood of finding jobs through personal contacts? Emphasis again moves, relatively
speaking, from micro to macro levels. In Chapter 7 I will attempt to
draw together the threads of these chapters to arrive at a somewhat
integrated idea of the causal sequences involved. Figure 1 summarizes
the conceptual scheme that has guided the organization of these
chapters.

Figure 1. Dimensions of causality in the transmission of job
information.

Scale	Time-frame	
	Short-term	Long-term
Micro	Chapter 1: Situation in which job-information was transmitted	Chapter 5: Origins of respondent-contact tie; how it was maintained
	Chapter 2: Relation of contact to respondent and to job information	
Macro	Chapter 3: Characteristics of relations and networks that facilitated information flow	Chapter 6: Influence of overall career pattern on current job-finding experiences.
	Chapter 4: Causes of vacancy	

Chapter

"Job Search" and Economic Theory

There is some overlap between the subject matter of the present study and that of labor-market theory in economics. In the classical conception, labor is a commodity, like wheat or shoes, and is hence subject to market analysis: employers are the buyers, and employees the sellers of labor. Wages (or, in more refined formulations, the total benefits accruing to a worker by virtue of holding a given job) are analogized to price. Supply and demand operate in the usual way to establish equilibrium: the price of labor fluctuates in the short run until that single price is arrived at which clears the market. For homogeneous work, wage dispersion and unemployment are not possible; firms paying more than the equilibrium price for labor will thereby attract workers from firms paying less. This excess of supply over demand will drive down the price. Firms losing employees will similarly be constrained to raise wages. Workers unemployed in the short run may bid for work, driving down wages to the point where they, and those currently working, will all be employed at the new, lower equilibrium wage. This elegant package ties together wages, unemployment, and labor mobility.

Like perfect commodity markets, however, perfect labor markets exist only in textbooks. Unemployment, obviously, persists. On wage dispersion, a recent text on labor economics summarizes a number of empirical studies by saying that even "in the absence of collective bargaining, employers will continue indefinitely to pay diverse rates for the same grade of labor in the same locality under strictly comparable job conditions . . . There is no wage which will clear the market" (Bloom and Northrup, 1969:232). Reynolds, in a detailed empirical study of New Haven, concluded that labor mobility and wage determination are more or less independent; the movement of labor has little effect on wages, and "voluntary movement of labor . . . seems to depend more largely on differences in availability of jobs than on differences in wage levels" (1951:230, 233). Brown, in his study of college professors, divided disciplines into those with excess supply and excess demand for teachers. He naturally assumed that job-changers in excess-demand disciplines would have received more job offers than those in fields with excess supply. Though there was some tendency in this direction, he reports that it was "not decisive," and that "repeated attempts to explain the differentials in market behavior by dividing the disciplines into excess supply and excess demand have not produced any conclusive evidence of the expected, usual relationships" (1965b: 117, 118n; for the basis of the excess supply and demand index see pages 87-91, 354, 361).

Several factors militate against perfect labor markets. Inertia as well as social and institutional pressures exert constraints on the free movement of labor contemplated in economic theory (cf. Kerr 1954; Parnes, 1954). Union agreements and community restraints discourage employers from adjusting wages to meet supply and demand (cf. Reynolds, chs. 7-9). The factor most relevant to the present discussion is imperfection of information.

The neoclassical theory of commodity markets generally takes the possession of complete information by market participants as one requirement of a perfect market. In Stigler's widely cited treatment of price theory, this is described as a *sufficient* condition (1952:56). But it is not simple to say exactly what complete information *means*, as Shubik noticed (1959), in trying to construct game-theoretic models for the behavior of actors in commodity markets. Alfred Marshall, a founder of the neoclassical synthesis, hedged on the issue, saying that it was not "necessary for our argument that any dealers [buyers or sellers] should have a thorough knowledge of the circumstances of the market" (1930:334). He felt that so long as each participant behaved strictly in accord with his supply or demand schedule, the equilibrium price would ultimately be reached. He does seem, in this argument, to assume that

buyers and sellers are at least aware of the *identities* of all those
they might transact business with and even their current bid (or
price)—only not necessarily their entire supply or demand schedules.
Stigler comments that the "New York City market for domestic
service is imperfect because some maids are working at wages less
than some prospective employers would be willing to pay, and some
maids are receiving more than unemployed maids would be willing
to work for" (Stigler, 1952:56). This is caused primarily, one would
guess, because the underpaid maids do not know the identity of
very many potential employers, nor do the overpaying employers
know who is available at a lower wage. Clearly, knowledge of the
identities of these people is prerequisite to determining under what
conditions they will offer (or purchase) services.

While there is disagreement on just how much information
actually is possessed by workers in various labor markets, it seems
clear that there is considerable ignorance. Reynolds holds that
workers' "knowledge of wage and nonwage terms of employment
in other companies [than their own] is very meager . . . much of
what workers purport to know about other companies is inaccurate"
(1951:213). Even less is known about the general state of knowledge
of employers; all would agree, however, that few employers know of
all or most individuals who could potentially fill vacancies they
have open.

Only in the last ten years have economists begun to suggest how
information is obtained and diffused in markets. Most of the models
presented deal with "search" behavior, the active attempts of
buyers and sellers to determine each others' identities and offers;
maximization of utility by rational actors using marginal principles
pervades these models. Stigler, the first to present such analyses,
asserted that if "the cost of search is equated to its expected
marginal return, the optimum amount of search will be found"
(1961:216). In his conception, cost of search, for a consumer, is
approximately measured by the number of sellers approached,
"for the chief cost is time" (1961:216). He does not consider how
buyers and sellers determine one anothers' identities, an issue of
particular importance in labor markets, but also with some applica-

bility to general commodity markets. Indeed, one might want to
make a clear distinction between two stages of search: 1) finding
the buyers (or sellers), and 2) determining their offers. Adapting
some comments of Rees (1966), we might call the first part the
extensive aspect of search, and the second, the intensive. This
dichotomy applies less to markets in highly standardized commodities, where the nature of an offer is as straightforward as the identity
of the person making it. But in, for example, labor markets, there
are many subtleties in the nature of a bid to employ or to offer
services, and gathering information about each such bid may be
much more time-consuming than finding out who is making bids.
In practice, a job-searcher must make a tradeoff between the
two aspects: the more people he discovers who are bidding, the less
he will be able to find out about each bid.

Of course, *some* intensive activity will precede hiring, especially
in higher level jobs. In commodity markets, the knowledge that
a given person is offering wheat at K dollars per bushel ordinarily
suffices to be sure that *you* will be able to buy it from him. At
worst, he might sell you less than you want (wheat being entirely
divisible, as classical commodities should be). But having specified
an employer offering an acceptable wage, or having found an
employee offering his labor at a price one is willing to pay, does
not by any means guarantee the consummation of the transaction.
Especially in higher-level jobs, a direct inquiry is generally felt
to be necessary, in which prospective employer and employee learn
more about each other and decide whether a job should be offered,
and if offered, accepted.

In general, measuring the costs and benefits of search poses quite
difficult problems. The proposal to consider time as the main cost
(see also McCall, 1970) is more appropriate for blue-collar workers
who cannot easily search during 9-to-5 jobs, than for PTM workers.
A very important cost for them, on the other hand, involves their
frequent use of personal contacts. In my sample, more than 80
percent of the personal contacts used not only told the respondent
about his new job, but also "put in a good word" for him. Contacts
cannot be asked to do this too often without the respondents'

using up their "credit" with them, straining the relationship. There are, moreover, as Brown points out, opportunity costs in searching for a particular job (or employee): one may necessarily forego searching for others (Brown, 1965b:187). Brown's model, similar to Stigler's in its assumptions of optimal search behavior, allows for these other costs (1965b:185-198). His formulation, however, could be operationalized only via extensive survey data.

Similar difficulties arise on the benefit side; all models found measured benefits in money terms (Stigler, 1962; Brown, 1965b; McCall, 1965, 1970). Stigler and McCall recognize that the future benefits of the present search must be taken into account. McCall interprets this primarily in terms of expected length of employment in a job; Stigler's more general formulation points out that if current price offers are correlated with future ones, information now found also has future benefits. Each suggests appropriate discounting procedures. No attempts are made, however, to specify the value in the future of holding a particularly *prestigious* job now. More relevant, even, from the point of view of my study, no attempt is made to assess the value of contacts acquired in a particular position. This may be psychologically a minor factor; many of my respondents had never realized, until the time of interview, how much of their career was mediated by personal contacts acquired in previous jobs; but the actual benefits may be considerable, as discussed later on in Chapters 5 and 6.

The primary contribution of the present study to this discussion lies in an analysis of the notion of "search," as viewed from the supply side of labor markets. Of the authors surveyed, only Brown tries to work into his theory the idea that different methods of search yield different amounts of information. Brown's idea is that job-seekers, in effect, compute costs and benefits for *each method* they might use. That method with the highest expected net benefit is used first; then all calculations are repeated, and the searcher chooses a method for his second try. Search continues until marginal benefits equal marginal cost. Time, in this model, is effectively omitted as a parameter, since after any method is used, the next time period is assumed to begin (1965b:191-198).

While this account is closer than others to my empirical findings on labor-market behavior, it is nevertheless inadequate. One of my original motives in choosing a PTM sample for study was, in fact, my interest in observing sophisticated search procedures; I assumed that if anyone would be likely to search in a careful, effective way, it would be people in PTM jobs. My results, however, lead me to doubt that information in labor markets, at least in PTM markets, *is* diffused primarily by "search."

For blue-collar markets, Reynolds holds that "the core of the effective labor supply at any time . . . consists of . . . people who are entering the market for the first time, who have been discharged, who have quit their previous jobs because of dissatisfaction, or who have been unemployed long enough for their benefit rights to be exhausted" (1951:106). It is reasonable that all such people *will* be searching for jobs, whereas those employed full-time at the blue-collar level would do so only with difficulty. Yet, Reynolds reports that 25 percent of those in his sample who changed jobs had lined up a new job before quitting, and moved to better jobs than those who quit or were discharged without having set up a new job first (1951:215). Given the 9-to-5 character of most blue-collar work it seems doubtful that those who found a new job before leaving the old one did much searching.

While PTM workers probably have more time to search, evidence indicates that this is often not the route to job-change. Brown reports that 26 percent of his sample of college professors, when asked how they found their present job, said that they "did nothing and were recruited" (1967:119). In my PTM sample, 29 percent of the respondents answered "no" to the question of whether there was a "period of time when you were actively *searching* for a new job" (before finding the current one).

Moreover, whether a respondent actively searched is systematically related to the method by which he found his job, and to the nature and quality of job obtained. Stage of career is of some importance in predicting search behavior. Table 7 indicates that those in their first job, or in sixth or subsequent jobs were most likely to have searched; the latter cases are individuals changing jobs

Table 7. Job-search activity, by career length of respondent.

Searched for present job?	Number of (full-time) jobs held in career				
	1	2–3	4–5	6–10	Total
Yes	93.3%	79.1%	62.1%	81.8%	76.5%
No	6.7%	20.9%	37.9%	18.2%	23.5%
N^{a}	15	43	29	11	98
			$p = 0.11$		

[a]Interview sample only.

Table 8. Job-search activity, by prestige of college attended by respondent.

Searched for present job?	Prestige of college granting B.A. or B.S.[a]			
	Lowest 60%	Top 10–40%	Top 10%	Total
Yes	85.1%	50.0%	63.6%	69.6%
No	14.9%	50.0%	36.4%	30.4%
N	47	24	44	115
		$p = 0.006$		

[a]The college reported by each respondent was ranked according to the index provided by Brown (1965b:333–352), based on eight factors, including percent of faculty with Ph.D.'s, faculty-student ratio, average faculty salaries, and similar measures. Since any such index is somewhat arbitrary, it seemed sensible to use one recently employed in a related study.

frequently on account of dissatisfaction. The tendency to search decreases with age; those under 34 searched in 78.6 percent of the cases, those 34 or over in 63.9 percent ($p = 0.01$).

Amount of education is unrelated to search behavior, but a measure of the prestige and quality of college attended for bachelor's degree shows interesting results. Table 8 shows that far fewer of those who attended colleges in the "top" 40 percent searched for their jobs than those in lower prestige colleges. A very similar table could be produced for the ranking of institutions granting graduate degrees to these respondents.

A first temptation is to conclude that the quality of education received in better colleges makes one more desirable afterwards; it is also possible is that those attending better schools are pre-selected, regardless of educational quality of the schools, so that they would be more likely to be sought out later. While there may be some truth in each of these ideas, I would also suggest that contacts acquired at higher prestige colleges are generally better placed in the occupational structure and will ultimately be of more help to their protegés—more likely to be in a position from which they can seek them out to offer or inform them of a job.

It is of special interest that, as shown in Table 9, higher-income jobs are less likely to go to those searching for them. Moreover, in the PTM group (see Table 10), managers are least likely to find their jobs through search, and technical workers most likely. This is

Table 9. Job-search activity, by level of income of respondent from present job.

Searched for present job?	Income				
	Less than $10,000	$10,000– 14,999	$15,000– 24,999	$25,000 or more	Total
Yes	75.7%	81.8%	61.0%	56.7%	71.4%
No	24.3%	18.2%	39.0%	43.3%	28.6%
N	74	88	77	30	269
			$p = 0.006$		

Table 10. Job-search activity, by occupational category of respondent.

Searched for present job?	Occupation			
	Professional	Technical	Managerial	Total
Yes	71.3%	85.1%	58.7%	71.0%
No	28.7%	14.9%	41.2%	29.0%
N	129	67	80	276
		$p = 0.002$		

a logical result of the greater reliance of the latter on formal means
and direct application.

How one's job was found is closely related to search behavior.
The use of formal means or direct application implies active search;
in such cases, the search does lead to the information that yields
a new job. For those finding a new job through contacts, however,
the situation is more complex. First, only 57.4 percent of these
individuals report having actively searched. Moreover, in many cases,
the job taken was not found as a result of this search. When a contact
was the source of job information, therefore, it is interesting to ask
on whose *initiative*—respondent's or contact's—the job-information
was passed. If the respondent was not searching, his contact is likely
to have taken the initiative; but this is often true also when the
respondent *was* searching, as when the contact heard through the
"grapevine" of the search, or passed the information without
knowing that any search was in progress.

For 57.9 percent of the individuals finding their new job through
contacts ($N = 157$), the interaction during which job information
was passed was, in fact, initiated by the contact. In about half *these*
cases, he knew that the respondent was looking for a new job; this
means that a little over a quarter of the time, initiative came from
someone who had not been approached and did not know whether
his friend would even be *interested*. In another 20.9 percent of the
instances, the respondent contacted his friend, asked him if he
knew of anything, and was told about the job he subsequently took;
8.3 percent of the respondents were contacted by someone they
did not know and were told that they had been recommended for a
job. The person doing the recommending turned out to be a personal
contact of the respondent. In 13.4 percent of the cases, the respondent and his personal contact were interacting for some purpose
unrelated to job information; in the course of this meeting, the
information happened to be transmitted. Some of these were
instances of "bumping into" friends on the street or at professional
meetings; others involved prearranged meetings, but for other
purposes. (The "interaction unrelated to job information" category
is probably underestimated since it was not available as a choice in

the mail sample—a few cases would be coded that way from written-in comments. Over 24 percent of interview cases fall in this classification, but only 5.5 percent of mail surveys.)

Several cases will illustrate situations in which interaction was not initiated for the purpose of passing job information:

> Case #2: Carl Y. was doing commission sales for an encyclopedia firm, but was not doing well. He decided he would have to find a different job; meanwhile, he started driving a cab to bring in extra money. One passenger asked to be taken to the train station where he had to meet a friend. This friend turned out to be an old friend of Carl Y's, and asked him "what're you doing driving a cab?" When Mr. Y. explained, the friend offered him the job he now holds—labor relations manager for a small company, owned by his friend.

> Case #3: Edward A. had graduated from high school and been in the service. After returning, he resumed his practice of driving to the local park, in the evening, where his friends hung around; bars and restaurants in the vicinity made the area a popular teen-age hangout. The usual procedure was to drive by and see if anyone was there that you knew. On one such occasion he ran into an older friend employed by an engineering firm. The friend told him that there was an opening for a draftsman in this firm; Mr. A. applied and accepted this job.

> Case #4: Franklin B. was an executive in a Philadelphia brokerage firm, which he had decided to leave. Through a contact, he received an offer in the Boston area, and was considering it. Meanwhile, he and another executive from the Philadelphia firm came to the Boston area on other business; Mr. B.'s companion suggested that they have lunch with Robert M., president of a Boston brokerage firm, simply because he would be a pleasant lunch companion. Both Mr. B. and his companion knew Mr. M. slightly from business. During lunch, Mr. B. mentioned that he might be taking a new job in Boston; afterward, Mr. M. collared him privately and made a better offer, which he subsequently accepted.

To see the relation between the various categories of initiative and the respondents' search behavior, we must ask what proportion of respondents in each initiative category reported having searched actively. These are as follows: 67.3 percent of respondents contacted by a friend who "knew" they were searching; 19.5 percent of those whose contact didn't know whether they wanted a new job; 65.0 percent in cases where respondent and contact were meeting for other purposes; 84.6 percent of respondents who were recommended by people they knew, and 75.0 percent of those who asked a friend, who then told them about the job. Two contradictions are apparent; 1) in one-third of the cases where a respondent was contacted by a friend who "knew he was looking for something new" the respondent reported he had *not* been actively searching; 2) in one-quarter of the cases where respondent *asked* a friend who told him about a job, he reported himself as not having actively searched. The difficulty apparently lies in the perception of the word "actively"; a PTM worker who is on the lookout for a new job may not consider himself to be "actively" searching—merely keeping his ears open and asking an occasional question. In contrast to blue-collar workers, it is difficult to tell when a PTM worker is "in the market."

This ambiguity may cast doubt on results obtained by use of the subjective appraisal of the respondent as to whether he was searching. It would be more objective to consider whether a given respondent received information about the job he took as the result of a search or not. We may count information as resulting from a search if the respondent used formal means or direct application, asked a friend who told him about the job, or if he was contacted by a friend who knew he was searching. If the respondent was contacted by a friend who didn't know whether he wanted a new job, learned of the job in the course of interaction with a different original purpose, or heard from someone he didn't know (to whom he had been recommended by a personal contact), then no search was involved in producing the information.

A crucial earlier finding was that those in higher-income jobs were less likely to have searched actively for them. Table 11 shows that the correlation is even stronger if we use the relatively more objective measure outlined here: the higher the income, the less likely that information about the job was found through a search.

Table 11. Relation of locating job through a search to level of income of respondent from present job.

	Income				
Information from search	Less than $10,000	$10,000– 14,999	$15,000– 24,999	$25,000 or more	Total
Yes	82.7%	80.2%	57.4%	44.4%	71.1%
No	17.3%	19.8%	42.6%	55.6%	28.9%
N	75	86	68	27	256

$$p < 0.001$$

Thus, the finding holds up under two somewhat independent measures of the significance of job search.[1]

A difficult conceptual issue here boils down to what is to be characterized as the object of "search." Presumably, a job-hunter is searching for elements of the set of all jobs which he might be invited, potentially, to fill. The employer is searching for elements of the set of all those who might be willing and able to fill the job(s) he has to offer. But do such sets exist? In certain important ways, the answer is "no." It is not generally possible to define in PTM work, who is "in the market." Partly this is because it is considered a liability to seem to be very obviously looking for something new. Many PTM workers play what Brown (1967) calls "reluctant maiden": it is suspected that those who are searching would not if they didn't *have* to, and wouldn't have to if they were good enough. But beyond this, many PTM workers cannot *say* whether they are in the market for a new job. I asked each respondent in my interview sample, "Have you recently thought about looking for a different job?" Although 38.4 percent answered that

1. Two arguments can be made against Table 11. One is that those using personal contacts are over-represented among those with high incomes and also among those not using information from a search; thus, the finding may be an artifact. It is not, however, since it holds nearly as strongly when we construct the same table, confining it to those who used contacts. The other is that those contacted by people they didn't know, to whom they had been recommended, may have been so contacted because they were searching. But when these respondents are shifted over to the "yes" category, the result remains substantially the same.

they had, only half of these indicated that they had "actually done anything along these lines." A frequent answer went something like: "Sure. You always *think* about different jobs. If you didn't, you'd be a vegetable." Nearly one in five of my sample, then, are definitely *not* searching for a new job, but are keeping their ears open for possibilities; if the right job came along, they might be convinced to take it. But how could we identify in advance which of these would be interested in a given job? Could we have identified in advance, for example, the one-third of newly hired faculty in American colleges in 1964–65 who, according to Brown (1967:47), "would not be teaching in higher education if an active recruiter had not interested them with a specific offer?"

Comparable to those not quite "in the market" but who might be drawn in under the right circumstances, are those jobs which have not been created, but could be if the right person were available to fill them. I will refer to such people and such potential jobs as quasi-searchers and quasi-jobs. In my sample, 35.3 percent of respondents reported filling jobs which had not previously existed and which represented work not being done previously, or not previously combined in the same job. Interviews suggest that roughly half of these were designed because of a specific need and that some search went on to fill them, but that about half would not have existed had the right person not come along to fill them. Little or no recruiting was done for these jobs.[2]

Is it a coincidence that the proportion of jobs being filled which are quasi-jobs is about the same as the proportion of PTM workers who are quasi-searchers—about 20 percent? If quasi-jobs which become actual ones are filled by quasi-searchers, it would be a great help for "search" models, since such jobs and men could then be segregated from the rest of the normal search process in labor markets, and their peculiar behavior analyzed separately. Evidence does not support this hypothesis, however. Sixty-five percent of

2. Of course, the numbers here are too small to be taken as more than suggestive, and the fact that this information about the demand side of the labor market came from employees rather than employers gives a further reason for caution.

those holding newly created jobs (N = 94) reported that they were
searching actively for a job before taking this one.

A very important part of labor-market behavior is thus described
inadequately by search models. This is especially significant in
view of the finding that those least involved in search behavior
are over-represented in jobs of the highest income level. Even if
search models were adequate, the habit, ingrained in economic
theory, of looking separately at the supply and demand sides of a
market would make them difficult to apply. Between jobs and
men, a *matching* process goes on, which search models do not treat
explicitly (see White 1970, ch. 8). How is the "search" of suppliers
supposed to be coordinated with that of demanders? Stigler dis-
cusses both types, while Brown and McCall confine themselves to
the problem of the workers seeking jobs. In traditional economic
analysis, supply and demand *may* be analyzed separately because
they are united via the medium of price; equilibrium prices clear
the market and render superfluous a discussion of how buyers and
sellers find one another. Of the authors surveyed, only Holt and
David (1966) attempted to explain how the searches of employees
and employers are brought together; to do so, they fell back on
the notion of price. Their idea is that those who are unemployed,
and those who control vacancies, each engage in "random" search.
Each starts out knowing what wage he will offer or accept. Those
who encounter one another are matched if the wage offered is
within the range of the acceptable wage. As workers continue to
search, they are said to reduce their wage demands, and as job-
controllers continue to search, they increase their offers (and/or
lower standards). "Stochastic equilibrium" is ultimately reached.

Unhappily, the model fails even from the standpoint of economics. Price is well-known not to behave empirically in labor
markets as described. Lester concludes that the theory "applies
rather widely to the pre-1940 situation and to some industries
still, such as agriculture, domestic service and other types of small-
scale enterprise, where seniority, promotion ladders and unions
are absent. Otherwise the theory lacks relevance" (1966a:119).
That is, employers are generally prevented by a host of institutional

constraints from adjusting wages upward and downward as jobs are easier or harder to fill.

If price does not match men with jobs, we are left with the question of what does. The argument of the present study is that the relevant factors are social; that job-finding behavior is more than a rational economic process—it is heavily embedded in other social processes that closely constrain and determine its course and results. It is the purpose of the present study to elucidate such processes. Even if these *are* exogeneous to the economic frame of reference, of course, there is no reason why they could not be used as input to an economic model.

Chapter

Contacts and Their Information

Further analysis of the use of personal contacts requires that we move beyond the respondents themselves, to ask: 1) what kind of relationships typically existed between respondents and their contacts, and 2) how these contacts were connected to the job information that they offered.

Where respondents found their current job through a personal contact, I asked: "How did you happen to know this friend?" Though responses were highly disparate, they can be reduced to two categories: 1) the person was a relative, a friend of the family, or a social friend; these I will call "family-social" contacts; 2) he was a person known from a work situation. Logically, of course, the two categories are not mutually exclusive; in practice, however, they are nearly so. In the interview survey, respondents were asked whether they ever saw their personal contact socially. In cases where the primary relationship was a working one, 88.9 percent answered "never" or "rarely." The few ambiguous cases have been coded in accordance with what seemed to be the primary aspect of the relationship—occupational or social. The issue was nearly always clearcut. "Teacher" is somewhat of an intermediate category, but is actually much closer to "work contacts," because two-thirds of those who reported using teachers as contacts are currently college professors. When high school teachers were used as contacts, some specialized field, such as art, was usually involved, and the contact again seemed primarily occupational. Hence, teachers have been classified as work contacts.

Of the individuals who found their job through a contact, 31.4 percent indicated that the contact was a family or social one; 68.7

percent named a work contact—11.8 percent a teacher, 56.9
percent other work contacts ($N = 153$). In the interview sample,
respondents were asked whether *they* had recently told anyone
they knew about a job; those who had, indicated, similarly, that
the person told was a family or social contact of *theirs* in 34.1
percent of the cases ($N = 44$). Thus, the figure for family-social
contacts seems to be fairly stable, though this is hardly a conclusive
test.

While this result may be congruent with a general expectation
that, in PTM work, family and social contacts are not as useful as in
less "modernized" sectors of the economy, such a conclusion should
not be drawn until comparable data are available for blue-collar
workers. Actually, it is hard to know what baseline to use for
comparison, since the sociological or economic theories currently
in use afford only vague predictions on such matters.

Some insight may be gained, however, by comparing the incidence of various categories of contact in different subgroups of
the sample. Table 12 shows that those who are younger, who grew
up in Massachusetts, and whose job is located in Newton or a contiguous town, are considerably more likely to use family-social
contacts. All three groups are comparatively badly placed in the
metropolitan Boston job market.

Younger workers, whose careers are still taking shape, have not
yet acquired as large a number of professional colleagues who can be
of assistance as have those who have been working fifteen or thirty
years. In Chapter 1 we saw that younger PTM workers are less likely,
in general, to use personal contacts. Now we see that when they do,
the contacts are more likely to be friends and relatives than professional ones. The effect is even stronger if we divide the sample
into those holding first jobs, and those holding subsequent ones:
63.6 percent of the former used family-social contacts; for the latter,
the figure is 26.8 percent ($N = 67$, interview sample only).

That natives of Massachusetts are more likely to have used
family-social contacts seems plausible; those who have left their
home state may have left most of their extended family behind,
and not yet established firm social ties in Newton. This is especially

Table 12. Proportion of sample subgroups finding job through family-social contacts.

Subgroup	Used family-social contacts	Total	N^a	p
Those whose age is—		31.6%	152	0.15
Under 34	38.0%			
34 or over	25.9%			
Those who grew up in—		31.6%	152	0.004
Massachusetts	47.6%			
Other states in North	17.8%			
South and West	28.6%			
Outside U.S.	11.1%			
Those whose job is—		31.4%	153	n.s.[b]
In Newton or contiguous	41.0%			
In Boston-Cambridge	30.0%			
In another community in Massachusetts	25.0%			
Outside Massachusetts	0.0%			

[a]Includes only respondents finding current job through contacts.
[b]Significance levels of 0.20 or less are reported; otherwise n.s. (= not significant) is indicated.

likely since most non-natives in this sample are recent migrants. Nevertheless, literature on working-class patterns might lead us to expect something different. In "chain migration" (MacDonald and MacDonald, 1964), individuals move to another area in the train of others—family and social contacts—who have moved there before them, and who smooth the way in finding housing and employment. This kind of migration appears, then, to be atypical of the upper-middle class.[1]

I would argue that what this finding reflects is the tendency of the more provincial members of the sample, in the sense of being

1. Controlling age and income does not affect the tendency of Massachusetts natives to use such contacts more often: it is nearly as strong in the older half of the sample as the younger, and even stronger among the upper half in income than the lower half. It can therefore, not be an artifact of heavy incidence of Massachusetts birth among the young or low-income members of the sample, though such incidence exists.

tied to a local area, to make use of family and social contacts. This suggestion is further supported by the finding that those working locally are most likely to have been channeled to their job via this route. An important question is whether this provincialism is related to the desirability of one's labor-market position.

First, it is of interest that 38.8 percent of those who reported searching actively for their present job used family-social contacts, as compared to 21.2 percent of those who reported no such search ($p = 0.03$).[2] This suggests that the use of family or social contacts is less natural than that of other types; it is more likely to be resorted to in situations where there is time pressure. Those who searched actively probably had some good reason to do so; it can be assumed that, compared to those who found their present job without a search, they were more reluctant to remain in their previous job, or did not have the option. (For example, only 11 percent of the sample reported a period of time between their previous and current jobs when they were not working. Of those who searched, however, 15.4 percent reported such a period, but only 1.4 percent of those who did not search ($N = 237; p = 0.003$). More directly, 70.0 percent of those who reported this period of unemployment, compared to 28.6 percent of those who did not, had used family-social contacts ($N = 136; p = 0.02$; counting only those who used contacts). Under the circumstances it is not surprising that they would turn to individuals closer to them, who would be more motivated to help. When there is less pressure, information through work contacts is more common.

Two further findings support the hypothesis that those with access to better jobs are more likely to use work contacts: these concern education and income. Educational level makes no difference until we reach the people who hold doctorates or law degrees; 18.9 percent of them, but 38.0 percent of others, used family-social contacts ($N = 153$, $p = 0.007$). There is also a strong tendency for the use of family-social contacts to decrease as the prestige of college

2. Alternatively, 70.2 percent of those using family-social contacts were actively searching compared to 50.0 percent of those using work contacts.

Table 13. Type of personal contact, by level of income of respondent from present job.

Type of contact	Income				
	$10,000 or less	$10,000– 14,999	$15,000– 24,999	$25,000 or more	Total
Family-social	42.9%	28.6%	30.4%	20.0%	31.3%
Work	57.1%	71.4%	69.6%	80.0%	68.7%
N	35	49	46	20	150
		p = n.s.[a]			

[a]Significance levels of 0.20 or less are reported; otherwise n.s. (= not significant) is indicated.

awarding B.A. increases. (For the basis of prestige measurements, see Table 8.) Table 13 shows that jobs in the lowest income category are most likely, and those in the highest, least likely to have been found through family-social contacts.[3]

Having established some findings concerning the relationship between respondent and contact, I will now trace the connection between contact and job information, but it will first be useful to make further distinctions within the category "work contacts." This category can be subclassified into: 1) employers, including

3. One interesting finding may be added to the above discussion—it seems unrelated. I indicated in the previous chapter that none of the major three religious groups was more likely than the others to use personal contacts. However, when we confine ourselves to those who found their jobs through contacts, Jewish respondents are more likely to use family-social contacts than are Protestants or Catholics (36.5 percent as against 30.2 percent and 27.1 percent). Common assumptions about the importance of family ties and close-knit community structure in Jewish culture may help explain this. It is all the more remarkable when one considers that Jews in this sample are generally *over*-represented in those categories of people prone to use work-contacts; they are the least likely of the religious groups to work in Newton (and contiguous cities), least likely to be holding first jobs, most likely to hold a Ph.D. or LL.B., most likely to have earned a B.A. from a high-prestige college, and, as a group, show the highest average income and age of the three. Only in the proportion who have grown up in Massachusetts (50.0 percent, compared to 27.3 percent of Protestants and 60.2 percent of Catholics,) do Jews not fall into the category that leads one to expect heavy use of work contacts.

direct supervisors; for the mail survey, this was coded from the
response "I once worked under him"; 2) colleagues within the
same company; 3) colleagues in different companies and 4) teachers.
These accounted for 21, 36, 25.7 and 17.3 percent, ($N = 105$)
respectively, of all work contacts.[4]

Respondents were asked, in all cases where contacts were used,
how the contact knew about the job. 33.1 percent indicated that
the contact was the new employer himself; 37.7 percent said that
the contact knew by virtue of working in the same firm where
the job opened up, though not as employer; 19.9 percent described
his knowledge as resulting from being a "business friend of the
employer." Other answers accounted for 9.3 percent remaining.
Table 14 shows, for each type of personal contact, how the contact
knew about the job. Important sequences can be partially reconstructed from this table. Consider first those whose contacts were
employers (in some job previous to the current one). It is clear
enough in such cases how the respondent was initially related to the
contact person. It can also be seen that in two-thirds of such cases,
compared to less than one-third, in general, these former employers
knew about the new job because they were again the employer. This
is sensible enough, since former employers are likely to be of higher
status and position than other kinds of contacts, and thus more
likely to be in a position to offer new jobs. The question of how the
new employer knew about the new job does not, by definition,
arise, making this the most straightforward possible sequence.[5]

Colleagues from different companies are also especially likely to
transmit job information *qua* employer. While this finding is

4. This may be misleading, however; in the mail survey, the answer "I once
worked with him" was interpreted to mean as colleague in the same company.
In only 10.4 percent of the cases of work contacts did a mail respondent
make it clear that the person was working in a different company; in the
interview survey, by contrast, 50 percent of work contacts were colleagues
from different firms. Thus, the figure given here probably underestimates the
proportion of work contacts not working in the same company as the
respondent, when the relationship was operative.

5. This situation is different from the category "returned to previous
employer" often found in blue-collar studies, in that respondents here are not
returning to a *company* previously worked for; rather, the former employer
has changed companies.

Table 14. Contact's connection to job information, by type of contact.

Contact's connection	Family-social	Work				Total
		Contact was teacher	Contact was employer	Colleague in same company	Colleague in different company	
Worked in company where job opened up	47.8%	11.1%	4.8%	62.9%	38.5%	39.0%
Was employer	17.4%	33.3%	66.7%	14.3%	50.0%	31.5%
Was business friend of employer	19.6%	44.4%	23.8%	11.4%	11.5%	19.9%
Other	15.2%	11.1%	4.8%	11.4%	0 %	9.6%
N	46	18	21	35	26	146

$p < 0.001$

somewhat problematical, it may be that higher status people are more likely to be the ones who develop contacts outside their own company. Their concerns are more general, requiring them to deal with the environment of the organization more frequently than those with a more restricted purview. This would accord with a general finding in sociological studies that individuals of higher status have wider social contacts (Homans, 1950:144–145).

Former teachers of my respondents were especially likely to pass information gained by being "business colleagues" of the employer. Since "former teachers" consists mostly of college teachers, this is readily explicable in terms of the tendency of professors to align themselves more with members of their own field than with any particular institution at which they happen currently to find themselves. Thus their awareness of the employment situation in other departments in their field is much greater than is the knowledge of the members of most organizations about the situation in other organizations. Research on "professionalization" might lead us to expect this pattern generally for professionals, more than for technical or managerial personnel. (See Blau and Scott, 1962:60–74, 244–247.)

Especially interesting in Table 14 is the strong tendency of family-social contacts to be passing on job information obtained more because of proximity to the situation—working in the same company—than because of any particular control over it. This accords with my argument above that use of family and social contacts is, in some sense, a less natural method than use of work contacts. One winds up, even when the method works, having to settle for information that is not really from the "inside," and may eventuate in a less lucrative placement than if work contacts had been available.

While family-social contacts may not, *in general*, lead to the best jobs or be the most efficient type of contact, they do appear to be highly satisfactory in some cases. There is evidence, for instance, that such contacts are especially likely to have been used when an individual has made a major change in his *type* of work. (Because of the small number of such cases in this sample, this relationship is

reported only as being suggestive.) The following cases, which
resulted in satisfying outcomes for the respondents, illustrate the
point:

Case #5 (Pilot Study): George C. was working as a technician for an
electrical firm, with a salary of about $8000, and little apparent
chance for advancement. While courting his future wife, he met her
downstairs neighbor, the manager of a candy shop, a concession
leased from a national chain. After they were married, Mr. C.
continued to see him when visiting his mother-in-law. The neighbor
finally talked him into entering a trainee program for the chain,
and arranged an interview for him. Within three years, Mr. C. was
earning nearly $30,000, in this business. (He found his story as
remarkable as I did, saying: "Every morning I pinch myself to see if
it's still true!")

Case #6: Herman D. was the owner of a fruit and vegetable store,
which he sold (at age 45) because of ill health. He took a vacation;
meanwhile his brother, a business executive, attended a meeting
where a colleague mentioned that he was looking for someone to do
inventory management. Mr. D. had done similar work before buying
his store, and his brother therefore suggested him. He was hired
several days later.

Case #7: Gerald F. was a salesman for a wholesale liquor distributor.
A friend who was a doctor asked him if we would be interested in
managing a nursing home, and if so, to put together a resume. One
of the references Mr. F. used for the resume was his wife's cousin,
owner of a fashionable antique shop. When the nursing home job
didn't come through, the wife's cousin, now aware that Mr. F.
was considering changing jobs, offered him a job as business manager
of his shop, which he accepted.

It is not surprising that a major change in type of work would
not be mediated through work contacts. The people one meets in
the course of his work are naturally those in roughly similar or
perhaps complementary lines of work. Opportunities they are able
to make possible are highly likely to involve more or less similar
activities to those one already is engaged in. Social and family
contacts, on the other hand, may have little in common occupa-
tionally. Laumann found, for instance, in an intensive study of

friendship patterns in Cambridge, Massachusetts, that "a relative reported as a friend is more likely to be higher or lower in status (not in the same occupational category) than the respondent, whereas a nonrelative reported as a friend is more likely to be in the same occupational category as the respondent" (1966:70).

The most general formulation would suggest that one's probability of making a major occupational change is roughly proportional to the percentage of one's personal contacts who are in occupations different, in a major way, from one's own. Any basis for personal relationship other than occupational activity increases the proportion of such friends; kinship is one example of this phenomenon, and as such, it may remain rather important in a society where the common assumption is that kinship has declined in its economic functions. Social acquaintance on any basis other than occupational should serve a similar function. Friends from fraternal organizations, sports, recreational or hobby groups, neighborhood, college or summer vacations, to name a few possibilities, may all be expected to be over-represented as the operative personal contacts in major changes of work type.

Chapter

3

The Dynamics of Information Flow

Having described the nature of the connections between respondent and contact, and between contact and job-information,
I must now pay closer attention to those factors that activate
and/or facilitate the flow of information through these channels.
The economist S. Ozga (1960) has proposed the model of information flow in market structures which comes closest to my findings.
His assumptions are quite different from those of other economists
described in Chapter 1, who posit that information moves via
search: he assumes, rather, that it moves entirely by diffusion
through social processes *unrelated* to market behavior. Each person is
assumed to pass the relevant information to some fixed proportion
of all those with whom he has contact; random mixing is assumed
in the population—that is, the probability of telling someone who
already "knows" is exactly equal to the proportion in the group
who already do "know" (1960:31). (This implies that the people
who have told *you* are no more likely to have told your friends
than anyone else in the population; but since people who are
friends have more overlap in their acquaintance circles than those
who are not, the assumption is an idealization [See Rapoport
1963] .) Given this fixed proportion, and the number who "know"
initially, it is easy to compute, by differential equations, the
number who will "know" after a given time period. Under these
assumptions, the entire group will ultimately receive the piece of
information in question, the time elapsed before this depending on
values of the two parameters.

The model is made more realistic by adding population growth
and attrition to the analysis. Ozga shows that even if advertising

is introduced to offset the influx of new, ignorant members and the outflow of those *with* the information, imperfect markets *necessarily* result—that is, in the more realistic model, there is no tendency for the information, even theoretically, to reach the entire population. The proportion reached depends on the relative values of the four rates: population growth and attrition, information spread, and advertising. He proceeds to indicate how his ideas can be integrated into the standard supply-demand, marginal analysis of neoclassical economics.

This account agrees with mine in that rather than being mediated by search, I find that much labor-market information actually *is* transmitted as a byproduct of other social processes. But the model probably would work better (and is, indeed, intended) for commodity markets than for labor. There, one can make rough assumptions like that of people passing on information about commodities to a fixed proportion of all contacts; in labor markets, however, it seems clear that much of the information passed is clearly earmarked for a given person, rather than being spread at random. In labor markets, moreover, the time dimension in Ozga's process is truncated. Most products continue over a substantial period to be offered at a similar price, so that his equations, predicting the ultimate proportion hearing of them, may run their course. But once a *job* is taken, information about it no longer is of interest or value, and, in practice, only a tiny proportion of those who might plausibly fill any given job ever hear of it.

We must, therefore, begin to ask specific questions about under what circumstances people are *motivated* to give job information to their friends, and whether some of one's contacts are more "strategically" placed to provide information than others. These two questions interact. A natural *a priori* idea might be, for instance, that those with whom one has strong ties would be more motivated to help with job information. There is, however, a structural tendency for those to whom one is only *weakly* tied, to have better access to job information one does not already have. Acquaintances, as compared to close friends, are more prone to move in different circles than one's self. Those to whom one is closest are likely to have the greatest overlap in contact with those one already knows, so that the information to which they are privy is likely to be much the same as that which one already has (Laumann and Schuman, 1967; Rapoport and Horvath, 1961).

Rapoport and Horvath (1961) have shown that, other things being equal, information transmitted via weak ties would ultimately reach a larger number of people than if sent through strong ties; people strongly tied to each other would pass the information to the same people, given their greater overlap of contacts. The point is not that job information passed through weak ties reaches a larger number of people; usually it is earmarked fairly specifically for one person. But the number of people who are *potential* recipients of job information is greater when weak ties are involved, so that we would expect such ties to be especially useful.

Although it is difficult to talk precisely about the strength of an interpersonal tie, we may take as a crude measure of that strength the amount of time spent together by the two people.[1] Respondents in my survey were asked how often they saw their personal contact around the time that he passed on job information to them. (It is possible, of course, that someone who is not seen very often *now* was once a close friend, and that the tie is still perceived as much stronger than a contact-frequency measure would suggest. Relations of adults with parents are typical of this situation. My impression from interviews, however, is that few or none of the cases reported here fall into this category.)

I have used the following categories for frequency of contact: "often"—at least twice a week; "occasionally"—more than once a year but less than twice a week; "rarely"—once a year or less. Of those in the interview sample who found their job through contacts, 16.7 percent reported that they were seeing their contact "often," 55.6 percent "occasionally," while 27.8 percent saw him "rarely" ($N = 54$). The skew is to the weak side of the continuum. Moreover, those who found their job through weaker ties reported much more

1. A more comprehensive definition, and discussion of the relation of weak ties to information flow is given in my paper "The Strength of Weak Ties" (1973).

often that their contacts "put in a good word" for them, as well as telling them about the job. *All* of those who saw their contact "rarely;" 89.7 percent of those who saw him occasionally; and 66.7 percent of those who saw him often indicated that he did so ($N = 53, p = 0.04$). This is a clear indication of the primacy of structure over motivation; close friends might indeed have been more *disposed* than acquaintances to use influence, but were simply less often in a position to do so.

The paradox that acquaintances are more likely to pass job information than close friends is partly resolved by the finding that when weak ties are used, respondents are not likely to be under any particular pressure. None of those who saw their contact rarely reported a period of unemployment between their present and previous job; but 4.2 percent of those seeing him occasionally and 20 percent of those seeing him often report such a period ($N = 50$, $p = .07$). When a respondent was in real job trouble, therefore, close friends were more likely than acquaintances to have helped him with job-information. Users of strong ties are also likely to be younger than those using weak ties. Partly this is because they are more prone to family-social contacts, which are generally stronger than work contacts.

Aside from other reasons so far cited, there may also be a general reluctance to find work through close friends because it would complicate and strain the relationship too much. One respondent who, after being urged for some years, did finally take a job in a close friend's company, explained that he had held off for so long because his new boss "was a friend, and I wanted to keep it that way."[2]

2. An alternative reason to expect predominance of weak ties in transfer of job information has been suggested to me by Donald Light. He points out that if most of the people one knows are acquaintances, we would expect, on a random model, that most of those passing job information would also be acquaintances. Base-line data on acquaintance nets of individuals are lacking, so that this must remain inconclusive. But even if the premise is correct, one might expect nevertheless that greater motivation of close friends would overcome their being outnumbered. Different assumptions would yield different "random models"; it is not clear which one should be accepted as a starting point.

One might, at this point, reasonably wonder what *does* motivate the passing of job information, if not the strength of interpersonal ties. Respondents did not really know what to say to this question; usually they simply felt their informant was just "being nice"; one asked: "didn't you ever want to do a favor for somebody?" There is no reason to doubt that such motivations do exist; but they exist in a context. At the minimal level of self-interest, those offering information about jobs related to their own are presumably offering them to individuals they would *like* to work with. If, as in many organizations, there is internal factionalism, those passing job information may be attempting to recruit allies.

More generally, those who are able to recruit competent personnel may find their reputations enhanced; they will appear to be people who know how to get things done. Tangible rewards may sometimes be involved: in times of short labor supply, employees often receive "bounties" for recruitment. One respondent reported that his informant was fund-raising for a large organization, and that if the employer to whom he had referred him (the respondent) was happy with his work, and that of others sent to him by this route, he would be more easily convinced to make a substantial contribution. Aside from reputation and reward, a general sense of efficacy is involved; one person who makes a habit of passing on job information was referred to as the "kind of guy who likes to put people in places."

The above discussion can be put in a more macroscopic perspective by looking at the flow of a particular piece of information from its origins—in this case, with a prospective employer—to its destination, the subsequent job-incumbent. We can imagine tracing, for each person finding his job through personal contacts, the chain through which the information reached him; that is, if the employer told A that there was a job opening, and A told B who told C who told D who told my respondent, we have a chain with four intermediaries between origin and destination. I will argue that the number of intermediaries is an important parameter in the process, and will henceforth designate it by the expression "chain length."

(Coding rules for chain length must deal with certain ambiguities. An account of these, and of the rules adopted, may be found in Appendix B.)

In the first instance, chain length gives a rough, conservative estimate of how many people have *ever* heard of the job opening filled by my respondent. If we assume that each person in such an information chain tells some fixed number of other people about the job he has heard about—call this number "N"—and if the chain is of length L, as defined above, then the number of people who finally hear about the job, including the employer, is the partial sum of a geometric series: $1 + N + N^2 + N^3 + \ldots N^{L+1} = (1 - N^{(L+2)})/(1 - N)$. This increases very fast, so that if the chain is of length five, and each person tells three others *who have not already heard* (a crucial assumption), more than a thousand people will have heard. If four people are told by each person, the total exceeds 5000. With $L = 8$ and $N = 5$, more than a million people receive the information. In real social networks, of course, some of the people told will have already heard from others. In addition, since, as I have argued, job information tends to be specifically earmarked for particular people, the assumption of a fixed number hearing at each remove is dubious. But if (as I will show below) the degree of "earmarking" is substantially less in long chains, the overall qualitative conclusion will still be correct: job information in long chains will reach much larger numbers of people than that passed through short chains.[3]

One reason to be interested in how many people hear about given job openings is that some comparisons then become possible with the perfect labor market of economic theory. That theory proposes no mechanism to account for the presumed wide spread of information in the labor market. Only two possibilities seem open: 1) mass media—including newspapers, radio-television, and public employ-

3. It was beyond my scope to attempt directly to find out, for particular jobs, how many such people there were; this would not be a simple number to find. The present measure is conservative because, as shown below, few individuals actually *find* their jobs through long chains; thus a study considering only chains by which people do find jobs has a built-in bias against long ones, as well as against any other unsuccessful ones.

ment services; and 2) diffusion of information through long chains of personal contact. In the United States, the mass media clearly do not fulfill this role. It is therefore interesting to ask to what extent long chains might.

A priori, it is perfectly plausible to suppose that many cases resemble the following one:

Case #8f: Karl E. is an engineer just out of college. His father, also an engineer, heard from a colleague that there was an opening in a nearby company. The colleague had heard about this opening from a salesman who had visited that company and heard of it from a secretary. The secretary had heard from the employer. K.E. applied, and was later accepted for the job.

This is an example of a chain of length four; it is fabricated, however, since *no chains as long as four were found in my study* (interview data only). Chains of length zero accounted for 39.1 percent of the cases; 45.3 percent had length one, and 12.5 percent length two; chains longer than two accounted for 3.1 percent of the cases ($N = 64$).[4]

It is interesting to examine the characteristics of search procedure and jobs obtained according to length of information chain; if perfect labor markets actually could be achieved via long chains, as the predominant case, this analysis would give us some inkling of

4. Since all information was collected from the respondents themselves, and not from their personal contacts, or others along the chains, some bias against the finding of long chains is introduced. If a chain were actually of length six, for instance, it is unlikely that a respondent would know more details than the identity of the person from whom his personal contact got the information. The exact length could not be coded without interviewing further along this chain of information flow; I have coded such chains as simply "greater than two." In a pilot study, I found that it was possible to interview, by telephone, everyone along the information chain until the actual employer was reached. A complete account of information flow, along with many interesting details not otherwise available, can be gotten in this way; at each step, respondents are surprisingly unreluctant to divulge the name of the next link. But I did not have the time or resources to follow this procedure in my overall study. It is likely that the bias introduced is small, since in nearly all cases respondents were able to supply enough detail to leave no doubt that almost all information chains are of length 0–2; in such cases, it seems reasonable that respondents *would* be able to give a detailed and accurate account.

Table 15. Relation of length of information chain to certain characteristics of respondents.

Proportion of each chain-length category who–	Chain length				
	0	1	2 or more	*N*	*p*
Are under age 34	28.0	48.3	60.0	64	0.15
Are very satisfied with job	76.0	53.6	40.0	63	0.08
Are in lowest income group (less than $10,000)	16.0	25.0	30.0	63	n.s.[a]
Searched for job	48.0	72.4	77.8	63	0.11
Have recently thought about looking for a new job	20.0	34.5	70.0	64	0.02
Are unemployed between jobs	0.0	8.7	20.0	55	0.12

[a]Significance levels of 0.20 or less are reported; otherwise n.s. (= not significant) is indicated.

what such markets would look like. Table 15 shows that those in longer chains are younger, more dissatisfied, more poorly paid, more likely to have searched for the job held (and to be considering leaving it), and more likely to have been unemployed before taking the present job.

As these differences might lead us to suspect, different kinds of processes are involved in chains of different lengths. In one-chains or longer, for instance, family-social contacts are much more likely to have been used than in zero-chains; moreover, personal influence is more likely to be exerted in short chains. All of those in zero-chains said that their contact had "put in a good word" for them, 96.3 percent of those in one-chains, but only 60.0 percent of those in two-chains or more ($N = 62, p = 0.001$). This is partly tautological: a zero-chain means that the respondent's contact was the employer, who is here counted as having "put in a good word" with himself. But the large difference between one-chains and others is not attributable to this definition. Nor is it surprising that those contacts who have gotten information in a more roundabout way are less likely to be in a position to exert any influence.

This situation is indeed closer to the ideal market of economic theory: information is transmitted free of influence on the recruiting process.

In brief, those using long information chains are less well placed in the labor market than those using short ones. As we put together their profile, it seems that finding jobs through long chains is more like finding them by formal means than by contacts. In an important sense, we can say that formal means are the limiting case of long chains of contacts; the longer the chains, the more people hear, and the less important any particular tie between individuals is in the transmission of the information. As with rumors, which move through long chains, it matters little from *whom* I hear the rumor since it is being so widely transmitted that I am likely to hear it from others even if I don't hear from some *particular* person. It becomes like formal means also because the process is less likely to involve influence. Just as reading about a job in the newspaper affords me no recommendation in applying for it, neither does it to have heard about it fifth-hand.

Thus, the two ways suggested earlier as mechanisms for labor markets to approach perfection—mass media and long chains—both entail similar search procedures and degrees of job satisfaction for those using them. Unless radical steps were taken to eliminate features attendant to those mechanisms that *could* establish perfection of markets, few in those markets would find the situation to their liking.

Chains of length two present an interesting intermediate case between those of length zero and one, where the direct contacts of the respondent are of prime importance, and the longer chains that are not so different from formal means. As such they deserve closer scrutiny. The following cases of two-chains present useful illustrative material:

Case #9: Lawrence F. was a pediatrician in private practice. A small hospital decided that it wanted to open a pediatrics section, and asked a doctor who occasionally consulted with them on related problems to recommend someone to head such a section. He didn't know of anyone, but suggested that they ask a friend of his,

teaching at a large hospital nearby. The friend recommended
Lawrence F., and urged him to take the job; (Dr. F. had been
trained under him). He did so.

Case #10: Norman H. was about to finish a Ph.D degree in land
economics. A Boston area university had received a foundation grant
with which to hire several faculty members in this area. When a
foundation representative came for a site visit, they asked him if he
could suggest potential candidates. He suggested that they contact
an acquaintance of his who was chairman of the economics department at Mr. H.'s university, as he would be familiar with younger
candidates. The chairman recommended Norman H., who subsequently took one of these positions.

Organizations moving into new areas are less closely connected,
socially, to the relevant networks of individuals for the positions
to be filled; they are thus likely to need more intermediaries to
bridge the social-structural gaps. To the extent that their information
chains become longer, the procedure comes to resemble the use of,
say, advertising. The two-chain produces candidates about whom
their information can be trusted better than if the candidates came
with no introduction at all, but about whom more could be known
with confidence if they had come recommended directly by the
person initially asked. One knows roughly how well to trust the
recommendation of the person one initially asks for one, and also
to what extent that person is likely to feel obligated to recommend
only someone especially well qualified. One knows neither of these
for friends of the first person, with the same degree of confidence.
With still another intermediary—chain length three—the feeling of
confidence in a recommendation might well be little more than if
the candidate had answered an advertisement.

Similar comments apply to the individual hearing of a job-opening
through a two-chain: the degree of confidence he has in what he is
told about the job may be more than if he had found it through
an impersonal intermediary, but the fact remains that no one whom
he knows personally has direct inside information to offer him in
this case. (This will be mitigated, to some extent, if the organization
is well-known and can be judged by "objective" criteria.)

The strength of one's tie to one's personal contact is also related to chain length. Of those using contacts they had seen rarely, none reported chains of length greater than one, whereas 14.3 percent of those who saw their contacts occasionally, and 37.5 percent of those seeing them often, reported two-chains or more ($N = 51$, $p = .09$). If it is correct that one has a greater potential exposure to information through weak ties than through strong ones, this pattern would be expected. The following examples are suggestive:

Case #11: While a graduate student in chemistry, Mark G. heard from a close friend that a local junior college was opening a natural sciences department. His friend had heard this from a girl he knew slightly, at a party; the girl taught English at the junior college. He applied, was interviewed and hired.

Case #12: Robert K. was an engineer at firm X. A close friend of his, also working at X, told him that an acquaintance working at firm W had said that anyone who wanted to switch jobs should contact him, and he would set up an interview with the employer. Mr. K. did so, and later took a job at W.

In both cases, information was passed through an acquaintance of a close friend of the respondent. If we consider those strongly tied to each other to be roughly in the same information pool, an equivalence class with respect to the diffusion of information, and those weakly tied to one another to be in different information pools, it would follow that those receiving information from close friends would tend to be in longer chains. In a certain structural sense, these two-chains can be considered one-chains, if we count as a link only the transmission of information between acquaintances and not between close friends.[5]

This reduction scheme is a reasonable device if we want to use chain length to estimate the number of people who ultimately hear

5. Ideally one would want to make this distinction according to whether one's friend had a substantial number of ties to individuals one did not know, or was mostly tied to the same people as one's self. The strength of tie is merely an indicator of this, but may be useful since it is generally impractical to collect the necessary detailed social network data.

about a given job, since it takes into account the fact that telling
some close friend will result in much less spread of the information
than if an acquaintance were informed. Such a method might be
one way to handle the difficult problem of estimating the damping
effect of an overlap of friendship circles on the otherwise exponential
growth of number of people entering some diffusion process. Chain
length, conceived in this way, bears an interesting and perhaps useful
relation to "social distance," as this is usually thought of.

Chapter

The Dynamics of Vacancy Structure

In this last chapter on short-term causation, it is useful to shift attention to the fact that one cannot enter a job that is already filled. We can ask, therefore, how the jobs filled by my respondents came to be vacated, or if new jobs, created. Broadly speaking, such an analysis need not be confined to the short term. Whether there exist vacancies or new jobs in a given industry depends on economic conditions over varying periods of time—especially on patterns of demand, investment, and training. These general trends, however, are unlikely to predict the existence of a vacancy in any *specific* job. This problem is attacked by White (1970) in a monograph on "vacancy chains." He conceives the appearance of a job-vacancy to draw in a new incumbent, who thus generates another vacancy in his previous job, which in turn draws in another incumbent, and so on, until some vacancy is filled by someone who, for whatever reason, does not leave one behind; the chain of vacancies is then ended. The model assumes that each position has as unique an identity as does the man who fills it. The creation of a job or the death (or retirement) of a man begins a vacancy chain; the "death" of a job or recruitment of a man from outside the system of jobs in question ends one.

The opening of any vacancy in the chain is due, in a clear causal sense, to the initial event in the chain; yet, it is highly unlikely that those filling such vacancies will be aware of this sequence. One may know that he is replacing K, and may even know that K left that job to replace L. The identity of M, the person replaced by L, is highly unlikely to be known. Similarly, one may know who replaces him in the job left, but probably not who replaces the

63

replacement, and so on. A specific analytical effort is thus required
to reconstruct these chains of causality.

It would have been possible, in principle, to trace in detail the
vacancy chains in which my respondents were involved, especially
to see where they began, thus determining, in one sense of immediate cause, how their current job was opened. This procedure was
beyond my scope, however, and I will thus limit myself to a discussion of the jobs that they took and the ones that they left.

Each respondent was asked about the vacancy status of his
current job; the answers fell into three categories: 1) the respondent was replacing a particular person; 2) there were several jobs
of the same type and the respondent's job was still another which
was added on to these; and 3) the respondent was the first person
to hold this particular job. Only in the first case can the respondent's
mobility be said to have been caused by events in a vacancy chain.
Proportions falling into each of the three categories are 44.9
percent, and 19.9 percent and 35.3 percent, respectively ($N = 272$).
Brown, in his study of all college professors entering jobs in 1964–
65, found similar figures: He found that 41 percent of vacancies
were due to a predecessor's leaving, while 43 percent of jobs were
newly created (1967:28). Such figures may be especially dependent
on general economic conditions. One would guess, for instance,
that the lower the level of aggregate demand, the higher the proportion of jobs that would be direct replacements. The proportion
of new jobs in a system would also depend on the rate of technological change; the field of computer science has, for example,
generated a new type of expertise, and thus continues to provide
new types of jobs.

Certain properties of jobs and incumbents also affect the
incidence of new-job creating. Table 16 shows that managers are
more likely than technical or professional personnel to have new
jobs created for them, and that professionals are most likely to be
directly replacing individuals in a distinct position. White's data are
drawn entirely from professionals—clergymen—and it may be that
vacancy-chain analysis is especially relevant for professionals.
Tables 17 through 19 show that the older the respondent, the

Table 16. Origin of job, by occupational category of respondent.

| | Occupation | | | |
Origin of job	Professional	Technical	Managerial	Total
Direct replacement	53.8%	26.2%	45.5%	44.9%
Added on	16.9%	40.0%	7.8%	19.9%
Newly created	29.2%	33.8%	46.8%	35.3%
N	130	65	77	272
	$p < 0.001$			

Table 17. Origin of job, by age of respondent.

| | Age | | |
Origin of job	Under 34	34 or over	Total
Direct replacement	51.5%	38.1%	44.8%
Added on	26.5%	13.4%	20.0%
Newly created	22.1%	48.5%	35.2%
N	136	134	270
	$p < 0.001$		

smaller his firm, and the higher his income, the more likely he is, in each case, to be holding a newly created job. The way a respondent found out about his new job tells us a surprising amount about its vacancy status. The most likely way to find a job involving direct replacement is to apply directly to a company: 58 percent of jobs found this way are replacement jobs. Jobs added on can most probably be found by formal means: 31.4 percent of jobs found formally are added on. One's best chance of finding a job newly created is by using personal contacts: 43.8 percent of jobs found through contacts are newly created. (Cf. Table 3 and the discussion on pp. 12–13).

Table 20 analyzes, for those who found their job through personal contacts, the effect of the occasion upon which information was passed. New jobs were most likely to be created either when the personal contact took the initiative and didn't know

Table 18. Origin of job, by size of firm in which respondent is employed.

| Origin of job | Number of employees in firm | | | |
	Less than 20	20–99	100 or more	Total
Direct replacement	37.3%	46.3%	45.1%	43.1%
Added on	13.4%	17.9%	29.7%	21.3%
Newly created	49.3%	35.8%	25.3%	35.6%
N	67	67	91	225

$$p = 0.02$$

Table 19. Origin of job, by level of income from present job of respondent.

| Origin of job | Income | | | | |
	Less than $10,000	$10,000–14,999	$15,000–24,999	$25,000 or more	Total
Direct replacement	62.3%	40.4%	37.7%	36.7%	44.9%
Added on	21.7%	25.8%	16.9%	0 %	19.2%
Newly created	15.9%	33.7%	45.5%	63.3%	35.8%
N	69	89	77	30	265

$$p < 0.001$$

whether the respondent was looking for a new job, or when the respondent and his contact were meeting for purposes *other* than the exchange of job information (including accidental meetings). This corresponds roughly to the category of people, discussed in Chapter 1, who received job information not connected to a search.[1]

We may guess that when an employer has a *new* job in mind, one involving work not currently being done, or being done by several

---

1. The "roughness" of the correspondence is due to ambiguity as to whether to classify those in category 5 as having information related to a search or not. This point is discussed on p. 36 above.

Table 20. Origin of job, by nature of information–passing occasion.

Origin of job	Category of occasion[a]					Total
	(1)	(2)	(3)	(4)	(5)	
Direct replacement	55.1%	39.0%	21.1%	25.8%	53.8%	40.5%
Added on	8.2%	14.6%	10.5%	35.5%	7.7%	15.7%
Newly created	36.7%	46.3%	68.4%	38.7%	38.5%	43.8%
N	49	41	19	31	13	153

$$p = 0.009$$

[a]Categories are as follows:

(1) Contact approached respondent; knew he was searching.

(2) Contact approached respondent; didn't know he wanted new job.

(3) Contact and respondent met for purpose other than exchange of job information.

(4) Respondent asked contact about job.

(5) Stranger approached respondent on recommendation of contact.

different people, he may be more likely than otherwise to conceive the job *in terms of* the people with whom he is acquainted who might possibly fill it. Since most people are not actively seeking a new job at any given time, he is thus likely to think of people who are not actively in the market, and contact them. Alternatively, as occurred for several of my respondents, a meeting unrelated to an exchange of job information may crystallize, for an employer, an idea he has had in the *back* of his mind for some time, to start up a new type of work or a new branch of his company. In these cases, a showing of enthusiasm by the respondent, for the idea, redirected the purpose of the meeting and created a new job for himself.

Also, as Brown points out for college teachers (1965a:50–51) there is more pressure on an employer to hire a replacement for work that *was* actually being done until someone retired or left; new jobs, by contrast, can be left unfilled and uncreated until the employer is satisfied that he has found the right person. The procedure can then be more leisurely and is less likely to result from the search activity of potential employees. Some support for these speculations derives from the finding that for those finding jobs through contacts and taking jobs newly created, the most common case is that in which the personal contact is the new employer himself. This occurs in 50 percent of the 64 cases.

Each respondent was also asked about the filling of the vacancy which *he* left behind, in taking his current job. Analysis of data resulting from this question does not apply directly to the question of how *these* respondents' mobility became possible. It will provide some general insight, however, into causal issues involving entire systems of jobs. Their responses fall into three categories: 1) the respondent was replaced by someone who does more or less the same work he did; 2) he was not replaced (in some cases the job was parcelled out to other employees; in others, simply dropped); 3) respondent does not know what happened. The proportions in each category are 55.1, 30.4 and 14.5 percent, respectively (N = 214).

Comparing these figures to those found when respondents were asked about the vacancy status of jobs they were filling, we may conceive a "demography" of jobs, where the "birth rate" is the proportion of newly occupied jobs which had no previous incumbent (that is, the sum of the jobs newly created and those "added on"), and the "death rate" is the proportion of jobs vacated that are left unfilled. In this sample, the respective rates are 55.2 and 30.4 percent. If jobs were dying faster than being born, the overall system would reach a rather depressed and stagnant state. As in population demography, given constant rates, the population size (that is, number of jobs) would fall toward zero, and unless the labor force fell similarly in size, unemployment would increase.[2]

But more is needed for a "healthy" economy than for the net increase in jobs to exactly parallel the number of new labor force entrants. It should be recalled that each job born triggers off a

2. To be exact, if J_i is the number of jobs existing at the beginning of time period i, D is the proportion of jobs vacated during this period which are left unfilled, and B is the proportion of jobs taken which are newly created or added on, then:

$J_i = (J_{i-1} - DJ_{i-1}) + B(J_i)$, so that $J_i = J_{i-1} (1-D) / (1-B)$, and $J_i = J_0 [(1-D)/(1-B)]^i$,

where J_0 is the number of jobs in the initial time period.

vacancy chain, and thus has a multiplier effect on mobility; the
death of a job ends one, having a damping effect (see White 1970,
chs. 2, 9). Thus, quite different levels of mobility are consistent
with similar evolutions of system size, since these levels depend on
both parameters (as well as on the tightness or looseness of labor
markets). Readings on the birth and death rate taken periodically
could indicate forthcoming changes in mobility rates.

In general, the issues are complex, and it is impossible, here,
to offer a detailed account of the relation between these numbers
and mobility trends. Empirical research would be necessary to
determine the value of these suggestions. It may be that general
economic trends could be related to a time series of the proposed
index, in a useful predictive way. The relevant information could
easily enough be collected as I have done; the appropriate sample is,
as here, a random one of all those moving from one job to another
over a given period of time. Such a group could be extracted as
a subsample of the general population samples taken by various
government agencies. A few coding rules would suffice: a job could
be ruled "dead," for example, if unoccupied for a year or more.[3]

A more thorough idea about the nature of the vacancy chains
in which my respondents are involved can be achieved by cross-
tabulating the vacancy status of a current job with that of the
previous one. In 26.2 percent of the cases, respondents are in the
middle of vacancy chains: that is—they are replacing someone
definite *and* being replaced in their former job; 20.9 percent and
7.6 percent, respectively, took newly created or added-on jobs,
and were replaced in previous jobs, thus starting off a vacancy
chain; 5.2 percent replaced someone but do not know if they were
replaced (they are in a vacancy chain, but in an indeterminate
position); 12.4 percent end vacancy chains by replacing someone
but not being themselves replaced. No vacancy chains arise from
the 13.4 percent and 4.8 percent of the cases where respondents

3. In a symposium on job vacancies sponsored by the National Bureau of
Economic Research in 1966, a number of suggestions are made on the possible
use of surveys of *vacancies* to indicate conditions in various sectors of the
economy. But many "vacancies" have no real existence until they are filled;
the present suggestion avoids this dilemma.

take new or added-on jobs but are not replaced in their old ones; 9.6 percent take new or added-on jobs but do not know whether they were replaced; thus we cannot say whether chains are generated or not ($N = 210$).

Adding up all those who are involved in vacancy chains in one way or another, we have 72.3 percent (over two-thirds).[4] If it is generally true that such a large proportion of mobility in PTM work involves these chains, then the tools developed in White's monograph (1970) should have application far wider than the particular, narrow empirical frame (national churches and their clergy) that he chose for the initial testing and specification of the model. Note, however, that not all of those in chains are directly dependent on them for mobility: only those 43.8 percent ($26.2 + 12.4 + 5.2$) who replaced someone definite are. The rest are *generating* chains, thereby affecting the mobility of others.

It is of interest that those who *are* dependent on vacancy chains for mobility tend to receive lower salaries than those who are not. This trend is shown in Table 21 where those directly replacing someone are the ones dependent on vacancy chains. This finding is discussed further in the chapter on career structure.

My attempt to determine which *kinds* of jobs tend not to be filled after their incumbent leaves them found few consistent patterns. Partly, little can be said because my focus was on respondents' current jobs, and much less information was gathered on previous ones. One clear relationship is that technical jobs are least likely to be reported as having been re-filled; only about a third of such jobs are so reported, compared to about 60 percent of other jobs. This is probably due to the sensitivity of technical work to

4. White's coding rules would actually require all reported cases to be counted in vacancy chains. I have diverged in my usage of the term to include only those which involve the contingency of one man's mobility on another's. To code those taking newly created or added-on jobs and not being replaced as in vacancy chains may be appropriate in a system of definite jobs, such as the clergy studied by White. But the coding rule rests on the assumptions: 1) that the new or added-on job existed in a vacant form before it was filled, and 2) that the job left had a definite identity and was thus fillable, though not filled. I believe from my data on general PTM work that the first assumption is generally false; the second remains to be tested. (See White, 1970: Appendix C.)

Table 21. Income of respondent from present job, by dependence on vacancy chain.

| Income | Dependent on vacancy chain for mobility? | | Total |
	Yes	No	
Less than $10,000	36.1%	17.8%	26.0%
$10,000–14,999	30.3%	36.3%	33.6%
$15,000–24,999	24.4%	32.9%	29.1%
$25,000 or more	9.2%	13.0%	11.3%
N	119	146	265
	$p = 0.009$		

fluctuations in aggregate and government demand. Many technical workers are involved on projects stemming from particular contracts; when these expire, they move on to a new project, derived from another contract. If the overall number of such contracts diminishes, many jobs may ultimately be abolished.

When a job concerns several different *functional* areas, it can more easily be split up and parceled out among various existing personnel; the person need not be replaced. One respondent referred to this as the "elevator-operator syndrome": if the elevator operator quits (assuming the elevator is not automatic), the work can't be parceled out. One either hires a new operator or uses the stairs. If, on the other hand, someone is doing both technical and sales work, two people can absorb the job, one the technical and one the sales part, without having each to double their current load. Other combinations appeared in my sample—technical + managerial work, and sales + managerial work—in which respondents indicated that the job was split along functional lines and parceled out to existing employees.

We can also imagine cases where one's work is undifferentiated but also easily split. One such case was reported by a respondent who had been responsible for supervising the research of ten individuals in an industrial laboratory; when he left, these ten were simply parceled out to other supervisors. But relatively few PTM jobs involve "piece work" of this kind.

A relevant strategy, then, for investigating this type of short-term cause of individual mobility would be, for a substantial number of cases, to trace the vacancy chains through which mobility became possible. To the extent that such chains are long and move far beyond the acquaintance circles of respondents, a more macroscopic level of causation is introduced here than I have discussed previously. What correlation would exist between distance in a vacancy chain and social distance in a more general sense (as measured, for example, by the shortest path of personal contacts needed to connect the two people in question) is far from clear on general principles, though some relation would likely be found.

Certain ambiguities could arise in our tracing procedure. One respondent reported, for example, that his job was one of *two* junior positions created when an older man retired; another said that he was able to enter his job only because another man, in an unrelated position, had left and freed vital facilities. In both cases the causal influence is clear, but does not fit cleanly into the framework of White's vacancy chains.

A more general strategy may be needed to cope with systems in which large numbers of jobs do not have identities as stable as those of particular men. One could then analyze the total number of tasks that organizations decide to perform, the total resources at their disposal, and determine how these two sets become partitioned into a structure of jobs, and how such a structure evolves over time. To a limited degree, this problem is tackled in an important but difficult operations-research issue called the "assignment problem" (March and Simon, 1958:23–25, 158). Such a procedure might be too complex to yield useful results; however, only further work will determine this.

Chapter

Contacts: Acquisition and Maintenance

In this chapter and the next I will take cognizance of the fact
that some of the causes influencing respondents' current mobility
extend back in time beyond the immediate period of that mobility.
Discussions of mobility processes over time often involve "stochastic" models—that is, they deal with the probability of individuals
in a given status changing to some other status during a specified
time period. The question of "stochastic independence" arises:
a system in which the probability of moving to any other given
status is entirely unrelated to one's present status exhibits such
independence. Not surprisingly, this situation is rare, since one's present status is likely to exert a considerable shaping influence on
what possibilities will arise. The search for it stems from the
analytical fact that it is mathematically simple; many theorems and
formulas apply only if it can be assumed. The next simplest model
is that which assumes a "Markov process."[1] In a Markov process, the
outcome at each step is not independent of the previous one, but
depends at *most* on its outcome; earlier outcomes have no influence.
(Technically, this is "one-step" Markovian dependence; while it is
possible to construct models which allow dependence two or more
steps in the past, such models are very complex and have generally
been avoided. Two recent attacks on this problem are McGinnis,
1968 and McFarland, 1970.)

Intergenerational mobility affords a useful example. Imagine a
system of occupational statuses whose definitions are stable over a

1. A nontechnical account can be found in Kemeny et al., 1957: 171-177;
more thorough treatments are given in Kemeny and Snell, 1960, and in Feller,
1957: 338-396.

long period of time; we may examine sequences of statuses in the male line. That is, consider the status of every male in the present population at age 35, say, and compare it to that of his father at this age, that of his father's father, and so on. Independence would require that one's present status be uncorrelated with that of his father or any preceding ancestor. The Markovian assumption is more realistic here: it would specify dependence on father's status but not on that of previous ancestors. There could, of course, be indirect dependence on previous ancestors, insofar as they helped determine father's status; but the question is one of whether all previous dependence can be "rolled up" into the status of the father. If knowing father's father's status affords predictive power *beyond* that known from father's, then neither the assumption of independence nor that of a Markovian process is satisfied.

Substantively, the question is one of how far into the past one need look to find causes of present events; to what extent are ongoing processes in a system limited by the history of that system. In the present case, the issue can be posed as follows; consider a career as a chain of events—a sequence of job-enterings by an individual. At each time when someone enters a job, there exist simultaneously a large number of other jobs he might also have entered, had he been properly connected. The assumption of independence would require that one's previous positions exert no influence on which of these jobs is taken. The extensive use of personal contacts acquired in the course of work casts considerable doubt on the independence assumption. Those who use formal means and direct application come closest to stochastic independence, but even for them, there is no guarantee that present or past jobs will not play an important role in whether they are *hired* for future jobs, however they hear about them.

The Markovian assumption would permit the identity of one's next job in a career to depend, at most, on one's present position. If it were correct, the present chapter would be superfluous. One way to examine the assumption, for my data, is to ask how long ago the personal contacts used in acquiring one's present job were met.[2]

2. The usual test requires that jobs be arranged into categories, such that the set of possible categories occupied does not change over time. Only then can

Few of these contacts were of recent vintage: 30.3 percent had been met within two years of the time of the respondent's mobility, 39.4 percent within three to seven years, and 30.3 percent were known eight or more years (*N*-66, interview subsample).

It is of special interest that one's likelihood of being "very satisfied" with his job rises as contacts are of longer standing: the percentages are 45, 60 and 80 for the three categories of contact length ($p = 0.06$; $N = 65$). Income figures show a similar though less strong relation. We can also ask whether the contact was met in the course of the job held immediately prior to the most recent mobility, or earlier than this. Excluding those holding first jobs, 47.2 percent of remaining respondents had met that contact in their immediately previous job, and 52.8 percent earlier ($N = 53$). Of those met earlier, 61 percent were met before one's first job, 39 percent during a job earlier than one's immediately prior one. These percentages remain quite constant across age groups and different stage of career. Intensive attempts to find subgroups in the sample which differed markedly on this variable failed. The only apparent relationship is that work contacts are much more likely than family-social ones to have been acquired during the immediately previous job (56.8 percent compared to 5.3 percent; $N = 63$; $p = 0.001$).

Since the contacts named by respondents were not necessarily, or even typically, individuals recently met in straightforward job-related interaction, the question of how and when they were acquired as friends becomes problematic, as does that of how the contact was maintained over the time between first acquaintance and passage of job-information. Investigation of these questions constitutes an important aspect of the causal analysis attempted here, since the acquisition and maintenance of these contacts is a direct cause of subsequent mobility.

---

stable probabilities be computed for the movement from one category to another. Single jobs cannot constitute such categories because they are born and die with some frequency, and because there would be too many, each being unique. It might be desirable to divide up the jobs according to some measure of their location in the social structure, to facilitate the type of question I am asking, but no clear criterion of "location" in this sense is available; thus I have avoided the usual categorizing.

In Chapter 1 I divided personal contacts into family/social and
work-related ones. In the interview subsample, more detailed
information was obtained, from which we can reconstruct the
origins and maintenance of contacts. Of the 31.4 percent of
contacts who were family/social, 16.5 percent were met because
they were relatives or friends of relatives, 9 percent were fellow
students of the respondent at some stage of his educational career,
and 5.9 percent were social friends met in miscellaneous ways
(grew up in same neighborhood, friend of friend, neighbor). Of the
68.7 percent who were work contacts, 13.7 percent had been
teachers, 27.5 percent had worked in the same company, and 27.5
percent in different companies, at the time of first meeting. These
figures are based on a sample of 66 and, as such, can hardly be
taken as more than suggestive.[3] Accordingly, I will present, here, an
extended series of case abstracts, illustrating the content of these
various categories. This detail will suggest hypotheses for further
testing. This method is particularly useful for discussion of how
contacts are *maintained*. This question, though important, has been
thoroughly neglected by sociologists, and it is not even clear what
the appropriate categories would *be* for a statistical breakdown,
were the data more complete. The following four cases illustrate
how kinship ties affect the flow of information and influence:

Case #3 (see also p. 34): Edward A., during high school, went to a
party given by a girl he knew. There, he met her older sister's boy
friend, who was ten years older than himself. Three years later,
when he had just gotten out of the service, he ran into him in a local
hangout. In conversation, the boy friend mentioned to Mr. A. that
his company had an opening for a draftsman; Mr. A. applied for this
job and was hired.

Case #13: While Michael E.'s older sister (by five or six years) was
in high school, he met George W., a friend of hers. Some years later,

3. The proportion of family/social contacts in the interview subsample is
almost identical to that in the overall sample. In the mail survey, however,
only 5.8 percent of contacts were met via the family, and 24.4 percent as
social friends (N=86). Some of this difference must result from the alternatives offered in question 7 on the mail survey: none mention the family.

after he had graduated from college and decided against teaching (his previous plan), he happened to be at a baseball game with his sister, her husband, and George W. The latter asked what Michael was working at, and when told he was "up in the air," asked if he would be interested in being assistant manager of the real estate office where he was manager. After the formality of an interview, he was hired.

Case # 14: Dominick F's father worked in an engineering firm, and introduced him to Robert M., the son of a workmate of his. The two did not become particularly friendly, but years later, when Mr. F. had graduated from high school, his father suggested that he ask Robert if he knew of any jobs. He did so, and was told of an opening in his company which he subsequently filled.

Case #15: Kenneth E. is now produce manager of a supermarket. Six years ago, he had worked under his present employer, but in a different store. He changed jobs and did not see the employer for five years. But it happened that both had mutual friends in the same family: the employer knew the oldest brother in this family, because he had sponsored him to come to the U.S. from Germany, where he had also known the parents. Mr. E. knew the *youngest* brother because the latter had married a cousin of his wife. When the sister of these two brothers got married, in 1968, Mr. E. and his former employer both attended the wedding; they got to talking, and he was offered his current job. (He adds that he had once worked with the employer's sister, which reinforced the relationship.)

A fundamental demographic fact is that a wide span of ages is represented within any nuclear family. For relatively young people, the only personal contacts which will be useful will be those somewhat older than themselves; they must have some way of getting connected to such people. Three of the examples above show that this can be accomplished by the age spread among siblings. One's own siblings need not be involved; anyone one knows may have older siblings who have friends. Indeed, the case of Michael E., whose own sibling is involved, may be less common, since one can have many friends with older siblings, but a limited number of one's own siblings. The case of Dominick F. shows that even members of one's *own* generation may be reached through older relatives. The general point, that relatives and friends' relatives may serve as connectors to the rest of the community has been made especially well by Young and Willmott (1962). As one would expect from their study, this phenomenon is associated with low residential mobility. Respondents in the first three cases had all grown up in Newton. Kenneth E. had not, but his case is different. The actual initial contact was not due to the connective power of siblings' age differences (and was not, in fact, even a family or social contact), but the maintenance of the tie and the ultimate job offer stem clearly from this.

The following case offers still another variation on the connective power of family age-spread:

Case #16: Norman G.'s daughter was in nursery school, where she met the daughter of a lawyer who consequently became friendly with him. When Mr. G. quit his job, the lawyer told him of an opening in the accounting area of a firm which was one of his clients. He applied, and was hired.

In cases of respondents who knew their contacts because they had been students together, the interesting question is not how they met, which is fairly straightforward, but how the contact was maintained. The following three examples are suggestive:

Case #17: Nicholas L., originally from Czechoslovakia, attended engineering school in London from 1941–1945. He wanted to come to the United States after the war, but this was difficult. He applied to emigrate to several countries from which it would ultimately be easier to enter the U.S., and went to the first one which accepted him. In Bolivia he found an engineering job which he held for ten years. Before leaving London, he had told a friend about a notice he had seen on a bulletin board, about an opening for someone to teach engineering at a midwestern American university; it was too late for him to follow this up, but his friend did and was hired. During his ten years in Bolivia, Mr. L. sent his friend two letters, to keep in touch, and received two back. The second informed him of another opening in the midwestern university, which he successfully applied for. After three years there, he became bored; while visiting

San Francisco for a vacation, he met a friend of his wife's brother, who got his engineering firm to take him on.

After three years in California, he felt again that he would like to try something new, and went to Boston to look around. He first looked up a friend with whom he had worked in Bolivia; this friend told him that there was an engineer in Boston who had attended the same school as Mr. L. This turned out to be an old friend, whom he had not seen in twenty years. When Mr. L. went to see him, he suggested that he apply to his current firm. He did so and was hired. After two years, a senior member of that firm formed a spin-off company, and asked Mr. L. to join him. This is his current job.

Case #18: William P. was a graduate student in French literature when he met Mark W., a fellow student, in the dining commons. They roomed together in 1951 and 1952. From 1953 to 1955 they both still lived in the college town and saw each other occasionally. After receiving his M.A., Mr. P. went to a small women's college in New England to teach. From 1957–59, his friend Mr. W. taught nearby at a state college, and visited him a few times. In 1960, Mr. P. received his Ph.D. and went to a larger school in upstate New York. His friend's family lived in a nearby town, and so, in 1962, while visiting them, he also stopped by to see Mr. P. In 1964, the latter took a better job in a large university in Pennsylvania. Mr. W., meanwhile, was teaching in a university near the one where he and Mr. P. had been students. During the summers, Mr. P started returning to that university for research, since their library facilities were unusually good for his particular scholarly interest. He saw Mark W. about once each summer between 1964 and 1967. On one of these occasions, he was asked by him whether he would be interested in teaching in his own department. Two years later when Mr. P. realized that he would not receive tenure where he was, he contacted his friend and asked if there was still an opening. There was, and he took it.

Case #19: David M. had been, as a boy, bat boy for the Brooklyn Dodgers, and later became manager of the food concession at Ebbets Field (their ballpark). Meanwhile he worked his way through a local college, graduating in 1940. He then took a marketing position with one of the food distributors he had dealt with at Ebbets Field; in 1961, he decided to go into business for himself, and opened a restaurant on the Massachusetts North Shore, where he had relatives. In mid-1966, a customer saw Mr. M's name on the liquor license, and asked him if he was the same David M. he had known 27 years earlier in college; he was.

They got to talking, and the friend became a regular customer. He was director of a large, private social welfare program in northern Massachusetts, and, after several months of discussions, decided that Mr. M. would be the right person to manage one of his programs: re-training handicapped workers. After several months, Mr. M. accepted the job.

Mr. M. stressed that he had been only "acquaintances" in college with his new employer, and admitted that he began the new job with no expertise whatever. He asserted, however, that expertise did not really exist in this field, so that a layman could, in fact, work successfully at it.

These cases illustrate the argument (made in chapter 3) that the ties to those who help one find a job may be rather weak ones. In two of these cases, a twenty-year or more hiatus separated one occasion of contact from another. Cases like this are particularly damaging to Markovian assumptions. The case of David M. also is an example of a major change of work-type being mediated by a nonwork contact. (Cf. Ch. 2, 48–50). It may be that, in general, major changes of work type are less likely to follow the Markovian model. Most work contacts, as noted above, are acquired on one's immediately previous job.

The cases cited so far in this chapter here involved, almost exclusively, family or social contacts. There are some interesting findings concerning how respondents became connected to work contacts in companies *other than their own*. Discussion of these will be found in Chapter 8, on interorganizational relationships. When work contacts are established within the same company, there is little to be explained about how the contact was made.[4]

Given prevailing rates of mobility, the set of people one meets during any given job (whether they were in one's own company or not) will, in the future, be distributed over a number of firms and areas, in which they may act as personal contacts, "inducing" or at

4. This would be a subject of interest, however, if I were to put more emphasis on the internal dynamics of formal organizations.

least facilitating one's mobility to that location. As with family social contacts, we may ask how these relationships are maintained in the intervening period. Professional meetings and activities appear to be important in this respect, as is the information people secure about one another from mutual friends. The question is less problematical for work contacts since the average intervening period is much shorter.

Important theoretical issues are implicit in the discussion of how job contacts are acquired and maintained. Of special interest is the question of whether the mechanisms involved are substantially different from those which people use to acquire and maintain social contacts in general. Unfortunately (and remarkably) baseline data are lacking; there are no systematic studies of social contact formation and maintenance for general populations. I would guess that acquisition is somewhat different, here, since the tie created is likely to be to individuals with access to a substantially different information pool; hence, those mechanisms which bridge social distance (in the sense specified in Chapter 3) should be over-represented. This point is especially clear in the cases where young men were connected to older ones via family age-spreads. The general formulation here might be that we should analyze formation of the ties individuals have with others whose status is substantially different from their own, since such ties will connect them, potentially, to *others* of different status.

The mechanisms for maintenance are not unexpected ones. The custom of visiting friends when passing through their area is common to all cultures and periods. The same is true of weddings, funerals and other ritual occasions. Kinship ties often not only generate a contact, but, given some residential immobility, provide occasions for its renewal. Some methods are more contrived; many tribal societies have periodic events involving considerable travel, and the ceremonial exchange of symbolic objects; the Kula ring of the Trobriand Islanders is a famous example (Malinowski, 1922). Professional meetings serve a similar function for us; the exchange of papers is widely acknowledged to be secondary to keeping in touch with others in one's field at a personal level, and keeping up with the góssip—a good part of which concerns who is now working where; hence, even those who do not attend may be affected by having knowledge of their whereabouts spread among former friends, via mutual acquaintances (Katz 1958, Granovetter 1973).

What is perhaps more surprising, though consistent with the emphasis on weak ties in Chapter 3, is that some ties which are used had barely *been* maintained at all over long periods. It is a remarkable fact that one may receive crucial information from individuals whose existence one has nearly forgotten. The paucity of "maintenance events" makes the following hypothetical research project imaginable: for each individual under study, construct a chart to keep track of his total social interaction. Let each column represent a given time period, and each row one individual he knows. Construct enough columns for his entire lifetime and enough rows for every person he has ever known on a first-name basis (over some minimal period of interaction). In each cell of this box enter the amount, type and occasions of interaction for the time period chosen; we would then have a lifetime record of which ties the individual has maintained, and how. The cases cited in this chapter may be seen as subsets of rows on these hypothetical charts.

The problem, of course, is that these cases are chosen *post hoc* after we know which particular contact has been relevant. Causal chains must, naturally, be constructed so that we can pick out the important elements *before* the event at the end of the chain actually occurs (cf. Hempel 1965). Operationally, some version of these charts can be imagined. Over some time period, ten years, say, individuals could keep charts like those suggested. Gurevitch's study (1961) shows that people are capable of an even more complex task—keeping a record of every person with whom they come in contact every single day. Time periods for the study proposed here could be easier to manage, perhaps as long as a quarter-year, and entries for those frequently seen during the quarter could give merely rough estimates of amounts of interaction. Much could be learned from such a demonstration project since we could find out not only who does offer useful job information, but who offers no information and who offers information which turns out not to be used. (The present study suffers from inability to collect these last two types of data.) Interviews with these three groups of people could be quite illuminating. Ultimately, one would hope that the relevant causal chains could be constructed with the help of only short-term data, once it was clear what the important variables were. Though the method proposed may seem wasteful of effort, I find it hard to imagine how else one could find out whether there was anything unusual about those who provide job information, as compared, say, to a random sample of one's everyday contacts.

Chapter

Career Structure

The previous chapter showed that careers are not made up of random jumps from one job to another, but rather that individuals rely on contacts acquired at various stages of their work-life, and before. One important result of this finding is that mobility appears to be self-generating: the more different social and work settings one moves through, the larger the reservoir of personal contacts he has who may mediate further mobility. It is because ties from past jobs and from before work are about as likely to be used as more recent ones that we have a cumulative effect, as if individuals "stockpile" their contacts. If only strong or recent ties mediated mobility, this could not be true; but since relatively weak ones may be crucial, working on a job for two or three years may be sufficient to build a tie which will later be useful (though this is generally unanticipated). Too short a time may not be enough, since one's contact must have a definite impression of one's abilities and personality; staying too long in one's jobs, on the other hand, may foreclose future mobility by truncating the pool of personal contacts one might otherwise have built up.

In the interview subsample, I collected some details on each job in the respondent's career.[1] The mean of the average job tenure (per career) reported was 4.7 years. Of these, 14.1 percent had average tenures of less than two years, 51.3 percent 2–5 years, and 34.6 percent five or more years ($N = 78$).[2] If my comments above

1. Only full-time jobs of at least a year in duration were counted. Briefer ones seemed unlikely to have much impact on careers, though this may be unnecessarily restrictive.
2. Current job was excluded from this tabulation, since the length of time it will be held is indeterminate. This implies that those holding their first full-time job do not appear at all in these figures.

are correct, we might expect those in the middle group to be best placed with regard to personal contacts, and the other two groups to be at a disadvantage. There is some evidence for this assertion, though the results are ambiguous. Those with average tenures of five or more years reported finding their present job by contacts in 58.3 percent of the cases, compared to the two-to-five year groups 67.5 percent and the 0–2 year group's 72.7 percent. The difference is not statistically significant; there may be two reasons for this lack of significance. The more obvious one is the small numbers involved; this should be kept in mind when reading the tables in this chapter. Whatever relationships are demonstrated with such numbers must be of primarily heuristic interest. The other, more difficult problem, is that most of the arguments here implicitly apply more to work contacts than to social ones. Each person moves in two sets of social circles, occupational and social, which are only imperfectly correlated. Informal questioning of my respondents suggested that many make a clear distinction between work and social contacts, though I have no systematic formulation to explain who does and does not. The question requires further investigation. To the extent that one *has* a considerable amount of social contact unrelated to work, the present arguments apply only with some slippage; though work contacts in general are more important for mobility, I have catalogued various important exceptions.

Each respondent was asked how he found every job in his career. Excluding present job, I have, in Table 22, arranged respondents into groups based on the proportion of career jobs found by contacts. Those with intermediate job tenures *are* more likely than those with short or long ones to have found two-thirds or more of their jobs through contacts, though the difference is not over-whelming. The tendency displayed might well be stronger were it not for the fact that managers and older individuals are over-represented among those with long tenures, and both groups are unusually likely to use contacts. If the number in this subsample permitted control of age and occupation, the postulated effect might show up more strongly.

Table 22. Proportion of jobs found through contacts, by average job tenure of respondent.

Jobs found through contacts	Average job tenure			
	Less than 2 years	2–4.999 years	5 years or more	Total
None	20%	20%	11.1%	16.9%
0.1–66.6%	50%	25%	48.2%	36.4%
66.7–99.9%	0%	35%	14.7%	23.4%
All	30%	20%	26.0%	23.4%
N[a]	10	40	27	77
		$p = 0.15$		

[a]Interview sample only; excludes those holding first job.

Table 23. Proportion of respondents who gave friend job information, by average job tenure of respondent.

Recently told friend about a job?	Average job tenure			
	Less than 2 years	2–4.999 years	5 years or more	Total
Yes	36.4%	70.0%	46.2%	57.1%
No	63.6%	30.0%	53.8%	42.9%
N	11	40	26	77
		$p = 0.05$		

I also asked respondents if they had told anyone *they* knew personally about a job in the last year or so. We may assume that those answering "yes" are more in touch with job information than others; Table 23 shows that the respondents with average tenures of 2–5 years are much more likely than the other groups to be able to offer job information to their friends.

As suggested in Chapter 3, chain length through which one finds his current job, when using personal contacts, is a measure of how well placed one is in the labor market. Table 24 shows that this

Table 24. Length of information chain, by average job tenure of respondent.

| Chain length | Average job tenure | | | |
	Less than 2 years	2–4.999 years	5 years or more	Total
Zero	25.0%	61.5%	31.2%	46.0%
One	37.5%	30.8%	56.2%	40.0%
Two or more	37.5%	7.7%	12.5%	14.0%
N	8	26	16	50
		$p = 0.08$		

group of 2–5 year tenure respondents is far more likely than other groups to have used zero-length chains in finding their current job; the data also reveal this group to be more likely to be satisfied with their current job than other groups, whereas respondents with average tenure of five or more years are most dissatisfied with their current jobs.

Certain cases in my sample attuned me to the notion that staying too long in a job might have the effect of cutting off one's future mobility by retarding the cumulation of personal contacts. The case of Victor O. is especially striking:

Case #20: Victor O. is a chemical engineer. When he got out of the army he talked to a friend who told him about a job at his former college. He left this after two years, answering an advertisement to work in a small company near Buffalo. He held this job for 18½ years; many of his workmates also stayed there the whole time. The company was then bought out in a conglomerate acquisition, and Mr. O.'s position was eliminated. He began searching by contacting friends and acquaintances and by answering ads. He wrote to 115 companies; as time passed and his frustration mounted, he began keeping a scrapbook of the ads and his letters along with the responses (hence the exact count). Four or five of these letters resulted in interviews. He began systematically varying the form of the résumes he sent, to see if it made a difference; it didn't. Finally, he was called to give a reference for someone he knew, who was applying for a job at another company; he made it clear that he was also available, and when his friend didn't take this job, he was hired instead. He is very unhappy with this job, however, and has begun writing to companies again.

As I examined Mr. O's scrapbook I was struck by the amount of care and angry frustration which had gone into its construction. His case was the most extreme, though not unrepresentative, of a number of initially puzzling interviews in which I talked to people who seemed personable and intelligent, who had stayed in one job for fifteen or more years, and had then had remarkable difficulty in job search.[3]

The overall results, then, for job tenure suggest that an average of 2–5 years is optimal for future career prospects; managers may be the primary exception in that the nature of their work requires them to stay in an organization longer before being able to work effectively. Technical and professional men, on the other hand, are less coupled with organizational arrangements and can demonstrate their competence within a few years to a considerable number of people and then move on. The effects of excessive tenure can perhaps also be overcome by extensive contacts outside one's own organization; managers might be expected to be most likely to have these (as noted in Chapter 8). My claim is that other things being equal, long job tenure cuts off the cumulation of personal contacts and thus reduces the chances for mobility opportunity.

None of the results cited would be inconsistent with the hypothesis that a selection factor operates; that those with long tenures may be precisely those with minimal contacts, so that tenure-length is result rather than cause of contact structure. With the small sample here I cannot settle the direction of causality; but I would argue that while some selection may operate, it is at least equally plausible for causality to run the other way. Most of those in my sample who fell into this category indicated that they had stayed in their

3. Without standardized measures of ability, we cannot rule out the possibility that people having long tenures are less competent, and hence have more difficulty in the job market. The difficulty of constructing such measures is discussed by Rees and Shultz, 1970.

Table 25. Search behavior of respondents, by proportion of past jobs found through contacts.

Searched for present job?	Past jobs found through contacts				
	None	0.1–66.6%	66.7–99.9%	All	Total
Yes	90.5%	77.8%	72.7%	50.0%	72.8%
No	9.5%	22.2%	27.3%	50.0%	27.2%
N	21	27	11	22	81
		$p = 0.02$			

Table 26. Method of finding present job, by proportion of past jobs found through contacts.

Method used for present job	Past jobs found through contacts				
	None	0.1–66.6%	66.7–99.9%	All	Total
Formal means	18.2%	22.2%	9.1%	4.5%	14.6%
Personal contacts	40.9%	63.0%	90.9%	77.3%	64.6%
Direct application	36.4%	14.8%	0 %	9.1%	17.1%
Other	4.5%	0 %	0 %	9.1%	3.7%
N	22	27	11	22	82
		$p = 0.04$			

jobs for a long time because they had wanted to; moreover, the long tenures tended to start at the beginnings of their careers, and since most contacts are generated *after* this stage, it is reasonable to assume that these long tenures cut off some of the possibilities.

Further evidence that present job-finding activity is heavily dependent on one's previous career is presented in Tables 25 and 26, which divide up the sample according to proportion of *past* jobs found through contacts (therefore excluding those currently in first jobs). Table 25 shows that over 90 percent of those who had found none of their previous jobs through personal contacts had to search for their present one, and that this proportion steadily decreases with increase in likelihood of having found past jobs via contacts. Table 26 makes it clear that those who had found most previous jobs by contacts again found their current one by this means. As might be expected from these two results, the proportion "very satisfied" with their current job increases with proportion of past jobs found through contacts, from 35 percent of those who had found none of their jobs through contacts to 68.2 percent of those who had found all of them that way.

Still another way of viewing the situation is to point out that if career events *were* independent of each other (and if the probability of finding a job through contacts did not change over time-older studies suggest this is approximately true), then the expected proportion of jobs found by contacts during the average career should equal the probability of finding any single job by contacts. In my interview subsample 66 percent found their present job through contacts. But the probability of a respondent having found between 60 and 70 percent of his jobs by contacts is only 12.0 percent; the modal categories (where categories are deciles, plus "all" or "none") are, instead, "all" (30 percent) and "none" (19 percent). That is, people find jobs by contacts through their entire career or none of it, as the most likely cases.

This is statistically deceptive, since the 100 respondents have careers of varying lengths, and those with shorter ones are more likely to find none or all of their jobs by contacts; in the extreme case, those whose present job is their first ($N = 18$), no other possibility exists. We may construct a simple model to allow for this truncation effect. Consider all those with a career of length C jobs as taking part in a binomial experiment with probability of success $= 0.66$ (the probability of finding a job through contacts), and C trials. If the trials are independent, we may easily derive, for each C, the number who are expected to find $0, 1, \ldots, C$ jobs by contacts, and compare these to the observed numbers, to see whether the bimodal tendency is greater than expected on this null hypothesis. The results are not unambiguous, but do suggest that "all" or "none" are more likely than the assumption of independence would permit.

This may result from the way contacts are generated. A few initial contacts, however acquired, facilitate mobility, which increases the number of contacts, making further mobility more probable, and so on. Moreover, each new contact is able to introduce one to *his* contacts. If the overall process has a weak beginning, very few total contacts may be acquired. In probability theory, such situations are called "branching processes," and often yield bimodal results. Feller, for example, shows that after a relatively few generations, the probability distribution for number of descendants in a male line behaves in this way, taking into account only fixed probabilities of birth of male children; that is, either very few *or* very many descendants carrying the last name of the founder can be expected after (say) ten or more generations, but not a moderate number (Feller, 1957:274-276). An analogous process may be at work to produce the bimodal tendency in my data.[4]

4. This analogy will be presented with more mathematical detail and more data from the present study, in a forthcoming article.

Chapter
7
Some Theoretical Implications

The past six chapters have focussed on various factors affecting the mobility of the individuals in my sample, with particular though not exclusive emphasis on those making use of personal contacts. Before considering the relation of my data to larger structures, I want to pause to summarize the findings for individuals and to make some theoretical comments.

The findings do not lend themselves to easy summary or integrated discussion. In particular, it is hard to put short-term and long-term influences, at both micro and macro levels, together into a coherent account. I have not tried to do so in any detail, therefore, but have, instead, developed the following general comments, which are too abstract to be satisfactory, but which may stimulate some lines of investigation which strike me as fruitful. These comments progress from micro to macro level.

Causal Effects on Individuals

I begin with a crude summary of the data in Chapters 1-6: Individuals do sometimes search for the information that enables them to be mobile, but will have found a better job, in general, if they have not done so, or if job information was unconnected to their search. Those who do best are those whose contacts are occupational rather than social, whose ties to contacts are weak rather than strong, and who are in information chains that are short. About half of the respondents took vacancies which were left behind by previous incumbents, while the rest, for various reasons, were not dependent on someone else's mobility in this way.

Analysis of career-length time-sequences showed that respondents' experience in current job-finding was not independent of immediately previous jobs, nor could the dependence, in many cases, be limited to that time span. In particular, the most successful respondents were heavily dependent on past contacts and career patterns.

What general conclusions can be drawn from this collection of findings? Roughly speaking, the analysis of causation in social systems suffers from an insufficiently refined notion of a distance metric. In any system, we want to know how extensively events occurring in one part affect other parts, and how "far" the influence travels. It is equally important to identify those system aspects that remain more or less invariant under transformations effected elsewhere, or which change more on the basis of some inner logic than through external forces.

One relevant place to apply such notions is in the analysis of influences that affect the behavior and choices of particular individuals. Implicit in my discussion during the past six chapters have been concepts of causal distance. One was distance in network structures—represented by the measure of chain length. Another would have been, had there been sufficient data, the length of vacancy chains. (Cf. White, 1970:chs. 1, 5.) Both measures represent ideas of causal distance on the micro-macro continuum, at one instant of time.

Another dimension of causal distance is temporal: how far into the past must one go to find direct causal influence on present events? In this sense, the difference between long- and short-term causes is analogous to that between distant (macro) and nearby (micro) causes. Much more discussion would be needed to flesh out these vague theoretical images.

A few things can be said, however, on the basis of the present findings, for the problem at hand—the causes of mobility opportunity. Where short-term causes are concerned, it appears that those individuals who have the most autonomy and most desirable choices to make are those least affected by events socially distant from them. This point is especially clear from the discussion in Ch. 3 on the length of information chains, and can also be related to the analysis of vacancy chains: those least subject to causes distant from themselves would presumably be individuals whose mobility did not depend on a vacancy chain. If we had measured the length of chains for those involved, it might be that distinctions could be made according to the length—expectations being that those at the end of longer chains would show lower incomes and less job-satisfaction. This would be consistent with White's theoretical idea, empirically verified for his data, that each step in the life of a vacancy chain is from higher to lower status, since most job-mobility is upward. Hence, the number of steps in the vacancy-chain before one's self may be somewhat of a status-indicator.[1] Here we can make only the either-or comparison: those affected by vacancy chains are those taking jobs previously held, while those taking newly created or added-on jobs are not so affected. In this limited comparison, it was shown in Chapter 4 that those affected by the chains did report lower incomes.

When we enter the realm of causal influences over time, some-what the opposite effect is found. Those who are most insulated from effects in their past life, who have fewest contacts over a long-term in the occupational community, who approach the market-place at each new job with a clean slate—as in the "perfect market" of economic theory—are the most disadvantaged, have the fewest choices and achieve the least desirable positions. It is interesting which prediction economic theory gives us in both directions: in present time, it assumes that the norm consists of being involved in long chains of job-information: across the time dimension, it involves being independent of past events. Economic man exists, in both ways, but is hardly an object for emulation. The two predic-tions are related: it is precisely *because* of past connections and contacts, forged particularly in certain types of career patterns, that search processes in present time are truncated, so that information chains are short. For given individuals, then, an inverse relation

---

1. This argument is not conclusive; White actually suggests an opposite one—that sharp prestige differentials might inhibit mobility and result in short chains (1970: 19–20). His data involved chains *within* rather than between organizations, however. In the more open and vaguely defined systems which my data involve, I lean toward my version.

exists between the depth of causal influence in time and its breadth at present.

To argue that success may be defined as independence of distant events is by no means original; the point here is rather to suggest that this commonsense idea may be dealt with in a systematic way, by constructing structural measures of such influences, and relating them to individuals' current experiences in social systems. The exploratory nature of the present discussion should be obvious; the data necessary to develop these ideas are not those of my study, since the ideas are a product of that study.

Rationality and Information-Processing

A key problem in economic and social theory is the extent to which individuals behave "rationally." For my respondents, two somewhat contradictory threads emerge. Given their goals and possibilities, they do seem to have chosen courses of action that would serve their purposes; their contacts and employers did the same. At the same time, enormous constraints narrowed the range of actual alternatives from which they chose—chance meetings, past mobility history, dimly remembered acquaintances—and the mobility and information-spreading of strangers.

There is no real contradiction here, but sociological theories do tend to emphasize either voluntarism or determinism exclusively. To say that one should investigate both voluntary behavior *and* the constraints imposed on it sounds obvious once said, yet few analysts do both. My own imbalance in the present study has been to focus heavily on constraints—therefore I should say a few words about rationality.

Many of the findings reported here are, even if unexpected, easily explained in terms of rational behavior. I found, for instance, that better jobs were found by those not searching for a job. But these nonsearchers probably had better jobs to *remain* in than those searching actively, so that a job which would attract them would *have* to be an unusually good one. As in a recent commercial, such individuals can "select, not settle." On the demand side, an analogous factor operates for employers who want to create new positions: these positions can be filled at leisure since they are unlikely to involve currently vital work; replacements, on the other hand, must be sought more quickly lest other work be disrupted. Less qualified applicants may be settled for. But the fact that such relationships can be explained in terms of rational individual behavior does not make them less important, since they have an emergent reality at the macroscopic level of analysis. Ideologically, for instance, the fact that the best jobs may be filled without search by candidates must affect our idea of what the possibilities are for an "open" society.

A similar point can be made about why employers and employees prefer to make use of personal contacts in securing labor market information. They reason, correctly, that personal ties mean better information (see p. 11). By "better," I mean more "intensive" in the sense proposed by Rees: "information in any market has both an extensive and an intensive margin. A buyer can search at the extensive margin by getting a quotation from one more seller. He can search at the intensive margin by getting additional information concerning an offer already received" (1966:560). He goes on to say that the former strategy would be appropriate in searching for new cars, the latter for used cars and also in labor markets. The distinction is based on the degree of standardization of the item sought. The abstract categories of social theory discourage us from noticing that in many important situations, one has to obtain information about rather unstandardized alternatives.

Many have analyzed the fact that a cost attaches to the gathering of every bit of information (cf. Ch. 1, above). Less formal analysis has been given to the fact that people not only do not strive to secure complete information, but actually attempt to *filter out* some information which might otherwise be registered. "The problem facing the employer," as Rees puts it, "is not to get in touch with the largest number of potential applicants; rather it is to find a few applicants promising enough to be worth the investment of thorough investigation" (1966:561). He argues that frequently, "employer hiring standards can be viewed as devices to narrow the intensive field of search by reducing the number of applicants to manageable proportions." Thus, arbitrary rules are adopted: "clerical workers must be high school graduates; material handlers must weigh at least 150 pounds; janitors must have lived a year in the metropolitan area; . . . Each of these rules has some relevance to job-performance, but lack of the qualities specified could be compensated for by the presence of others" (1966:561–562). Job-seekers have a similar interest in keeping manageable the number of possibilities investigated and seriously considered.

Psychologists have written extensively on the need for individuals to filter out uninformative stimuli, and on the clear limits which exist in human information-processing capacity (Broadbent, 1958; G. Miller, 1956), but little attention has been paid to the sociological side of this activity. I would make the general observation that personal contacts are used simultaneously to gather information *and* screen out noise, and are, for many types of information, the most efficient device for so doing.

In the case of jobs, it would be a mistake to infer from my study that unqualified personnel typically fill PTM jobs because of labor-market "imperfections." Many criteria restrict the population from which the incumbents of most PTM positions may be chosen; the problem is that even when education, training, and experience are taken into account, the number available is still unmanageable. Personal contacts narrow the range *within* this already narrowed group, and do so at less cost than other methods.[2]

The filtering side of information processing is even more obviously central in other social processes: marriage may be the paradigmatic example. No study seems to attack directly the question of how spouses become aware of one another's existence. One would have to consider the activity of both bride and groom,

2. When naïve recruiters neglect the filtering process, they may be inundated. A *New York Times* article early in 1969 described a "talent search" of the new administration. Forms were sent to nearly 80,000 Americans. The result: "more than 30,000 solicited and unsolicited letters about jobs, swamping the Nixon administration" because of the extensive screening the FBI clearance checks necessitate for each applicant. One official was quoted as calling the search the "worst mistake of the Nixon administration to date" (*New York Times*, February 9, 1969).

and in most societies, that of their families. As with jobs, the range of possible spouses is narrowed initially by more or less arbitrary rules. These may be precise and formally stated, as in many tribal societies or informal but nevertheless clear as when, in modern societies, permissible status-differences between spouses are specified. Personal contacts and institutionalized intermediaries (for example, go-betweens) narrow the field still more.

Questions of interest comparable to those in my study would be: are those spouses found informally (that is, introduced by friends) preferred to those found by formal means?; what is the length and effect of information chains used (for example, do friends of one's friends friends become one's spouse)?; what is the significance of supply and demand (that is, fluctuations in the population sex ratio) on mode of finding a spouse?

One would expect that each side would want to maximize information about the prospective spouse; where marriage is an alliance between families, information about the respective families also is sought. Personal contacts probably give the most intensive information but (especially where there is local exogamy) such contacts may not suffice. Go-betweens may become quite skilled at developing good information (just as *some* "executive search" agencies are quite well regarded). In Japan, private detective agencies may even be hired to investigate the family and prospects of a potential spouse (Vogel, 1961:114).[3]

The general point is that information in any society is both costly and valuable; there is no reason why it should be expected to flow easily unless there is direct compensation or a personal tie. Formal intermediaries receive direct compensation; often, information cannot be secured in this way, and without personal ties to those who possess it, none is available. This is clearly demonstrated by a recent study of how women find abortionists (Lee, 1969). In

3. One of my respondents, in a high-status managerial job, reported that before he was hired, he had found out that his prospective employer had sent private investigators to his neighborhood to be sure that he was on good terms with the neighbors; it was felt that he might otherwise not get along well in the company. He did not think that this practice was uncommon, though he admitted that his superiors were a bit stodgy.

such a case (though less now than at the time of the study) there
are strong reasons *not* to pass information indiscriminately; to do so
could put one's self and the abortionist in danger. Similar studies
could be imagined on how people purchase marijuana, stolen
classified documents (intelligence work), and other objects. Borrow-
ing large sums of money on insufficient collateral could be analyzed
in this way. As with jobs, it could be expected that those who
find any of these through formal means or long information chains
would be less satisfied than those able to use more personal methods.
Abortionists and loan sharks found the wrong way are not infrequently lethal.

Again, to argue that the method employed is rational does not
imply that overall social welfare is optimized. Regardless of competence or merit, those without the right contacts are penalized.
Abortions, marijuana, loans, spouses, and jobs may be unsatisfactory
or unavailable to such individuals. Indeed, one of the main results
of my analysis is that routine social mechanisms which are quite
rational at the micro-level have the macro-level result of institu-
tionalizing social inequality, a result not necessarily intended by any
particular actor.

Modernization and Particularism

At the macro level of analysis, several themes are engaged by my
data. One obvious one is the relation between modernization and
structural differentiation. Most influential theorists have argued that
as societies "modernize," the various functions carried out within
them—economic, political, religious, socialization, and so on—
become separated from one another. Where families once did all
these things, specialized institutions and personnel now emerge.
Family firms disappear, government becomes centralized, schools
educate children, and priests explain the meaning of life. Religious,
political, and legal institutions become separated from one another.
As differentiation proceeds, ascriptive and particularistic procedures
fade. Differentiation can be viewed, we are told, as "a process of
'emancipation' from ascriptive ties" (Parsons, 1961:230). In their

place comes an emphasis on achievement and universalistic criteria in, for example, recruitment procedures.

Most theorists enter a *caveat* at this point. Levy points out that while "the emphasis on universalistic criteria can never be complete, it increases in the transition to and the maintenance of relatively modernized societies" (1966:54). In a sense, such *caveats* subsume my findings of extensive particularism in a modern economy, but they fail to appreciate the significance of this finding. If particularism is treated only as an "intrusion" or a kind of residual, frictional drag on generally universalistic processes, no grounds can be offered to account for its persistence. These grounds are related to my arguments above on the rationality of using personal contacts. The point is nicely put by Mayhew: "The source of the staying power and functional capacity of ascription (in modern society) can be summed up in three words: it is cheap. Ascription involves using an existent, pre-established structure as a resource rather than creating a new specialized structure for the same purpose" (1969:110).

A further question remains. Does the disjunction between my account and the usual theory result because universalism is not necessary in differentiated structures, or because these structures are less differentiated than usually supposed? I think both are true. Universalism has been expected because of its imputed superiority in dealing with complex situations. I have tried to show that in a purely technical sense this is incorrect, as it neglects the modes of acquisition and types of information necessary in such situations. (This point is amplified in Ch. 8, below). At the same time we should recognize that even when one recruits a business contact, some noneconomic factors enter motivation. Some of these are suggested above, in Chapter 3. Moreover, as detailed above, family and social contacts are by no means insignificant in modern recruitment. Attempts to construe individuals as rational actors or game theoretic "players" in a labor market founder not so much on the assumption of rationality as on that of the *closure* of the market, or game. Information comes to players even when they have done little or nothing to seek it, and from sources not previously known to be connected to the game. A more accurate image would be that of overlapping games, or in Norton Long's phrase, an "ecology of games," in which a given individual is involved. To conceive the situation in this way requires that we see activities previously supposed to be sharply differentiated as actually rather blurry at the boundaries.

Modern organizations other than businesses also have these complex relations to various social activities. Political groups and movements of various kinds, for instance, are likely to snowball their membership through personal contacts. Knowing which types of contacts are useful in which recruitments, the length of recruitment-information chains, the nature of the contact-recruit tie, would all shed light on political socialization. We might like to know which events early in the "careers" of individuals contributed to generating the personal contacts which eventually led to recruitment. It would be a fascinating though painfully difficult study to trace a revolutionary movement from the early, hard-core stage to more successful periods, by analysis of how contact networks generated more and more members. Comparison of unsuccessful and successful movements might be especially revealing. The structure of social networks in which an organization is embedded might provide crucial clues as to why large numbers could never be added.[4] As in the study of jobs, it would be important to specify the conditions under which recruitment is by other than personal contacts.

Issues similar to those in the economic sector arise—those of differentiation, particularism, and rationality of political activities. It is necessary to say at this stage, however, that these are blunt theoretical tools. Discussions of differentiation are particularly confounded because of disagreements, explicit or implicit, over exactly what the elements *are* whose differentiation from one another we are supposed to investigate. I have made no real attempt

4. In another paper (1973) I have sketched an analysis of this type for the organization described by Gans (1962), which attempted unsuccessfully to fight against urban renewal in Boston's West End.

to sort out this issue here. A more thorough theoretical discussion of macro-level problems related to this study can be carried out only in the context of a detailed empirical treatment of these problems. Such a treatment is sketched in Part II.

Part

Two

Mobility and Society

Thus far, most of my attention has been focused on the problem of explaining what the factors are that affect individual mobility. This mobility occurs, however, in a broader social context, which shapes it and is shaped by it in turn. In Chapter 8, I take note of the fact that since none of my respondents is self-employed, all of the mobility discussed takes place *between* formal organizations; implications for various aspects of organizational theory, especially that part dealing with interorganization relations, are considered. Chapter 9 broadens the perspective further by recognizing that the findings presented here are not necessarily those which would be found in all places at all times; it is important to ask what features of a society shape the channels of mobility. This is done by an attempt to compare the mechanics of the mobility process in radically different types of society. Chapter 10 considers whether or not this research may have practical implications.

Chapter

Mobility and Organizations

Most of the vast literature on formal organizations treats aspects of their internal structure. A few outstanding works, however, attempt to grapple with the fact that organizations exist in an environment, and must act accordingly (Selznick, 1949; Lawrence and Lorsch, 1967). Of particular interest from the point of view of the present study is the fact that organizations form a substantial part of the environment for *one another*. Most studies of inter-organizational relationships have noted this point primarily in the context of examining conflicts between organizations with (to some degree) mutually exclusive goals. (Levine and White, 1961; Litwak and Hylton, 1962; Warren, 1967) This issue is important because basic public services are often impeded by competition, duplication of function and other interorganizational difficulties. There has, however, been little attempt to generalize these ideas in a way corresponding to the general fact that routine, cooperative relations between organizations are also a crucial aspect of their everyday functioning.

Sets of organizations form complex networks of interaction, as do individuals; indeed, the magnitude of complexity is probably greater than that attaching to the study of networks of individuals or to that of single organizations. This complexity has discouraged attempts at theoretical elaboration, let alone empirical investigation. Evan (1966) provides some useful leads; J. Levine (1972) offers a new approach to interlocking directorates.

One fundamental area to be examined is the individual behavior constituting the interface between organizations. Thompson (1962) does this for individuals in "output roles"—that is, those engaged in distributing whatever it is that an organization produces. Similar study could be given to "input roles." Evan combines these ideas by suggesting that input-output analyses of information, influence, and personnel could be carried out for sets of organizations (1966, 186). Scrutiny of the flow of men between organizations is of particular interest to me. If my study had dealt with internal labor markets, we could have learned a good deal about the structure of given organizations by examining how personnel flowed from one department or division to another, and which units were thus linked. Similarly, if we consider a set of organizations as a system, study of *its* internal mobility patterns should reveal important details of its structure.

If comprehensive data could be collected enabling us to represent, in a square matrix, the flow of men between organizations, standard sociometric techniques could be applied to isolate "cliques" of organizations; asymmetry of flow between sets might then be used to index the prestige of different sets of organizations. (Davis and Leinhardt, 1972 use a similar method for small groups of individuals.) Categories arrived at by such methods would have more social reality than our standard industrial classifications.

The present data are obviously not suited to this design. Some of the details, however, may be useful in pointing up how, in many cases, mobility between two organizations is induced by the routine relationships which they maintain with each other.

Any personnel flow between two given organizations is significant in analyzing their overall pattern of interconnection. But for the purpose of specifying the causal influence of interorganizational relations, four varieties may be distinguished, which have somewhat different implications: 1) The move may be carried out via direct application or formal intermediaries. Here, little is revealed to us about relationships between the sending and receiving organizations since the mobility is probably not a result of such relationships. 2) The move may be made as a result of information supplied by a personal contact who is in some nonbusiness relationship with the mover, or who knows of the job-opening for some nonbusiness reason (is, for example, a social friend of the employer). As in the first case, little is implied about interorganizational relations, and so these two cases will not be treated further here. 3) The move may be made via information supplied to the mover by a business colleague in the receiving company; in such cases, the business relationship, presumably a necessary part of relations between the two companies, *has* led to an interchange of personnel. 4) The move is made on account of information supplied by someone in the other company, with whom connection is maintained not primarily due to company relations but because the individual had had a work relationship with him at some *previous* time. Here the implications for our topic are more complex.

The third pattern results from the fact that in a highly differentiated economy, hardly any firms are self-sufficient. Thus, it is necessary for almost any company to maintain face-to-face communication with other companies in similar or complementary fields. Various studies, especially those carried out in Sweden, suggest that *non* face-to-face contacts—those handled via telephone, letter and other modes, are "best suited to the transmission of simple, well-structured routine information. The more complicated or non-routine the information becomes, the greater the advantages of the direct personal contact" (Törnqvist, 1970:27). While this point is not surprising, it is important since it suggests that such interorganizational contacts, far from representing a carryover from "traditional" ways of doing business, actually are likely to become more rather than less important with the increasing technical complexity of our economic system. (Cf. the emphasis of J.K. Galbraith on the "technostructure," in his *New Industrial State*.) There has been little systematic research on the volume of these contacts; an exception is Törnqvist's report of two Swedish studies. Both showed not only a large volume, but also an almost linear tendency for the number of contacts per individual and the number of hours per week spent in such external contacts to increase in proportion to rank and income level within organizations. (Cf. here the finding of Homans, 1950, for primary groups, pp. 144–145.) Analysis of which functions were being carried out by those heavily engaged in external contacts showed that these were,

indeed, functions in which overall employment is expanding rather
than contracting (Törnqvist, 1970:90–91). This line of argument
complements the one in the previous chapter, in showing still
another way in which particularistic tendencies persist, for good
reasons, in modern, technically complex economic situations.

Perhaps the most obvious such interface between firms is that
having to do with sales and purchasing. Individuals who spend all
their time as sales agents for some company, and who travel from
one organization to another in this capacity, are especially likely
to become knowledgeable about the existence of job opportunities.
The career of Bruce S. shows this clearly:

Case #21: Mr. S. owned a bakery for 22 years in Germany. In 1963
he came to the United States to work for his uncle, with the
intention of buying out *his* bakery. They could not agree, however,
on terms. While working there, Mr. S. got to know the owner of a
food wholesaling company, who came around to the bakery selling.
He told Mr. S. to come to him if he ever needed a job. When he
fell out with his uncle, he did so, and became a salesman for the
wholesaler. Among others, he sold to the part-owner of a supermarket with an in-store bakery. When he bought the bakery out,
he invited Mr. S. to become manager. Another individual to whom
Bruce S. had sold food, meanwhile, became a salesman himself and
now sold to him. When the bakery showed signs of bankruptcy,
Mr. S. contacted him, and he, in turn, contacted the owner of a
store *he* had been selling to, where he knew there was an opening,
to arrange an interview for Mr. S. He was hired, and now holds
this job.

One respondent, manager of a jewelry store, said that salesmen
visiting such stores *intentionally* collect job information, and systematically exchange it at regional meetings. They thus help both
employers and employees fill jobs satisfactorily, enhancing their
relationships with both. They do so more effectively than a formal
intermediary because of their personal knowledge of the people
involved.

Contact brought about through buying and selling takes many
forms. One respondent found a job in a government agency because

of relationships made in the course of "contract peddling." Besides scientific work in the company at which he previously worked, he also had the assignment of travelling to government agencies to try to win contracts for his firm to carry out various technical projects. Since much government technical work is carried out on contracts of this kind, the liaison necessary to bid on these generates a large number of personal ties. The ideological term for transfer of personnel between industry and government based on previous ties of this kind is "military-industrial complex." Consistent exchange of personnel in this way may well have deleterious effects; it should be understood, however, that rather than resulting from conspiracy, such transfer is consonant with the way most PTM jobs are acquired.

Buying and selling generate contacts even after a sale has been decided on; one respondent reported that once the contract had been concluded for his company to supply certain equipment to a larger company, he was asked to help coordinate and settle various technical details between the two companies. Every couple of weeks he met with a representative of the relevant department in the other company; after four months, the latter indicated that he would like to have the respondent work in his department, as there was an opening to be filled. The respondent believed that his own company was "going down the drain," so he decided to accept the offer.

Other respondents reported that they had found jobs through contacts acquired while working on industry-wide committees which had the task of coordinating and calibrating standards to be observed in technical specifications. The purpose of such committees is partly to facilitate the buying and selling of equipment among companies; hence, still another aspect of buying and selling becomes relevant.

Another division of labor which creates personal contacts arises from the size distribution of firms in certain industries. Certain tasks cannot be handled efficiently by small units and are thus, in effect, subcontracted to larger ones of the same kind. In my sample, one example of this occurred several times: small banks often turn their investment accounts over to larger ones which specialize in

this activity. The larger banks must solicit these accounts, thus
sending representatives who act as salesmen for this purpose. To the
extent that there exists personnel transfer from larger to smaller
firms in an industry, some of it may be mediated by contacts created
in this way.

The situation of case 4), above, is more complex. Here, mobility
results from information supplied by someone in another company,
but the tie was not maintained primarily due to current work
relations but because the two individuals had had some *previous*
work relationship. At least seven subtypes of this case can be
described, depending on whether the two individuals worked in the
same or different firms when they first met, whether either present
firm was involved, and which worked where. As compared to case
3), additional complexity is introduced here primarily by the time
dimension; as indicated in Chapters 5 and 6, long-term relationships
may be quite important.

The most common subtype of case 4) may be that in which
people who used to work at the company (C_1) where the mobile
individual (P) has moved from, come to be scattered, over time,
through other companies; even the most marginal maintenance of
such contacts may be sufficient to be informed of job opportunities
in these other firms. That is, current flow of personnel between two
companies $(C_1$ and $C_2)$ may make future flow more likely. To find
out whether present mobility was induced by some previous personnel flow, a tracing procedure can be utilized. Determine, first,
how our individual's *contact* (O_1) happened to move from C_1 to
C_2. If this move was primarily mediated by a work relationship to
some third person (O_2) based on that person's tenure at C_2, the
trace would be ended. In the relation between the contact (O_1) and
his contact (O_2), we would see what facets of the operations of
the two companies facilitated both the movement of O_1 and P to
C_2. But if O_1 had moved to C_2 via some friend, O_3, whom he had
known at C_1, but who had *later* gone to C_2, then the causes of
O_3's move would need to be investigated. The trace would end
when: 1) someone was found who moved from C_1 to C_2 through
a personal contact he knew primarily because the latter was from

C_2, and there was some interorganizational process connecting the two individuals, or 2) someone was found who had moved primarily by direct application, formal means or social contacts. In the latter case, no interorganizational process would be causally implicated, directly or indirectly.[1]

Similar tracing procedures could be developed for the other sub-types of case 4). I omit them, both to avoid tedium and also because I was not able to carry out any such tracing procedures in my own study. Any further discussion would thus be excessively abstract, without the empirical detail necessary to demonstrate that such complex procedures would prove useful. The four cases described above are not exhaustive of the possibilities, as individuals may move through work contacts met through interorganizational processes, but who are employees of neither the sending nor receiving organization. This may be called case 5). Many such individuals are institutionalized liaisons. For example:

Case #22: Paul J. was commissioner of health in a Massachusetts town. He had a working relationship with an official from the U.S. Dept of HEW, who was assigned as liaison with his city and several others in the area. During a phone conversation, he mentioned to Mr. J. an opportunity that had arisen in another of the cities with which he was in contact. Suspecting that this would be a better job in terms of funds and leeway, Mr. J. investigated, and was hired.

Those who coordinate the activity of several organizations with that of their own, or who coordinate subdivisions within an organization, are likely to know more about opportunities in each location than those working entirely within one. Had I not excluded internal labor markets from this study, roles of this kind might have assumed much more importance.

The data which I have collected are not sufficiently extensive to attempt estimation of what proportion of the uses of personal contacts fall into cases 1)–5), let alone to try to sort out the number

1. Another possibility is that O_1 moved to C_2 through a contact, O_4, whom he had known at C_1, who had moved to a third company, C_3, and only *then* to C_2. There, the possibility exists of causal influence of a *chain* of inter-organizational relations.

in the various subtypes of 4). A general upper-bound can be suggested, however, for the proportion of cases where the relevant
interpersonal tie may have been generated by some interoganiza-
tional function. This can be done by computing the proportion of
cases where a new job was found through contacts, in which a
work contact was used who knew of the job for some work-related
reason. This number corresponds to those in Table 14 who are in
the last four columns and first three rows. The resulting figure is
93/146 or 63.6 percent. It is an upper bound, only, since the traces
suggested for case 4) instances may find for some cases that there
is no direct or indirect causation of interorganizational relations.
While this figure can only be considered a crude approximation,
then, it seems likely that the true figure is substantial.

The importance of all types of interorganizational mobility lies
in its effects. While it may seem from the point of view of some
individual firm to involve "pirating," and be greatly resented, it can
be seen from a larger perspective as effecting cohesion among those
firms exchanging personnel. The man who changes jobs not only
moves from one network of ties to another, but also, in so doing,
establishes a link between these two networks. Especially within
professional and technical specialties which are relatively well-
defined, this has the effect of generating an elaborate arrangement
of ties connecting the more coherent clusters of ties which constitute operative networks in particular locations.

Fields which do not possess unity of definition may move
toward it by such interchange of personnel. The inter-firm network
resulting from this allows information and ideas to move fairly
easily through a field, giving it some coherence and perhaps a
"sense of community." The man who has worked at company A
and now moves to B is likely to narrow the differences between
the two companies by virtue of bringing certain habits and styles
of work and thought learned there to the new setting.

An Application: The Outcome of Conglomerate Acquisition

The ideas of this chapter may be of value in attacking traditional
problems in organizational analysis. A common theme in recent

sociology, for example, is that of increasing bureaucratization and impersonality of work, as organizations pass into new and presumably more impersonal hands. Such mergers and takeovers can be seen as one species of interorganizational relations. One recalls Warner's description of the situation in "Yankee City" (Newburyport) when the local shoe industry passed into the hands of nonlocal owners; morale sank, as men complained that the new people had no personal interest in the operation, and unlike the old owners, saw it purely as a business (Warner and Low, 1947; see also Stein, 1960:70–93).

I noticed in the course of my interviews that a number of respondents used phrases that could easily have been cribbed out of Warner's account, to describe why their old job had been written out of existence. These people were the victims of reorganization attendant to one of the recent instances of conglomerate merger. They indicated that the new management (IT&T in several cases) was unpleasantly "impersonal," and that morale had sunk considerably; numerous jobs, notably their own, had been casualties of the reorganization.

But given my general results, it becomes plausible that the new management is not so much being impersonal as being personal in social networks different from those of the individuals who are presently in the organization. Those who had hired the present employees, usually on the basis of previous personal knowledge, have been removed as the operative leaders. Interpersonal networks which made the work situation seem friendly and personalized now lose those who have the authority to keep them intact; such networks must appear, also, somewhat threatening to the control of new managers. These individuals have, of course, careers of their own, during which they have acquired many personal contacts they would prefer to work with. By replacing current networks with members of the ones into which they are tied, they are in reality behaving no differently from those who set up the organization as it now stands.

Such incidents might occur whenever management changes hands. A number of cases differ however. If an organization is bought out by a close competitor, or by some firm which has maintained close relations with it for some other reason, then there may be, to start with, enough ties between the old and new managements, left over from previous inter-organizational relations, to stave off radical reorganization and resulting feelings of impersonality. Almost by definition, conglomerate acquisitions do not fall into this category; it is likely that the acquiring organization will be quite separate from the acquired one in the sense of not having any personal ties into it.

Firms related "vertically" will have been engaged in buying and selling to one another; those related "horizontally" will have had, at least, to set some standards in common, and perhaps will have come to informal agreements on prices and other policies. These contacts are a source of cohesion, as well as generating interorganizational mobility that further serves cohesion in ways suggested above. It would seem that horizontal and vertical mergers, then, would be less disruptive than conglomerate ones, in which the resulting dispersion of personal networks (if management takes seriously the idea of taking control of the firm) may have short-term effects on productivity exactly counter to that envisioned. This may be one reason that conglomerate performance has, thus far, been somewhat short of spectacular.

In any time period, some firms will change hands. It may be guessed that when such changes occur with more frequency than usual, some analysts will assert, as will many who are close to particular situations, that the economy is becoming more "impersonal." It is interesting that Warner's Yankee City research took place in the early 1930's, just after a five-year wave of mergers and acquisitions (1925-1929) which was not exceeded until 1965-1969 (1971 Statistical Abstract of the U.S., Table #743).

For Warner's case, there is a certain face validity to the thesis that when ownership of a firm passes out of the *community* into absentee ownership, an element of impersonality is introduced. But this is not at issue for PTM specialties, which rarely draw their labor force from what would be called a local community, in either a geographic or ethnographic sense. In such cases, "impersonality" can be seen as transitional; a new network of individuals has intruded on an older one. The situation is unstable and will tend toward a resolution which expels some of the older group and coopts others. "Impersonality" as a permanent feature of the economy or of any large number of firms is unlikely, at the PTM level, given the usual style by which such personnel are recruited into organizations—a style deriving in part from the necessity for interorganizational contact.

Chapter

Comparative Perspectives

In this chapter I want to consider to what extent my findings
are peculiar to higher white-collar workers in Massachusetts, rather
than being aspects of the human condition.[1] I will attempt comparison with other societies, past and present, simple and complex.
The question is whether all job systems operate as found here, or
if certain features in the economic or social structure may produce
different results.

The available relevant data, however, are extremely sparse.
Questions are not generally posed in such a way as to elicit the
amount of detail I have reported about interpersonal contacts.
Even after reading detailed treatises on the economies of various
types of societies one has little clear idea of how particular people
are recruited for particular kinds of work. This is not surprising
if we consider that the average layman in the United States, for
instance, would also be incapable of providing more than a small
part of the data presented in this study. Although he would have
personal experience in our system of work and jobs, he would
be unlikely to have detailed information about how *others* were
recruited (see Appendix A, below). Such information is available
only if specifically collected; it is not especially predictable from
other known characteristics of a society—at least in our present
state of knowledge. Hence, the present chapter is only a skeleton,
included more to indicate the importance of the problem than to
display the richness of data available to deal with it.

1. In Appendix A, I discuss the question of how representative the Newton
sample is likely to be of the United States; in the Introduction a summary
may be found of studies of American working-class patterns, which are, on
the whole, quite similar to those found in this study for PTM workers.

A first observation is that the questions of my study apply poorly to societies where most individuals do not hold "jobs" which are clearly differentiated from their other activities, or do not work in organizations created by others. Such societies do carry out work, of course, and a variety of recruitment techniques are used. These are nicely described by Udy (1959) under the headings of territorial, social (for example, by kinship), custodial (for example, serfdom, tenancy, slavery), reciprocal, and contractual.

Most work in industrial societies is "contractual"—that is, a contract is made between two parties, entered into voluntarily, specifying the type, duration, and recompense of work to be carried out. For work to be carried out by contract requires it to be more clearly differentiated from other elements of social life than it is in other types of recruitment. Where recruitment is territorial— that is, where all those in a given area pitch in—work is an integral part of everyday life and is not much thought of apart from it. Where recruitment is by kinship or other social criteria, the work done is seen in terms of fulfillment of obligations; the same is true when work is explicitly reciprocal. Work done under political duress is clearly embedded in a system of power differentials and political obligations. Given its greater differentiation from other social aspects, most theories of modernization would lead us to assume that contractual work would appear in modernized settings.

The typology leads us to suppose that there is a well-defined qualitative difference in types of recruitment, between contractual and other types, in that there is no predetermined social source, in contractual work, from which individuals are to be recruited. This is deceiving on both sides, however. For "pre-contractual" work, it may indeed be the case that some given familial, political, or religious group membership has been prescribed as requisite for recruitment to some type of work—yet a great deal of leeway is still available. In most cases only a small subset of those available on some given criterion is chosen; how these particular ones are singled out may involve factors similar to those considered in the present study. For contractual work, of course, much of my argument has consisted of showing that impersonal selection directed by abstract criteria is much less common than supposed.

If we limit our attention to societies with contractual labor, considerable continuity can be established between recruitment in pre-industrial and industrial societies. This continuity can be seen primarily in relatively impersonal modes of recruitment: shape-ups, guilds, and labor contractors.

The "shape-up" is used here as a generic term for any arrange-ment in which a particular physical place is known at which prospective employers and employees are to meet one another at a designated time for the purpose of matching job offers with job seekers. Depending on the type of work and the state of the economy, either employees or employers might have the upper hand; indeed, the shape-up almost looks to be a dramatization of the economists's perfect labor market.

The first shape-ups in England followed the bubonic plague, and seem to have been organized to prevent workers from taking excessive advantage of the severe labor shortage resulting from the epidemic. A law of 1351 required that agricultural workers should "bring openly in their hands to the merchant towns their instru-ments and there shall be hired in a common place and not pri-vately" (Mund, 1948:96). Annual "hiring fairs" developed from these shape-ups and were said to be treated by workers as general festivals once hiring was over.

Shape-ups have usually been, as their name suggests, less happy for workers. They are presently found universally in casual, un-skilled work, with marked fluctuations in the demand for labor. Longshoremen and seasonal farm laborers are especially familiar with the most degrading varieties. When, as is often the case, there is an excess of labor supply over demand, the institution comes to resemble a cattle market. Jensen (1964) describes such shape-ups for the dock work of New York, London, Liverpool, Rotterdam, and Marseilles, and Fisher (1953) for American migrant labor. These are typically early-morning affairs, beginning as early as 2 A.M. The local skid row is often the site chosen by employers, though innu-

merable ghetto and other street corners in American cities are
locally known as hiring sites for unskilled labor.

Shape-ups are easy to identify for the PTM workers in my
sample. At colleges and professional meetings, systematic interviewing arrangements are often made so that prospective employees
and employers can be matched up. This is a form of shape-up and
varies between the forms considered more or less pleasant. In
excess demand markets, for instance, college graduates may find
interviewing with various companies at their college as pleasant
as scarce workers in post-Bubonic-plague England found their
hiring fairs. When jobs are scarce, on the other hand the shape-up
at professional meetings is often referred to as the "slave-market."

Where work must be done at many different locations, especially
with heavy seasonal demand, the "labor contractor" tends to appear.
The contractor, a figure in both pre-industrial and industrial labor
markets, employs workers on subcontract; he may send individuals
or groups to particular employers. His responsibility may be
limited to supply of the men on a one-time basis, or may range all
the way to the situation in which he recruits, houses, supervises,
transports, and pays the men, then finds another employer to whom
he brings the same group and repeats the process. Generally contractors do not handle all these functions except in supplying
unskilled labor, as in the California harvest labor market (Fisher,
1953:49–56). The types of labor supplied by contractors range
from unskilled migrant farm labor through skilled craftsmen all the
way to workers with considerable technical training.

Many immigrants were brought to the United States as part of
a labor contracting arrangement. "Padrones," usually of the same
ethnic group as the people to be recruited, were paid by American
employers to supply laborers; Italians and Chinese immigrants were
often brought on this basis to work on railroads. Sometimes the
padrone's role ended there, sometimes he also acted as foreman for
the railroad. The U.S. Immigration Commission reported that this
system often resulted in a kind of "slavery," and was thus outlawed
in 1885; the law, however, was unenforceable (U.S. Immigration
Commission, 1911).

Particularly in economies with both feudal *and* industrial elements, the contractor system may take on strong paternalistic aspects. In the Japanese pattern, many contractors had highly stratified organizations which practiced elaborate ceremonies upon the entrance of new members. Ranks in the organization were patterned on kinship. In some cases the arrangement was lifelong, though this was variable. Unskilled as well as skilled labor (especially in construction where work is clearly divided into projects) was supplied until quite recently by labor contractors who took responsibility for finding work, assuring subsistence, and even caring for men in time of illness. Some contractors controlled as many as 50,000 workers (Bennett and Ishino, 1963:40–46; Yoshino, 1968:ch. 3). Employers liked the system as it freed them of obligations to employees and of the burden of recruiting. Employees were pleased with the security provided.

In the United States, contractors appeared in engineering and technical work after World War II. Their organizations are often known as "job-shops," and their employees as "job-shoppers" not to be confused with the style of production called the "jobshop method," or with chronic job-seekers. Nearly all of my respondents who did technical work reported that there were job-shoppers in their firm, though only a few were currently job-shopping or had been at some previous time. (Job-shoppers are called, from the point of view of the hiring company, "contract" or "per-diem" personnel.) Those who job-shop are paid considerably more than a company's "direct" employees, but generally receive none of the usual fringe benefits and can be dropped more easily. Often their work is limited to specific contracts which the company has received. The proportion of total employees in a company who are on loan from such labor contractors appears to reach 15–25 percent when there is an unexpected surge of work to be done. Industries like the automobile industry, where work is seasonal in nature, make especially heavy use of such employees.

Related to labor contracting is the practice of (pre-industrial) guilds, labor unions, and some professional organizations of controlling the number and identity of people who may work at a particular trade, and of regulating and specifying who may work for whom. Nearly all types of work are susceptible to arrangements of this kind. Even dock labor, usually mediated by haphazard shape-ups, can be controlled by guilds, as it was in Marseilles from the 14th century till nearly 1900, when shippers insisted on hiring their own men in a "free market" (Jensen 1964:254–255). Remnants of guild control of labor supply are found in PTM fields such as medicine, law, and college teaching. The hiring of Jewish Conservative rabbis follows the guild procedure quite closely.

Organizations involved in labor contracting may be placed on a continuum starting from employment agencies, ranging through guilds, job-shops, consulting-firms, to Japanese-style contracting organizations. The dimension of relevance is closeness of connection of the employee to the intermediary. Before and after an employment agency finds a job for someone, and the proper fees are paid, there is no connection. Job-shops and guilds hire out their members for job after job, thus holding certain claims on their loyalty; but since job-tenures may be long, this loyalty often shifts to the subcontractor. In the case of job-shops, employees often try to get themselves hired "direct," a more secure existence. Consultants and migrant laborers alike (in cases where labor is supplied by a closely knit contracting organization) carry out specific short-term assignments, maintaining loyalty to the consulting firm or contractor. Consultants may actually do the bulk of their work on the physical premises of the consulting firm rather than on that of the subcontractor. Naturally other types of firms may be found along the range which I have specified by these ideal types.

The main point of the discussion thus far is to show that there is a considerable similarity in recruitment between pre-industrial and industrial labor markets, despite the revolution supposedly wrought by modernization. In fact, given the impersonality usually imputed to *industrial* systems, it is interesting that one finds mainly relatively impersonal mechanisms like shape-ups and employment intermediaries to be common in pre-industrial situations, but little of the emphasis on personal contacts which I found in my survey of American PTM work.

This is misleading for two reasons, however. First, institutionalized mechanisms like the ones described are the ones which are likely to be recorded for posterity. The more personal arrangements are inherently private and may permanently elude the historian's search. Second, the incidence of labor contracting does not *necessarily* imply impersonality. When a labor contractor supplies a worker to a firm, the contractor, not the firm, in many cases, is the effective employer; for our purposes, then, the operational question becomes one of how one came to work for a given contractor. Personal contacts may well be involved at this stage, but this detail is rarely recorded. The safest conclusion we can reach on this matter, then, is that differences in recruitment between the most "rationalized" sector of our economy and pre-industrial contractual systems are almost certainly less than generally supposed, and not necessarily in the direction of increasing "impersonality."

It is also useful to ask whether important differences may exist in modes of job-finding among the various industrialized economies. No study which I have uncovered bears directly on this issue for a general sample in an economy other than the United States. I am reduced, therefore, to suggesting some factors which might make a difference. Kerr suggests that we conceive three general types of labor market: 1) "open"—the perfect labor market of classical economics; 2) "guild"—where the labor force is stratified horizontally; relatively free movement exists between firms but not between crafts; and 3) "manorial"—in which the labor force is stratified vertically; attachment is to place of work, and there may be "lifelong attachment of the worker to his plant" (1954:106). Kerr suggests Denmark (for skilled workers, at least) as typifying the guild economy, and Germany and Japan the manorial one. It is not clear whether there exists any industrialized economy in which professional, technical, and managerial work is heavily organized along guild lines. A general argument has been made for the case of Japan, however, that its labor force is characterized by the ideal and practice of "lifetime commitment" to a single firm. Abegglen's study of large Japanese factories (1958) popularized this argument, and supported it by asserting that the practice resulted from

Japanese cultural peculiarities—the emphasis in Japan on loyalty to the group, and the familiarity of paternal, feudalistic patterns.

In general, such an argument represents a major alternative to the patterns reported in my study. My respondents are preeminently economic men, acting to maximize their personal advantage, without weighing heavily the ultimate advantage of the firm to which they are currently attached. If they felt a moral obligation to stick with that firm, it is unlikely that personal contacts which they have, in fact utilized, would influence them to move. A "manorial" system would, moreover, be self-maintaining, in that so much American inter-firm mobility depends on previous inter-firm mobility. Having had a career in several different firms is what allowed many of my respondents to *have* a set of personal contacts scattered around in many firms through their field.

Mounting evidence of recent research, however, makes it doubtful that the Japanese economy can properly be characterized as "manorial," or that "lifetime commitment" is the norm. To begin with, Taira's detailed study of the history of the labor market in Japan shows that employer paternalism, "popularly attributed to unchanging Japanese traditions, was in fact a new institutional invention in response to the labor-market conditions that prevailed during the first cycle of Japan's industrialization." (1970:99). Until about 1920, employees shifted around at will from one firm to another, making long-range economic planning difficult for managers. (Taira, 1970:129-130; Yoshino, 1968:ch. 3). Especially during the 1920's, a pattern became institutionalized in which large firms hired boys out of school who were, in principle, to spend their entire career in that firm (Somers and Tsuda, 1966:203). Actual figures computed at various times, however, indicate that only a small proportion of Japanese workers do spend their entire career in this way (Taira, 1970:157; Marsh and Mannari, 1971:798).

One way the image of lifetime commitment is maintained is the practice of hiring temporary employees from labor contractors. The rapidly expanding auto industry as well as shipbuilding and electrical products uses many such workers; Toyota has 42 percent of all its employees on this basis (Somers and Tsuda, 1966:215).

Unlike American subcontract workers ("job-shoppers") such workers in Japan receive *lower* pay than regular employees, and no fringe benefits or job security. Taira suggests that firms under-report the number of such temporary workers, and that many are actually long-term employees, on whom companies are saving money (1970:161-162). This practice, common at least since the 1930's, contrasts sharply with the ideal of employer paternalism and lifetime commitment.

Despite these severe reservations, it does appear that inter-firm mobility in Japan is less common than in the United States (Marsh and Mannari, 1971:798). Among the nation's highest ranking executives, 46 percent spend their whole career in a single firm (Yoshino, 1968: 88-89). While this differs considerably from any monolithic idea about lifetime commitment, it is probably also quite different from the American pattern. This suggests that more high-level job-changes than here are taking place in internal labor markets, and would have to be analyzed with a framework appropriate to the dynamics of a single firm. A larger proportion of non internal-market cases than here would then be entry-level jobs. In my PTM sample, such jobs have tended heavily to be mediated through formal means and direct application, for reasons which ought to be general across cultures. One might guess, then, that to the extent that an economy *was* "manorial," such mechanisms would increase in importance.

Some evidence supports this notion: a recent student of Japanese labor markets suggests that the proportion finding jobs by personal contacts is about 30 percent, considerably lower than most American figures (Robert Cole, 1970: personal communication). Public employment services and school authorities are estimated, on the other hand, to place nearly 45 percent of all new hires (Somers and Tsuda, 1966:221, 230). Here we must note, however, that when a formal mechanism becomes heavily used by particular employers, the formal aspect wears off. Somers and Tsuda report that though employers list vacancies with public employment offices, "the cordial and informal relations between the employer and school authorities can play a more crucial role in the filling of the vacancy"

(1966:219). We may also surmise that the relation of students to
school authorities is somewhat less formal than it would be to an
employment agency.

For Germany, the other economy suggested by Kerr as "manorial," Lester estimates that "a quarter to a third of all new hires in
the professional managerial fields are handled through the . . . German Employment Service" (1966b:80). These figures and those
for Japan may be compared to the 10 percent of my PTM sample
finding jobs through agencies of various kinds. The figures cited,
however, are produced from the records of state agencies and from
surveys of employers. Until figures are available from a random
sample of *workers*, it will not be clear how accurate the statistics are.

One factor affecting the Japanese situation, which may be
important in general in determining the applicability of my findings,
is the size of firms. Abegglen's analysis (1958) was of large firms,
and it appears that to the extent that "lifetime commitment" does
obtain it may be limited to large firms (Somers and Tsuda 1966:
205; Marsh and Mannari 1971:799). Quite apart from cultural
reasons one could expect the rate of mobility out of large firms to
be smaller, and the average tenure longer simply because large
firms do possess an internal labor market in which individuals may
find an opportunity to advance. Those of *my* respondents who
worked in firms of size 100 or more were much less likely to find
their jobs through contacts than those working in smaller firms
(43 vs. 60 percent), and much more likely to use direct application
(31.2 vs. 13.3 percent; $N = 228$; $p = 0.06$). A similar finding was
reported by Malm for the San Francisco labor market (1954:225).
This may be partly a result of the tendency of jobs filled from
outside such firms to be "entry-level" jobs (which are, for PTM
workers, more likely than higher-level jobs to be filled by formal
means); also, large firms will be better known. This reputation will
generate a great deal of direct application, and may put small firms
at a disadvantage under some circumstances (Wilcock and Sobel,
1958:25).

The general point here is that a difference in the size distribution
of firms between two economies, however generated, would, if

my conjectures are correct, have, for purely structural reasons, the effect of reducing the rate of use of personal contacts in inter-firm mobility. This rate should be lower to the extent that workers are concentrated in large firms, other things being equal.

Unfortunately, comparison of the American and Japanese size-distributions do not support the argument. Marsh and Mannari report (1971:799) that in 1966, 16 percent of Japanese manufac-turing workers worked in establishments with 1000 or more employees. The 1970 figure for the U.S. is at least 24 percent (U.S. Department of Commerce 1971:29, 31).[2] Yet, both the overall inter-firm mobility rate and (probably) the rate at which such moves are initiated by contacts, are higher for the U.S. It may be that large Japanese firms comprise a more efficient labor market inter-nally because they gather more people over a smaller geographic space than do large U.S. firms. Other elements of the way large firms are organized would need to be analyzed here—such as the extent of independence of sub-units from one another. Where this is high, inter-firm mobility should be increased, since complementarity, and therefore personal contacts, will have to *cross* inter-firm boundaries. A detailed study would be necessary to determine the relative importance of these two factors and of presence or absence of a "lifetime commitment" ideology on American and Japanese mobility rates.

I have been unable to reach many general conclusions in this cursory discussion of non-American labor markets principally because there exist no studies strictly comparable to the present one. The main conclusion emerging from my analysis of factors affecting various kinds of labor markets is that there is no strong reason to expect processes in industrial non-American markets, or even in

2. This minimum was computed as follows: there are 19.8 million industrial workers, of whom 8.73 million work in establishments of 500 or more employees. No direct figures are given for larger size categories, but we do find that of the 6,265 manufacturing units with 500 or more employees, 3,799 have from 500–999 employees. If each such unit had exactly 999, they would employ 3.79 million workers, leaving 4.94 million in the larger estab-lishments, or a bit over 24 percent of the 19.8 million industrial workers. Since the average number in firms of the 500–999 class is surely under 999, the 24 percent estimate is low.

some pre-industrial ones, to be *radically* different from those
reported here, though the *relative frequency* of some processes may
vary because of structural differences across economies. Cultural
differences in attitudes towards work and employers may have a
substantial impact, but this is by no means obvious from existing
evidence. The main conclusion is negative then: it is not clear that
my results do not reflect the situation in a wide variety of economies.
Positive conclusions must await further research.

Chapter
10

Applications

In Chapters 4 and 7, I suggested some abstract applications of the concepts and ideas presented in this study—having to do with the "demography" of jobs, and with lines of sociological and political research analogous to the one pursued here. Now I want to suggest some more immediately practical applications—to programs which seek to find suitable jobs for designated groups. Some such programs deal mainly with the blue-collar unemployed, while others, currently tagged as "affirmative action," aim to upgrade the employment status of groups which have been discriminated against —women and blacks being the most frequently noted cases. Given the subject matter of my study, it may seem that I exceed my legitimate province by discussing women, blacks, and the blue-collar unemployed. But I doubt that this is actually so daring a step: with few exceptions, my findings are consistent with those of blue-collar studies, though these have not gone into the same amount of sociological detail. Comparable studies of women, blacks, and other ethnic or status groups are too few and rudimentary to allow evaluation of the appropriateness of these comments. Distinctions among groups will be necessary here, and further research may, naturally, invalidate some of these suggestions.

The improvement of employment opportunity has many ramifications; I will touch only on those which have some relation to the information channels by which people find work. The single prescription which has been made more often than any other is that public employment services be expanded so as to cover far more vacancies than presently. (See, for example, De Schweinetz, 1932: 153; Lester, 1966b:210; Brown, 1967:179; Lurie and Rayack,

1968:377-378.) Nationwide computerized matching systems have been proposed and are being tested in a preliminary way (U.S. Dept. of Labor, 1970:199-205; 1971:179-184; 1972:141-145).

These systems have appeal in attempts at affirmative action since they appear to offer the possibility of job placement via universalistic criteria. It is problematic, however, whether such matching can compete successfully with the preference of employers and employees for more personal methods. Two main issues arise. One is whether computerized systems can offer the kind of *intensive* information usually found only through contacts (cf. Chapter 7, above). Holt and Huber (1969) suggest that this problem can be handled by taking detailed information from employers and employees on their structure of preferences. It is probably worth attempting to do this, but my results support Ullman's more pessimistic conclusion that "there are some kinds of data that cannot be numerically reproduced and are thus beyond the ken of the computer. These are the factors that depend upon subtle differences in people and in their perceptions. The best examples involve the fit between individual personalities and the "personality" of the job and organization. Specifically, these factors include such things as the challenge of the job and relations with peers and superiors" (1969:51).

A second problem is closely related. Given the preference for personal methods, there is every reason to suppose that computer coverage of job vacancies will remain incomplete and that the better jobs and prospects will be matched by "word of mouth," as now, thus perpetuating the (probable) initial disadvantage of those using computer matching. Moreover, the "quasi-jobs" and "quasi-searchers" defined in Chapter 1, above, would be unlikely to be tapped by a centralized information system.

It is instructive to compare computer dating systems to those meant for job-matching. The same two problems obtain: matching is generally poor because information is not sufficiently intensive, and coverage of the population is heavily biassed toward those who have failed in more personalized attempts. Though many are intrigued by the idea and experiment with it, few marriages (but many dates) are likely to result. Similarly, jobs which are temporary and inter-changeable may be well-suited to recruitment by computer—as in longshoremen's work (Jensen 1967); such jobs are more like dates than marriages. Incompatibilities that would be intolerable over the long term can be written off as a temporary nuisance, so long as some minimum standard is met.

Analysts who recognize these points sometimes pursue them to the logical conclusion. Ullman advises job-seekers to "cultivate informal labor-market contacts rather than relying on intermediaries for their job-search" (1968:164). Lurie and Rayack suggest that it would "help considerably if the Negro community could develop an informal structure in some measure similar to the informal job information and placement services that other minority groups have used" (1968:378). This is easier said than done. If the suggestion means that one should acquire *new* labor-market contacts, the process could be a long one. In my sample, over 80 percent of those supplying job information had known my respondent for more than two years; nearly two-thirds had known them five or more years. Even more to the point is that it is all but impossible to arrange one's interaction in such an artificial way. The idea that one was being "cultivated" as a potential labor market contact would offer strong motivation to curtail a relationship. Such proposals can arise only through failure to recognize the extent to which labor-market behavior is embedded in other economic and social activity.

Especially important to recognize, moreover, is the self-maintaining aspect of personal contact systems. Blacks are at a disadvantage in using informal channels of job information not because they have failed to "develop an informal structure" suitable to the need, but because they are presently under-represented *in the structure of employment itself*. If those presently employed in a given industry or firm have no black friends, no blacks will enter those settings through personal contacts. Once a core of blacks (or whatever group is in question) has become established, however, a multiplier effect can be anticipated, as they recruit friends and relatives, who do the same, and so on. Once achieved, this situation is self-sustaining.

An experiment of the Rochester Employment Service suggests
one way this can be done efficiently. Its "outreach" efforts show
that it is feasible not only to recruit in pool-halls, snack-bars and
other public places, but also by going house-to-house (Adams
1969:118-152). The significance of this can be seen if we ask
abstractly how a multiplier effect can be best achieved. That is, if we
are to have a core of (say) black workers who will recruit their
friends, who will recruit *their* friends, and so forth, we may ask how
the core can be selected so as to maximize the total number
ultimately recruited. The primary damper on the multiplier effect
is the overlap of friendship circles. If everyone in a sizeable initial
core knew everyone else, for instance, the total number who could
be brought in by this group would be very much reduced since
there would be substantial overlap among the friendship circles of
the various individuals. When members of a group share many·
mutual friends, they are less likely to be effective as spreaders of
information (Granovetter, 1973); the multiplier is thus cut off early.

If detailed data of friendship circles were available, therefore,
the maximum multiplier would be achieved by selecting an initial
group whose members had a minimal number of friends in common.
This data would be extremely expensive to collect, however, and
the next best method would almost certainly be to use as the core
a random sample of the total population one hoped eventually to
recruit from. (Some justification for this assertion can be found in
the analysis of Rapoport and Horvath, 1961.) This would maximize
the number of different circles of friends eventually recruited,
given the constraint of not collecting data on friendships. In effect,
this is the (perhaps unwitting) strategy approximated by the
Rochester house-to-house method; results could be improved by
application of well-known techniques of random sampling in
surveys (cf., for example, M. Hansen et al, 1953).

It follows that insofar as current practices result in employing
individuals who are heavily enmeshed in similar groups of friends,
the effort is less efficient than it might be. "Creaming," the frequent
practice of selecting only the most promising applicants for various
programs, may be, in effect, doing just this. Quite aside from the

present injustice and inefficiency of the practice, therefore, the impact may be multiplied into the future. (These comments apply not only to employment programs, but to the whole range of programs which offer services to a community.)

One problem that plagues programs to train and/or place the unemployed is the high turnover of those placed. Employers, aware of this, often consider it not to their advantage to hire such individuals. Attempts to explain job turnover of the clients of poverty programs on the basis of wage rates and standard demographic variables have been less successful than might have been expected. (cf., for example, Doeringer 1969:250-253). It may be that route of entry to a job can explain a good deal of this problem. I found, in my sample of PTM workers, that those who had found their job through contacts were considerably less likely to have recently considered quitting than those who had entered by other means. One might attribute this partly to the better quality of jobs found through contacts. But Shapero et al. also found, in their rather homogeneous sample of aerospace engineering jobs, that quit rates were much higher for those who had not entered by personal contacts (1965:50).

The reasons for this are not hard to imagine: those entering a work situation through contacts have automatic entrée into the cliques and friendship circles of the workplace. Besides making daily work more pleasant, this access is likely to yield fringe benefits in "learning the ropes," finding out how to really get things done—information not contained in the company's personnel booklets. Those entering through agencies, advertisements, or programs will have a harder time fitting into this social structure; if they come from a different ethnic group and/or share few common experiences with the other workers, the difficulty will be accentuated. Even with good will from current workers, an isolated new recruit might face this problem. Needless to say, such good will is not always forthcoming.

Where social environment has been congenial, work has been efficient, with low turnover. In an IBM plant opened in Brooklyn's Bedford-Stuyvesant ghetto, for instance, turnover has been negligible.

"Having started it from scratch, the Beford-Stuyvesant workers feel that it is theirs. If they had been introduced into the labor force of a white plant, this pride of possession would be lacking, and in its place would be a certain resentment at having to adapt to a more or less alien and hostile environment" (Banfield 1969:55). Chernick and Smith report a low turnover rate in a pilot program run by Western Electric, which trained workers in a ghetto "feeder" plant, later transferring many to other plants. Though no analysis of the reasons for low turnover are yet available, it seems likely that substantial numbers who knew one another in training continued to maintain social ties when on the regular job, easing their transition (1969:14-25).

As long-range policies, however, these ideas may not be optimal. Putting in one workplace many who know one another may reduce turnover, but also goes at crosspurposes to the desired multiplier effect described above. Some balance would have to be struck between the benefits of high multiplier from randomly assembled work groups and that of low turnover from recruiting groups of friends.

Members of any group suffering an unusual degree of unemployment or underemployment have the problem that friends will be disproportionately un- or under-employed, and thus in a poor position to offer job information. Many engineers and technicians found themselves in this position from about 1970 on, with the shrinking defense-contract volume. This is not quite comparable to the situation of blacks, in that the total number of jobs actually available declined in this case; hence the strategies suggested above might be of little avail. What can be done for such highly skilled unemployed workers? It may simply be the case that jobs which they could fill do not exist; this at least is their feeling and that of the technical agencies unable to place them (Rice 1970:95). If so, one alternative suggested by my results would be for them to give careful thought to whether family and social contacts might be able to help them. Such contacts, it will be recalled, are especially likely to be useful to those who are unemployed or nearly so, and to mediate mobility involving a change of occupation. While

one might think, *a priori*, that the unemployed PTM worker would
have exhausted all such possibilities, it is not clear that all of them
would look at the problem in this way.

To find out whether there really *are* no openings in one's own
field is another problem—one which would indeed require a national,
computerized job-matching scheme. The difficulty with this is that,
as I have indicated, employers and employees do prefer knowledge
from personal contacts about one another, even if a computer
indicates a good match. Is there some way of adding this personal
dimension to a computerized system? Given any employer and
potential employee, matched—let us suppose—by a computer, there
presumably exists a chain of personal contacts connecting them—
that is, the employer knows someone who knows someone . . . who
knows the employee. Milgram (1967; also see Travers and Milgram,
1969) has developed a relatively low-cost method of *finding* such
chains between any two designated individuals. Suppose we know of
such a chain in some given case, in which the employer knows A who
knows B who knows C who knows the potential recruit. Let C give
B his assessment of the recruit; B then passes this along to A with
his assessment of C's qualification to recommend, and the likelihood
of his giving a frank opinion. A gives this to the employer, along
with his assessment of B. If such chains were long, the scheme would
not only be wildly impractical but would fail to mimic what
actually occurs in the labor market—where finding out about a job
through a long chain of contacts does not afford one much more
of a recommendation than if one simply came in off the street
(cf. Ch. 3, above). Even the recommendation-chain of length three,
described above, has a slightly implausible ring to it.

But Milgram's work holds out hope that short chains might be
the norm. He found that for *randomly chosen pairs of Americans*
(where one was chosen randomly from Massachusetts, one from
Nebraska), the average number of links needed to connect was only
six to eight. Between employees and workers in the same field
the average should be much lower. My results suggest that chains
of length two or one would be the most useful. Since people
actually *are* hired through recommendation chains of this length,

employers may well be more willing to hire on this basis than to take unknown individuals from employment offices or through direct application.

Such a plan might be difficult to institutionalize; people do not normally make recommendations of friends as part of a formal program but rather in the course of normal social and professional activity. If a new system led to the buying and selling of recommendations, this would be undesirable not only on principle, but also because the recommendations would not then be worthwhile. Details would have to be planned rather carefully.

When the problem is one of increasing the numbers of some under-represented group in the labor force of some industry or company, the technique of tracing minimal chains between employers and members of the target group would have the value of pointing out whether certain persons or types of person typically turn up as intermediaries in these chains. These people could be of special help in recruitment.

The suggestions in this chapter are extremely tentative. They are predicated on the assumption that one might do well to adopt strategies that mimic the most successful everyday ways people have of finding jobs. Whether this is a feasible proposition is unclear, but deserves some attention as a radical departure from usual thinking on the subject. Detailed studies of the ways in which a *given* target population normally obtains jobs may modify some of these ideas and suggest new ones whose application would be limited to the group in question. The main point that I have tried to establish here is simply that further attempts to understand and modify the patterns by which Americans find work cannot reasonably be inattentive to the fact that finding work is a social process.

Afterword 1994: Reconsiderations and a New Agenda

INTRODUCTION

In this Afterword,[1] I want to assess how the findings of *Getting a Job* hold up in light of twenty subsequent years of research, to summarize that research, and to suggest what empirical and theoretical agenda would most enrich our understanding of how people and jobs connect.

Though the research since 1974 is voluminous, most of it is narrowly focused; as in the past, research in economics and research in sociology proceed separately, like ships passing in the night. This mutual ignorance stems in part from differences in motivation. Sociological research has arisen especially from concerns about resource allocation through social networks, about inequality and labor markets, and in some cases as direct response to the research issues opened up by *Getting a Job* (hereafter in this Afterword, *GAJ*). Most economic research elaborates the theory of "job search," with its emphasis on whether allocative efficiency is achieved through reservation wages, job shopping, and information acquisition. The subset of economists and sociologists whose main concern is inequality is more akin to a research community, though differences in assumptions, methods, and rhetoric still strain communication.

I will comment further on these differences of approach. But first it is useful to review briefly the findings of large-scale survey research.

DESCRIPTIVE SURVEY RESULTS

A main premise of *GAJ* was that the finding of jobs via information supplied through a social network was widespread and important, and thus required much fuller analysis than it had previously received. Though there are variations in the survey results of the last twenty years, this premise is clearly sustained.

As always, differences in populations surveyed and in how questions are posed limit the comparability of results. For example, the January

[1] This Afterword has benefited from the thoughtful comments, graciously provided on unreasonably short notice, of Margaret Hivnor, Takehiko Kariya, Nan Lin, James Montgomery, James Rosenbaum, Roger Waldinger, and Shin Watanabe.

139

1973 Current Population Survey reports that of those male professional and technical workers who began their jobs in 1972, 35.7% found their job through formal means, 27.3% through direct application, and 27.4% through personal contacts (U.S. Dept. of Labor, 1975).[2] This is quite different from the figures of 18.8%, 18.8%, and 55.7% that I report in *GAJ* on page 19. One source of difference, which I comment on more fully below, is that like many surveys, this one did not pursue questions about how respondents found jobs if they *denied* having conducted a job search, as 34.4%, representing 5.5 million individuals, did. If we consider only job searchers in my original data, the figures on how jobs were found change to 26.0% formal means, 26.0% direct application, and 45.7% contacts, closing somewhat the apparent gap between the two surveys.

More generally, for the entire job-seeking population, this CPS survey found that 27.4% got their jobs through contacts. Higher proportions were found by the Panel Study on Income Dynamics (PSID), which followed 5,000 American families through a panel design; for household heads and their wives under 45 in 1978, 52% of white men, 47.1% of white women, 58.5% of black men, and 43% of black women found their current jobs through friends and relatives (Corcoran, Datcher and Duncan 1980:12). Another large panel survey with data on job finding was the 1982 wave of the National Longitudinal Survey of Youth (hereafter, NLSY), which asked its sample of 17- to 25-year-olds how they had found their current job. Staiger reports that even if one limits the definition of finding a job through contacts to cases where the respondents said there was someone who specifically helped them find their job and who worked for the prospective employer, almost 40% found their 1982 job this way (Staiger 1990:7).[3] The 1989 National Bureau of Economic Research's Study of Disadvantaged Youths, in three high-poverty Boston neighborhoods, found that 51% of whites and 42% of blacks found their jobs through friends and relatives. In a 1982 sample of employees of 52 manufacturing plants in the Indianapolis area, 51.4% of respondents reported having found the job through friends and relatives (Marsden and Campbell 1990:68).

Surveys in other countries also show substantial proportions using contacts. In Britain, the General Household Survey indicates that during the 1970's and 1980's between 30 and 40% of respondents found jobs through friends and relatives (Harris et al. 1987:94; Fevre 1989:92). In Japan, the 1982 Employment Status Survey showed that 34.7% of those aged fifteen

---

[2] These are not the categories reported. I have combined into "personal contacts" the categories "friends," "relatives," and "asked teacher or professor"; in "formal means" I include ads, agencies, school placement, civil service, and union hiring hall.

[3] Questions on job finding are not regular features of the PSID or NLSY, but were asked only for the years indicated in the text.

and above found jobs through contacts, though studies in specific cities have given figures as high as 70 to 75% (cited in Watanabe 1987:50–51). Watanabe's 1985 study of 2,003 male workers in the Tokyo metropolitan area, with questions broadly comparable and in some cases identical to those of *GAJ*, shows that of those who change jobs, 54.6% do so through personal contacts, 31.5% through formal means, 8.3% through direct application (1987:141). Boxman, DeGraaf, and Flap (1991), in their survey of 1,359 top Dutch managers, found that 61% had found their job through contacts.

So we may continue to pursue the original theme of *GAJ:* that despite modernization, technology, and the dizzying pace of social change, one constant in the world is that where and how we spend our working hours, the largest slice of life for most adults, depends very much on how we are embedded in networks of social contacts—the relatives, friends, and acquaintances that are not banished by the never-ending proposals to pair people to jobs by some automatic technical procedures such as national computerized matching. The research of the last twenty years has given us much more insight into how, why, and when contacts play this critical role, and in the rest of this Afterword I will review what we have learned. Then, I will step back and ask the crucial question of how networks in the labor market affect equality of opportunity, and whether there are groups of able people who lose out because they are not connected.

THE ECONOMIC THEORY OF JOB SEARCH

Further understanding of the mountain of findings we face requires us to explore first what economists mean by "job search," and how this meaning has shaped research. My account of job-search theory in *GAJ* (pp. 25–29) needs updating in 1994 (see the excellent theoretical review in Mortensen 1986, and the comprehensive review of empirical research conducted in the job-search framework in Devine and Kiefer 1991). The air of unreality that characterized early job-search theory is now more muted. Many constraining assumptions have been stretched or discarded, with considerable gain in sophistication. Thus, recent models treat not only employee, but also employer search, with some two-sided accounts (Mortensen 1986:913; Burdett and Wright 1994). The limitation of earlier models to search only while unemployed has been eased (Mortensen 1986:869ff.). A literature on "job shopping" has developed which relaxes the unrealistic assumption that once you find a job offer, all characteristics of the job are transparent to you (see my review of this literature in Granovetter 1988:190).

But job-search models still bypass important realities. As even two advocates note, "search theory itself is never tested. The models we can write down precisely enough to be subject to test are patently false. The question is whether one can write down models that are simple enough to be useful, yet not disastrously at odds with labor market data. As will be seen, the evidence is mixed" (Devine and Kiefer 1991:8).

For example, the continuing emphasis on reservation wage—that wage below which job offers would be unacceptable to the searcher—has a constricting effect on what can be achieved. Reservation wages are virtually never observed (Devine and Kiefer 1991:29), and data rarely report on the characteristics of offers accepted and rejected. In one of the few studies where all the relevant data are in place, Blau (1992) found that estimated reservation wage in fact predicted poorly which jobs workers would accept. There seem to be two reasons why reservation wage assumptions mislead. One is that it does not reflect the many nonpecuniary elements of jobs that concern prospective incumbents. Another is that contrary to the concern of traditional models with acceptance and rejection of job offers, "Workers almost always accept an offer—once an offer is received. . . . The action is in the arrival rates [of offers]" (Devine and Kiefer 1991:139). Devine and Kiefer sum up this issue by noting that "workers appear to search in markets in which almost all jobs are acceptable. Thus, variation in unemployment durations appear to arise primarily from variation in the likelihoods of receiving offers" (1991:302). They note that although models typically portray the arrival rates of offers as exogenous, it appears instead that they are endogenous—that is, driven by search intensity and search strategies. They conclude that there are "definite advances to be made in studying the process by which workers get offers" (1991:308), a proposal which the author of *GAJ* could hardly dispute.

Perhaps the way job-search theory has most adversely affected research has been in deflecting attention from the large number of jobs that, by almost any definition, are not found by search. On this subject, my critique in Chapter 1 of *GAJ* needs no revision. Historically, job-search theory has arisen in a context that gives it this particular blind spot. These models have not had as their main goal the understanding of all processes by which people are matched to jobs, but rather of the dynamics moving people between unemployed and employed status, with special reference to the impact of unemployment benefits on the efficient allocation of labor—whether benefits unduly discourage unemployed workers from search that would connect them with an appropriate new job. Mortensen comments that the theory "views the time spent searching for an acceptable job as a 'productive' activity, at least from the point of view of the searching worker. Hence, to the extent that non-employed workers who are classified as unemployed are searching, the theory suggests that 'un-

employment' is a productive state of labor force participation. This infer-
ence caused a lot of controversy in the early 1970's, particularly among
the then still dominant school of Keynesian macroeconomics. However,
for labor economists trained in the neoclassical tradition of Marshallian
microeconomics, this idea was not so objectionable" (1986:861).

Although job-search models now routinely contrast employed to unemployed search, and empirically discuss which is more efficient, the origins
of the ideas in the problem of unemployment may have made it difficult
to see the importance of nonsearch employment acquisition. Moreover,
such acquisition does not lend itself to easy modeling, as it is not obvious
what choices among scarce resources actors can be said to be making if
job offers arrive without conscious use of resources to obtain them.

That this is a serious issue was already suggested by the finding in *GAJ*
that nearly 30% of the sample denied having actively searched, a figure
close to the 34.4% in the 1973 Current Population Survey reported above.
Campbell and Rosenfeld took a sample from these CPS data of respondents aged twenty to fifty who had changed employers in the last five
years (also the time frame of *GAJ*) and found the following proportions of
nonsearchers: 36% of white males, 28% of black males, 37% of white females, and 30% of black females (1985:159). They comment that "not
searching is the most common method of search for all race/sex groups"
(161). In particular times and places, the proportions finding their job
without search rise higher. In Watanabe's male Tokyo sample, 49% of job
changers denied having actively searched, a figure that rose to 63.8% for
managers, and to 60.2% for jobs in the highest income category (1987:
255–258). In Hanson and Pratt's 1987 sample from Worcester, Massachusetts, 51% of men and 57% of women said they had not actively searched
for their current job (1991:236), leading Hanson and Pratt to assert that
the "fixation of the traditional job search model on the cost of acquiring information . . . seems misplaced, as, for the majority of cases in our
sample, the information leading to a new job came through existing social
networks at no cost to the worker at all" (237). Menon, studying job search
among migrants in Malaysia, could analyze only the 28% of his subjects
who had conducted such search; the majority reported, rather, that they
had prearranged employment before migration.

One might suspect that the luxury of finding jobs without search would
be reserved to those already comfortably employed, but Osberg (1993),
in his analysis of national data from Canada, reports that "many jobless
Canadians find jobs without recorded job search" (350). He reports, for
example, that in 1981, 68.7% of jobless males in the labor force did not
report active job search in January, but that one-eighth of these were employed in February. Using this measure of finding jobs without search, for

1981, 1983, and 1986 respectively, 8.6%, 5.5%, and 5.6% of male unemployed, and 9.9%, 7.8%, and 7.7% of female unemployed found their February jobs without January search (1993:351).[4] Callender's study of Welsh women put out of work by a partial closure of a clothing factory shows that the "majority denied that they were looking for work. But when offered a job they willingly accepted it; or if they heard of a vacancy they vigorously pursued it. Indeed, nearly half of the women who answered in the negative actually gained employment" (1987:26).[5]

Little is known about nonsearchers; the job-search perspective discourages interest in them since it provides no framework in which they can be understood. In Holzer's important work on the place of informal search in white and black youth unemployment, for example, based on NLSY data, he mentions briefly in a footnote that "those individuals who claim to have not been searching when they obtained their most recent jobs are omitted from the sample" (1987:447n). Because surveys oriented to job search ask few questions of those who deny this activity, we have little insight into their characteristics or how they were in fact connected to jobs. Campbell and Rosenfeld did explicitly analyze nonsearchers in the 1973 CPS data as having used the "nonsearch method" of job search, and found that not searching, and on-the-job search were more likely to produce wage gains than searching while voluntarily unemployed, and that men were much more likely than women to have wage gains by (finding a job while) not searching (1985:161–163). They also note that the longer one is out of the market, the more likely one is to find a job without active

[4] By merging two separate months Osberg estimates the numbers of unemployed finding jobs without search. This is a creative use of data not designed to answer this particular question. It would be preferable to have data on whether the actual job held in February had been found by search. Some of the jobs in his figures may have resulted from February search; conversely, some of those who searched in January may have found jobs in February unrelated to that search. The relative size of these errors cannot be estimated a priori.

[5] One of the needs in this research area is for standardization of questions. One might wonder whether it is reasonable to say of someone who vigorously pursues a vacancy she hears of that she is not looking for work, even though this is her understanding. Callender notes that most women in her sample thought that looking for work meant applying directly for jobs (1987:27). Still, if the process that led to a woman hearing of a vacancy was one in which she expended no effort, it is hard to see how to put this into the traditional cost-benefit framework of job-search models. In these models, the information that people are searching for is synonymous with offers; I do not know of variations in which the acquisition of information about vacancies is separate from the process of trying to acquire the job, although such a two-stage model is familiar enough in everyday life. Similarly, the respondents in Menon's Malaysian sample who had pre-arranged employment before migration may have engaged in some kind of systematic search behavior, but this is neither assured nor precluded by knowing that a job was prearranged.

search. This is one reason for the relatively low level of search among white women, for whom "reentering the market is often a fortuitous event. If there is economic urgency, women who have been out of the market may reenter, not after active search, but when they are approached about an appealing job" (169). One estimate of the frequency of finding jobs without search might be the proportion who go directly from outside the labor force to new jobs, without passing through unemployment. Such individuals are poorly explained by theories of job search, and to the extent that their number is substantial, they are likely to confound current macroeconomic forecasting models.

How are nonsearchers being connected to jobs? We have few clues about this, since most studies ignore the matching to jobs of nonsearchers, but the clues are consistent. In *GAJ*, 82.5% of nonsearchers found their jobs through personal contacts, compared to 45.4% of searchers (from unpublished tables prepared for *GAJ*, 1972). In Hanson and Pratt's Worcester sample, the comparable proportions were 73% and 32% (1991:237), and in Watanabe's Tokyo sample, 71% and 41% (1987:263). Thus, finding a job without a search may be close to a proxy for finding a job through personal contacts—not surprising, since jobs that "fall into your lap" are unlikely to do so without some personal intermediary. But then the inattention to those who find their jobs without a search amounts to a serious selection bias against cases where people are channeled into jobs through their position in an interpersonal network, a bias resulting from the distorting lens of search theory.

If workers can find jobs without search, so may employers fill them with similar nonchalance. But here also, the failure to search disappears from the view of survey data. Analyzing the 1980 Employer Opportunity Pilot Project survey of 3,100 employers, Barron, Bishop, and Dunkelberg (1985) note that employers were asked the length of time between the beginning of recruitment and the filling of the most recent position. They report that "twenty-eight percent responded that they did not recruit for the position. Unfortunately, the interviewer was instructed to skip questions on hiring activity if the employer responded that he did not recruit" (1985:45). They speculate that "did not recruit" "could mean that a job was created for an especially promising applicant. Or, it could mean that the position was filled by a friend or relative of a current employee" (1985:50n). In *GAJ*, I classified jobs into those where another person was directly replaced (a clear-cut vacancy); those where another person was added on, doing work similar to that of others; and jobs that were newly created and held for the first time by the respondent. The percentage of newly created jobs was 35.3%. Since I did not collect information on employer search, I cannot say anything definitive about this, but it is clear that in many cases, these new jobs were tailored for respondents by employers whom they knew; in this sense, they were not filled by a systematic search by employers over possible applicants. And 70.0% of newly created jobs were filled through personal contacts, a much higher rate than for direct replacements or add-on jobs (Table 3, p. 15, *GAJ*, repercentaged in the opposite direction). Thus it seems plausible that like nonsearching by workers, nonsearching by employers is closely linked to the use of contact networks. Fevre, drawing on his study of unemployed steel workers in Wales, argues that there is a forcible linkage between employer strategies and worker job search—that it is the "withdrawal of employers from the process of recruitment which leads to the use of informal methods by the workforce" (1989:104). That is, if employers do not advertise vacancies, this may be in part because they know they can be filled by friends and relatives of existing employees. Failure to search may be in full knowledge that workers then resort to their networks by default, and that this will be adequate for the job to be filled.

It follows that important aspects of how people are connected to jobs are missed by search theory and the orientation it conveys to empirical researchers. Part of this gap results from the fact that much of the information about jobs that one receives through contact networks is a by-product of other activities, and thus not appropriately costed out in a rational calculation of the costs and benefits of getting information. This is especially obvious when workers and/or employers make a match to positions without *any* explicit search activity. Such matches appear from existing evidence to result from people being embedded in ongoing networks of social interaction oriented to economic and noneconomic goals alike. It is hard to see how we can get a good grip on the matching of people to jobs when we miss such a central aspect of what is going on. The ambiguity about who is searching and who is "in the market" corresponds to uncertainty about when the filling of a job actually reflects an existing vacancy. This raises questions about whether employment, labor force, and job vacancy statistics, as we currently construct them, map closely enough onto the reality of how individuals and firms connect to give us insight into transitions among various states of labor force participation.

SOURCES OF LABOR-MARKET CONTINGENCY

In this section, I will review the main empirical findings on how matching of people to jobs is related to demographic variables such as race and gender, to type of social contacts used, and to job-finding methods. Some correlations recur frequently, and I will report those first. But most findings shift from one study to another, and thus most of this section will be devoted to analyzing how differences in context lead to different outcomes.

One finding that frequently recurs is a negative correlation between age, education, and occupational status and the likelihood of finding one's job through personal contacts. Although this finding does not surface in the 1973 CPS study, it is striking in the 1978 PSID results (Corcoran et al. 1980: 34), the Indianapolis study (Marsden and Campbell 1990; Marx and Leicht 1992), and the 1970 Detroit Area Study (Marsden and Hurlbert 1988). Although this is true in the aggregate, it is not inconsistent with the filling of some quite high-level jobs through contacts, especially insofar as high levels of trust and compatibility are required (see, for example, *GAJ;* Hanson and Pratt 1992: 389; Simon and Warner 1992; Boxman, DeGraaf, and Flap 1991).

There is evidence that finding jobs through contacts is efficient, in that more offers are received this way and are more likely to be accepted (Blau and Robins 1990: 646; Holzer 1987:447; Holzer 1988: 2; Wielgosz and Carpenter 1987:159). Reporting on the NLSY data with respect to unemployed youth, for example, Holzer notes how striking it is that 81% of all offers received through friends and relatives are accepted, a "percentage well above that of any other method listed" (1988:11). Those matched to jobs by contacts are also less likely to quit, as suggested in *GAJ* (Grieco 1987; Devine and Kiefer 1991: Chap. 8; Licht 1992:229; Wanous 1980: 32–34).

But most other major findings are challenged by other well-designed studies showing something quite different. The proportion using contacts shows no consistent pattern by race, ethnicity, or gender, and the correlation between contact use and the quality of job obtained, as measured by satisfaction or wages, also varies by study. Thus, Bridges and Villemez (1986) and Marsden and Hurlbert (1988) found little impact on wages of job-finding method. But see Corcoran, Datcher, and Duncan (1980) and Staiger (1990), using PSID and NLSY data respectively, for the finding that jobs found through contacts have an initial wage advantage that then declines over time, compared to those matched through other means, and for the argument that this means the original matches through contacts provided better information, which is not forthcoming for those matched without contacts until they have been observed on the job for some time, whereupon, if they remain in their jobs, they catch up in salary. Coverdill (1994), using data from the 1982 Employer Opportunity Pilot Project survey of employers, found that those using contacts had better wage growth and promotion opportunities during their first year of employment.

Different findings from different studies should not surprise us, considering the enormous variations in the circumstances under which people get job information through contact networks. It follows neither that the use of networks has no effect on outcomes nor that the effects are wholly unpredictable and depend on the intimate details of each case. Rather, I believe that the sources of variation, though complex, are identifiable and systematic, and I will now try to spell these out.

The Kind of Social Network Used

One fundamental source of variation is succinctly stated by Harris, Lee, and Brown: "Using networks of informal relationships will only be an effective method of job search if those networks connect the job seekers with employment opportunities" (1987:184). This near tautology immediately shows why it can only be a crude starting point to throw "informal methods" into a regression equation trying to predict wage growth between jobs. More than "formal means" or "direct application," "personal contacts" refers to a phenomenon whose detailed structure and social location make enormous differences in outcomes.

Several interconnected issues arise: the nature of the tie between job seeker and contact; the characteristics of the network of ties in which this tie is located, and the relation of this network to job information and opportunities.

The kind of tie between a job seeker and her contact has been explored almost entirely by sociologists (the exception being Montgomery 1991, 1992, 1994). In *GAJ* and in "The Strength of Weak Ties" (1973; see also a weak ties "revisited" piece, 1983), I proposed that "weak" ties were strong in connecting people to information beyond what they typically had access to through their strong ties, since our acquaintances are less likely than our close friends to know one another, and more likely to move in circles different from and beyond our own. Although close friends and relatives might be more motivated to help us with job information, I argued that "weak ties" were structurally located in such a way as to be more likely to offer help, and suggested that this was one reason why most of my respondents had found jobs through contacts they saw only infrequently at the time the job information was passed (*GAJ:* 52–54). I did not claim that jobs found through weak ties would necessarily be better in income or satisfaction than those found through strong ties or other methods. Such a claim would be suspect since knowing tie strength should not generally be enough to know the quality of job found through a tie. I did argue that strong ties, and ties of kinship and social (rather than work-related) origin were most likely to be used by job seekers who are unemployed or in great need of a new job.[6]

Bridges and Villemez (1986) in a 1981 Chicago survey found that workers obtained higher incomes in jobs through weak than through strong ties, but that the differences washed out when controls were added for race, gender, education, and experience. Marsden and Hurlbert, in their 1988 reanalysis of the 1970 Detroit Area Study data, also showed no net difference in income between weak- and strong-tie job finders, and neither study showed much effect of job-search method on income. In both, however, the question arises as to whether control variables used may unintentionally have been proxies for network phenomena of interest, in which case the disappearance of the zero-order relationship may be misleading. In the Marsden and Hurlbert study, characteristics of the job are added as a predictor, and they comment that my (1981) discussion of job matching might be taken to imply that wages are largely a "function of job characteristics, with social resources being important in explaining how persons are sorted into positions having particular characteristics" (1988:1048). In other words, if tie strength of contact determines nonpecuniary job characteristics that in turn determine income, controlling such characteristics may mask an indirect but valid causal relation between tie strength and income. Bridges and Villemez comment that their use of work experience as a control variable may be problematic if in fact this is in part a proxy for "social capital" presumably including some aspects of social networks (1986:579). This point is underscored by Montgomery (1992), who constructs a job-search model incorporating assumptions on tie strength. He argues that the net effect of tie strength on wages may be uninformative about the importance of tie strength because the entire network structure of individuals must be taken into account, rather than controlled away (1991:590–594). I would add that any cross-sectional analyses may miss the role of personal contacts in building a career. If the benefits of good early jobs found through contacts then translate into later labor market advantage, more variance is in fact attributable to social networks than can be captured in cross-section. I return to this theme below in discussing the internal structure of careers.

A more general set of issues about the kind of social ties and networks used has been raised by Nan Lin and his collaborators in the form of a theory of "social resources." Lin argues that valued resources are best protected by interaction with those similar to oneself, at similar hierarchical levels in a social structure, but that gaining new resources—such as

[6] This argument is elaborated in my "revisited" article (1983) under the heading "The Strength of Strong Ties."

better jobs—requires more explicitly instrumental action, since one must reach up to higher levels of social structure, and that this is most likely accomplished through weak ties (Lin 1990). On this argument, one would expect the use of weak ties to yield better jobs only if those ties linked people to others higher up in some hierarchical structure, a proposition confirmed empirically in Lin, Ensel, and Vaughn (1981). Whether one is able to make such a link may depend on how diversified one's network is in the first place, so that there is a general connection between network resources and the outcome achieved through a particular individual (Lai, Leung, and Lin 1994). Lin, Ensel, and Vaughn argued that on account of ceiling effects, there should be no advantage of weak ties for those at the top of a hierarchical structure, since there is not much distance above oneself that one can reach. Wegener (1991) agrees that within a network those high up cannot make much use of weak ties, but suggests that because there are distinct networks of individuals, this means only that those high in one network must access individuals of higher status by making contact with such people from a different network, most likely through weak ties. He also suggests that within distinct networks, although people vary in status level, there should be enough homogeneity on other nonvertical dimensions—for example, ethnicity—that people can reach upward through strong ties. It would then follow that weak ties should be of most advantage to those higher up and least to those at the bottom. This would explain why samples of high-status individuals overestimate the importance of weak ties and general samples yield no linear effects. In his German data, collected in 1987, he finds exactly the interaction effect he proposes. Similarly, Ericksen and Yancey (1980) found an income advantage for those using weak ties, but only for those with a high-school diploma or better, and increasing in size with education (1980:24–25). I believe that evidence from *GAJ* supports a third position—that weak ties used by those of high status can be beneficial if they reach individuals of comparably high status in other networks, whose resources are different, in that they pertain to organizational or institutional settings different from one's own. The evidence on this subject is mixed, and clarification awaits a more dynamic formulation of how network structure changes over time, and a better conception of network boundaries, so that we know what it means to say that a contact is inside or outside of one's network.

The social resources perspective requires us to think about where the network contacts of different individuals and groups might channel them, rather than making blanket assumptions about the payoff to use of contacts—too individualistic a viewpoint, as if individuals did not come to the labor market as part of well-defined groups. Thus, in particular groups, finding jobs through contacts may be one's best option, yet the jobs found may still be of poor quality by general standards if this is all the group can provide. You cannot get blood from a stone. Mostacci-Calzavara (1982:153), in her Toronto sample, found that working-class ethnic ties often led to jobs, but that the lower the average income in one's ethnic group, the less advantage in income from using one's same-group contacts, compared to other methods of finding jobs. Holzer, in his analysis of 1981 NLSY data, finds that more than 40% of the difference between black and white youths in probability of finding jobs is accounted for by the greater efficiency for whites than blacks of using friends and relatives (1987:449–452).

Korenman and Turner show, using data from the 1989 National Bureau of Economic Research (NBER) Study of Disadvantaged Youths (a study of young males and females from poor areas of Boston) that despite higher educational attainment and similar histories of welfare use, black youths had wages 15% lower than whites; the lower wages of black youths were largely explained by the fact that "jobs found through contacts did not pay as well for black youths as for white youths" (1994:3). They find no such general effect in the national NLSY data, but do cite evidence for lower returns to contacts among Hispanics. In the Boston sample, where 51% of whites and 42% of blacks found their jobs through contacts, white youths' wages through contacts were 24% higher than those of other methods, compared to 3% higher among blacks. Whites who found jobs through relatives earned 38% more per hour than blacks who did, and for blacks and whites who did not use contacts, whites' wages were only 5% higher (Korenman and Turner 1994:8). They speculate that jobs whites find through contacts are often union and/or construction jobs, which are relatively lucrative.

These findings lead naturally to the observation that it is not adequate to look only at the nature of the tie between job finder and her contact, but that various characteristics of the entire network affect outcomes. Montgomery (1992) points out that the strength-of-weak-tie argument is properly one about the structure of an ego-centered network rather than about the correlation between the type of a job seeker's tie and outcomes, even though most research has focused on the latter. It would also be natural, following Bott's classic distinction between "close-knit" and "loose-knit" networks (1957) to make distinctions about networks based on the structure of ties they display. Carson, for example, distinguishes among "isolated," "restricted," and "extended" networks for his unemployed respondents. Those in the first had little regular social contact. Those with restricted networks "regularly saw some friends, relatives and acquaintances, typically in each other's homes or while out shopping" while those with extended networks "had a wider social circle and . . .

regularly saw a wide range of friends, relatives and acquaintances either in their homes or institutional settings such as local clubs or sporting events" (1992:152). Although one might have concern about whether coding rules could be clear-cut with such categories, Carson finds (in a probit regression design) that extended, restricted, and isolated networks were associated with progressively less chance of being reemployed and with longer search for a new job in both time periods studied (1992: 152–156). Such a finding could not emerge from investigation, however close, of the particular tie used by a respondent.

Lydia Morris distinguishes among collective, individualistic, and dispersed networks. The collective type involves high levels of interconnectedness, pooling of information, shared identity, mutual trust and obligation, and involves frequent meetings in well-known public places (such as pubs). Dispersed networks have somewhat similar characteristics, but people see their friends individually, rather than in collective settings. The individualistic network is not interconnected, and its members are geographically dispersed. She suggests that in settings dominated by collective networks employers and workers will find it easier to set up short-term contracting, as in the Welsh steel mill area she and her colleagues studied (1984; Chris Harris et al. 1987). Men hear about this contracting work in their highly collectivized networks, and employers prefer to hire this way because the work is often unregulated and off the books, requiring that workers be under firm social control and not be spreading the word about it indiscreetly. As one Mr. Smith put it, "They know I'll always do it quietly. I don't shoot my mouth off bragging in the pubs and I only take work through people I know I can trust; tidy boys. You could cut their hands off and they wouldn't tell" (Morris 1984:349). Morris observes that men who do not have such an institutionally and collectively embedded network are much less likely to fall into short-term contracting work, and "tend either to acquire more secure employment through formal channels or to remain unemployed in the long term. A secure job is only usually achieved, however, after a relatively long spell without employment" (1987:134).

Details of one's work experience may also shape social networks in ways that have only barely begun to be explored; rather than take network structure as static and exogenous, it is important to look into how it is produced and reproduced by the details of everyday activity. One such study was carried out by Jung-Kyu Lee (1993), with data from a random sample of workers laid off from a Long Island (New York) aerospace facility, and also from the 1985 General Social Survey; Lee found that one's position in the firm—and in particular, the kinds of people with whom that position brought a worker into contact—had an important impact on the content and structure of the network of contacts. In particular, those in work roles that involve highly complex interactions with others are significantly more likely to have low-density networks dominated by weak ties (1993: Chap. 4). The low-density networks were associated with smaller income loss between jobs and short waiting periods for new employment. High-density, strong-tie networks often resulted in new jobs within a short time, but on the average with quite significant losses of income (1993: Chap. 6).

If even the relatively coarse-grained distinctions among network types made by Carson, Morris, and Lee show strong effects, it may be that more detailed accounts would do even more. Such accounts might link the many recent sophisticated measures for the structure of social networks (see, for example, Wasserman and Faust 1994) to the success of individual actions such as job finding, and to the matching processes typical of whole areas. This work might proceed from strategic analyses for individuals, such as those suggested by Burt (1992) for the utility of "structural holes" for corporate actors, or from the more global analyses of social networks suggested by classic anthropological work such as Nadel (1957) and by its sociological descendants in the algebraic and blockmodeling traditions (White, Boorman, and Breiger 1976; White 1992; Pattison 1993). But all such attempts would require more detailed measurement of egocentric and local networks than has been achieved to date.

Contingencies Within Individual Careers

A further source of variations in correlations measured at the individual level is the assumption in job-search models, typically carried over explicitly or implicitly into empirical research, of first-order Markov processes—that is, that all relevant causal information about an individual and his or her mobility is summed up in information about that person measured in the job immediately previous to the new one (see *GAJ*, Chapter 5). Devine and Kiefer note that this "assumption is typically untested. . . . Of course, there is no obvious tractable alternative assumption" (1991:195). Tractable or not, to the extent this assumption is incorrect, and there is causal influence over larger parts of an individual's career, measured correlations in cross-section will underestimate the causal impact of certain variables.

One aspect of this has to do with early labor market experience. In *GAJ* (Chap. 6) I argued from my data that early success, mediated through social networks, set a snowballing process in motion that led to more and more contacts being acquired, and that was self-sustaining. In a later paper I have elaborated this argument with reference to some disputes over youth unemployment (1988:196–197). Farber's investigation of NLSY data from 1979 to 1988 shows that recent mobility has only a "marginally stronger positive relationship with current mobility than earlier mobility" (1993:31), consistent with my argument about the snowballing of contacts. Though it is logically possible that frequent movers are simply different from others in some way, Farber notes that a pure heterogeneity model is easily dismissed, statistically. If the advantages of good jobs found through contacts any time in the career contribute to a cumulation of advantage over one's lifetime in the labor market, then the resources one uses to find a job even without contacts are partially the result of earlier networks. Because sample surveys typically ask only about the most recent job taken, such career dynamics become invisible.

A related point is made by Hagan: that if early connections lead young people into legal employment, the same should be true of criminal employment. Early experience is crucial, so that "successive criminal acts and contacts may further embed youths in criminal networks that are isolated from the personalized networks of job seeking" (1993:469). This has the ironic result that the usually cited causality from joblessness to crime is reversed. He reports on a long-term panel study in London of boys born in the early 1950's, showing that the "cumulation to age 18 of self-reported delinquency has a significant net effect . . . on the likelihood of a spell of unemployment at 21" (1993:482), whereas there is no lagged effect of unemployment on delinquency. He suggests that this "focus on criminal embeddedness helps to explain the sometimes surprising fact that the majority of youths, even in the most impoverished settings, become law-abiding, employed adults" (1993:487).

In general, despite the suggestive material in *GAJ* and a small number of other studies (such as Spilerman 1977; Rosenbaum 1984; DiPrete 1989), the coherence or lack thereof of careers has been little studied. This is somewhat surprising given the accumulation of longitudinal labor market data in recent years, although most of that data does not ask respondents about the means by which they moved from one job to another. Detailed interviewing of respondents on the details of their careers, such as I carried out in *GAJ*, seems the obvious remedy. Though it has not been pursued, it is a subject that respondents warm to quickly, as they rarely have the chance to review their entire career in one fell swoop. Their intimate knowledge of their own lives and histories allows them to provide the most unusual and unexpected yet apt and telling details that bring complex chains of contingencies into clearer focus. Until more of this open-ended interview material is collected, I am skeptical that we will be able to answer the most interesting questions through large-scale closed-ended survey data.

Goals and Activities of Employers

To use Alfred Marshall's apt metaphor, to analyze a market from only one side is like trying to cut with one blade of a scissors. While people are finding jobs, employers are finding people to fill them, and their behaviors, strategies, and purposes play a central but often neglected role in the process of matching people to jobs.

At the broadest level, changes in the way employing organizations view the future attachment of workers shape what strategies and actions will be effective in finding jobs. Markets characterized by widespread "lifetime employment," as in the stereotypical Japanese large firm (Abegglen 1958), would throw much job finding back to the point where students graduate from school and enter the firm that will define their career. In such a system, some of the job-finding action might be coordinated with the help of quasiformal relations between educational institutions and employing organizations, which I discuss more fully below.[7] At the other extreme is an economy in which firms have only a small core of permanent employees, and conduct most business with temporary help. The tendency to externalize employment (see Pfeffer and Baron 1988), or more specifically to shift employment back and forth between internal and external employees, results in increasingly complex networks of firms (see Granovetter 1994; Power and Smith-Doerr 1994) and the blurring of firm boundaries. Sabel refers to this condition as the development of "Moebius-strip organizations," after the topological trick of twisting a strip of paper one half-turn and joining the ends so that the inside and outside cannot be distinguished from one another. He suggests that such firms imply "open labor markets" in which "individuals secure their long-term employability through participation in neighborhood groups, hobby clubs, or other professional and social networks outside the firm. Only those who participate in such multiple, loosely connected networks are likely to know when their current jobs are in danger, where new opportunities lie, and what skills are required in order to seize these opportunities. The more open corporate labor markets become, the greater the burden these networks will have to bear and the greater will be the economic compulsion to participate in the social activities they organize" (1991:43). Saxenian's description of corporate life in Silicon Valley (1994) conveys something of what this means in a particular industry.

Within a particular regime of industrial organization, different kinds of employers have different goals under different circumstances, and these

[7] But no such system exists in pure form. Even at the peak of "lifetime employment" in Japan it seems unlikely that more than one-third of employees had such tenure. See Cole 1979; Granovetter 1984, 1986.

variations also are key in shaping what works or does not for job seekers. Empirically, research at the plant level, even in fairly homogeneous environments such as a sample of large manufacturing plants in central Indiana (conducted in 1982), indicates substantial variation across plants in how workers were recruited. On average, 51.4% of workers found their jobs through friends and relatives, but across the 52 plants, this varied from 23.1% to 89.3% (Marsden and Campbell 1990:68). Without more refined data it is hard to know what part of this striking across-plant variation derived from explicit employer recruitment policy and what part from the nature of job-seeker and employee networks.

Recruitment policy may be shaped in part by the overall strategy firms adopt to assure control of their workforce. As Tilly and I have argued (Granovetter and Tilly 1988:201–207), systems of control vary in the extent of coercion they employ, varying from direct surveillance and sanctions at one end to control via loyalty at the other, where loyalty systems are ones in which workers' commitment to the enterprise is encouraged above and beyond the material rewards they might receive, by both positive incentives and symbolic devices. Some loyalty systems build less on identification with the firm than on preexisting loyalties to groups that then serve to monitor performance and provide training and support. Such groups include such widely different entities as professions and ethnic networks. To the extent that control is built on primordial solidarities such as ethnicity, recruitment naturally takes the form of word-of-mouth through existing employees.

Grieco argues that employers often consciously recruit within families to build on the social control that comes with kinship ties, leading them to hire the "lads of dads" (1987:39). Then, she points out, the workplace intensifies rather than weakens kin linkages. She adds that to the extent employers want a workforce that is under social control by other workforce members, they are likely to recruit through strong rather than weak ties (1987:43). She also points out that when employers are especially concerned about social control, they may engage in long-distance recruitment through an ethnic and kinship network so as to get a workforce that is inexperienced in factory work, and therefore more likely to be docile than militant; her study of the Corby steelworks in England's Midlands and the Vauxhall car works in Luton, with their clear preference for Scottish labor, is an excellent case in point. Important also is the isolation of these ethnic networks in their new location, where they are regarded as foreign intruders and therefore have few alternatives to the firms that recruited them, which severely attenuates their bargaining power (1987: Chaps. 4–7). There are so many cases of this phenomenon in the research literature that they may be of much more theoretical importance than is usually supposed; this deserves systematic attention. Tilly and I, for example, pointed out that Henry Ford's decision during the labor shortage of World War I to "encourage black religious leaders to recruit southern blacks to work in segregated divisions of Ford's Detroit works established a system of migration, employment and unemployment that shaped Detroit's experience for 40 years" (1988:189; see also 202). Hanson and Pratt cite a Blackstone Valley (Massachusetts) wool-processing firm that eschews local workers in favor of Polish immigrants. The employer states that he has

> six Polish people working for us now—they have a good immigrant work ethic. They tend to live in the same area and drive to work together. A person will write home about his work experience. We take pictures of them in their uniforms and they send them home. They're proud; they're doing something that they're respected for. These men leave Poland for two or three years to work, and work they do—seven days, night jobs—and they send the money home. When they go back, we generally get a cousin or brother to take his spot. (Hanson and Pratt 1992:389)

Firms have goals other than workforce control. Windolf (1986), based on a study of English and German firms, relates recruitment strategies of organizations to their particular industry niches and general corporate goals. The question he asks is what kind of employees a firm requires to implement its goals. Most likely to recruit through networks, he suggests, are firms that are mainly trying to maintain the status quo—which are oriented to their traditional market segments. Many such firms enjoy a strong monopoly in the product market and have workers' representatives with strong input to recruitment. Least likely are firms he calls "autonomous," market leaders with rigid requirements about what sort of employees they want, which are dictated by technical standards and some version of scientific management. In between are "innovative" firms that want to attract as many potential innovators as possible, and so cast a wide net to catch many applicants whom they can then carefully screen; and "flexible/muddling through" firms, typically small- to medium-sized in a weak market position, with no clear profile of the ideal candidate. Although his data provide only limited confirmation of the hypotheses, the general point that recruitment should be seen as part of overall corporate strategy of firms in a particular niche is well worth pursuing.

Unemployment and Recession

It is natural to imagine that the situation of being unemployed, or the general rate of unemployment, would have an impact on how people find jobs, and on correlations between these methods and the quality of jobs found. In general, for example, one can expect to see better returns to

mobility, in wages and occupational prestige, when the mobility is voluntary, rather than the result of a layoff (some evidence on this point is summarized in Granovetter 1988:195). Thus, whether jobs found through contacts will result in better wages should be assessed net of the voluntary/
involuntary nature of the move, but the data required to permit this distinction are rarely available.

In *GAJ*, I offered evidence that people in great need of a new job, including the unemployed, are much more likely than others to have used
family and social rather than work contacts (44), and to have used strong
rather than weak ties (54). Subsequent studies have reported mixed results
on whether the unemployed are more or less likely than others to find
jobs through strong ties. In his Australian sample of laid-off meat packing
workers, Carson found that the majority who found new jobs did so
through weak ties, and that 69% of those who used weak ties had a "good
word" put in for them, as compared to 38% of those using strong ties
(1992:167). Lee, on the other hand, in his study of unemployed Welsh steel
workers, found a majority of the reemployed had used strong ties
(1987:120), and Grieco argues from her British ethnographic data that
strong ties are important in times of labor surplus (1987:48) because they
can certify skill and help ration scarce jobs to close friends and family
members. Carson suggests that the strong ties of kinship that Grieco
stresses might be relevant for "young job seekers, or immigrants . . . but
they can be outweighed where the worker has a specific reputation as a
worker in his or her own right" (212), and his respondents stressed the
importance of such a reputation (1992:220–221). My original point here
was simply that strong ties have more motivation to help out with job
information in a pinch, but that weak ties may be more likely to have
good information. There is no way to know a priori which of these factors
will be more important and how they will balance out. All that can be
said is that *ceteris paribus,* that is, holding constant the resources available through one's network of ties, one would expect more help from
strong ties the more desperate one's job situation. But even this is tenuous,
since a desperate job situation for one person often comes about in conjunction with one for many others, as in mass layoffs, so that the resources
of one's network may change dramatically.

Thus, the rate of unemployment and the consequent tightness or looseness of the labor market may have an impact on job-finding above and
beyond the situation of any particular person. In *GAJ*, I suggested that
since employers and employees alike consider recruitment through contacts to be low-cost and effective, the probability of such recruitment
might not be much subject to the business cycle. In tight labor markets
employers might have to use the more expensive and less preferred formal

methods, but since job seekers would have less motivation to do so under these conditions, the two tendencies should roughly "cancel out" (*GAJ:*12).

Many researchers have disagreed with this assessment, the most general argument being that in recessions, word-of-mouth recruitment increases. Based on studies in Britain and West Germany in 1980 and 1981, Wood reports managers as asserting that "with the current levels of unemployment, they did not need to use anything other than informal methods" and that many firms gave preference to friends and relatives, seeing it as a "kind of fringe benefit for their current employees, which was especially welcome when unemployment is high" (1985:111; similar views are voiced in Jenkins et al. 1983; Wial 1991:405). Other studies concur in showing that during labor shortages, as in World War II, informal methods had to be supplemented by the use of ads and agencies which had previously been considered to be last-resort measures (Licht 1992:42).

But Fevre cites General Household Survey data from Britain in the 1980's to show that informal job finding does not seem to increase systematically with recession, and points out that in fact numerous authors have argued that labor *shortages* would drive employers to more intensive use of informal recruiting (1989:92–95).

Conflicting findings like these suggest that we look for underlying contingencies whose balance drives the process, and I think that the previous two sections offer the obvious candidates. Whether people find jobs through contacts in recession depends not only on motivation but also on whether their contacts can connect them to jobs, which in turn may depend on whether contact networks cut across the boundary between employed and unemployed or whether people you know are all unemployed together, in which case they cannot offer much help. Thus, in mass layoffs that are geographically concentrated, especially in populations without contacts out of the area, formal means may be the only way back to employment, and indeed Osberg finds for Canada that although the public employment service provides "essentially no social benefits at the peak of the business cycle" it "pays off in a big way, in recessionary troughs" (1993:369) when it is used by people who would otherwise avoid it. My guess here would be that these are people who tried using contacts without success.

Lee argues not that recession has a definitive impact on how people find jobs, but rather that the "looser the market, the greater the importance of recruitment strategies by labor buyers relative to the labor market behavior of the sellers of labor power." Thus, in recession it is "employers' recruitment strategies rather than workers' job search strategies that require study" (1987:125). Thus, whatever way employers choose to recruit in a situation where they have all the bargaining power is likely to be the

way that prospective employees will find their jobs. Then all the considerations in the immediately previous section on employer strategy become
relevant.

Under all economic circumstances, some balance between the resources
in job seekers' networks and the recruitment strategies and actions of
employers will determine the extent to which people find jobs through
contacts. But in recession it is plausible that this balance will be dominated by employer action and in labor shortage by that of job seekers and
their networks. This argument is consistent with a variety of empirical
distributions over the business cycle, depending on the details of resources
and strategies on both sides of the labor market.

Institutional and Cultural Sources of Variation

A final source of contingency in the matching of people to jobs is variation
across settings in culture and institutions. It is not obvious at what scale
differences among settings lead to variations in matching. The central Indiana study cited above shows sharp variations among otherwise similar
manufacturing plants in recruitment techniques. Some evidence suggests
that the city may be a source of variation. Licht's historical study of finding work in Philadelphia stresses that its industrial organization made it
differ systematically from other cities in how jobs were found. Until the
mid twentieth century, it was characterized by a high level of product
diversity, and a preponderance of small- to medium-sized family-owned
and managed enterprises, with few branch plants of national corporations
and fewer immigrants than other cities (1992: Chap. 1). These factors may
have led to a higher proportion of job seekers finding jobs through their
social networks, given the relative absence of formalized procedures and
personnel departments and the greater involvement of localized management in selecting workers. This would be magnified by the shortness of
the distance to work for most workers until the Second World War, which
increased the importance of neighborhood-based networks (1992:54).
Hanson and Pratt stress that Worcester (Massachusetts) has a "higher
than average level of residential rootedness," which may then lead to more
extensive social networks, facilitating the use of contacts in job seeking
(1991:237).

There do not seem to be sharp variations by country in what proportion
of people find jobs through contacts, but institutional variations do lead
to differences in the detailed process. Some studies, for example, suggest
differences in the significance of tie strength. Based on some case studies,
Rogers and Kincaid stress the importance of strong ties in finding jobs

in Mexico (1981:245–247). In his Japanese probability sample, Watanabe found a preponderance of strong rather than weak ties among those who changed jobs through personal contacts. Looking at a subsample chosen to match that in *GAJ*, he found that only 6.3% of Japanese job changers, compared to 29.5% of the Americans, used weak ties.[8] One important source of the difference is that whereas work contacts tend to be weak ties for Americans they tend to be strong for Japanese. Another interesting difference is that contrary to the finding in *GAJ*, the longer the tenure in previous jobs the more likely was a respondent to find the current job through contacts (1987:342). Watanabe cites the patterns of reciprocity in Japan, where people tend to invest in ties over long periods of time. This is especially important in the large-firm sector where job tenures can be quite lengthy. Also, he argues that a contact connecting one to a job in Japan is like the traditional go-between in that the role of providing an introduction is linked to being a guarantor (1987: Chap. 11). But when blue-collar workers moved between different occupations, weak ties were especially useful, indicating that even in this setting the bridging role of weak ties occurs, if less frequently than elsewhere (1987:398).

Bian (1994) presents a different scenario in which strong ties are more valuable than weak: state assignment of individuals to jobs in China before the reforms of the late 1980's. His data come from a 1988 representative sample survey of 1,008 adults in Tianjin, in which slightly more than 45% of respondents indicated that there was someone who helped them get their first job. Bian points out that not all uses of personal exchange networks are permissible in the labor market. Assignment to work units was a state prerogative in this setting, and changing from one unit to another was not supposed to be accomplished by the use of contacts, which would be inconsistent with central planning of labor resources. Violators could, in principle, be severely punished. Thus, neither job seeker nor intermediary could afford to engage in such transactions unless there was considerable interpersonal trust between them, typical of stronger rather than weaker ties, and, consequently, most helpers were strong ties, sometimes accessed through family connections (Lin and Bian 1991:681).

Although all these cases are of great interest, it does not appear that there are fundamental *cultural* differences that dramatically reshape job-seeking behavior. While there may be somewhat more cultural emphasis on strong ties, for example, in Japan or Mexico or China than in some

---

[8] Watanabe used the frequency-of-contact tie-strength measures of *GAJ* for comparability, but also cross-validated the results using the emotional intensity measures suggested by Marsden and Campbell (1984). See his discussion in Watanabe 1987: Chap. 9.

Western countries, most of the reasons for differences seem to lie in institutional variation among countries. Thus we should expect to see more use of strong ties in countries with longer tenures within firms, as in Japan, or in settings where the use of contacts is proscribed, as in pre-reform China. The latter case is, in fact, reminiscent of the situation in South Wales, described above, where off-the-books contract workers were recruited through strong ties in localized communal networks, in part to insure that no one would blow the whistle on these illicit informal arrangements.

ARENAS FOR FORMAL MATCHING PROCESSES

Much of the discussion so far has treated circumstances where one might expect to see labor market matches made through personal contacts. Where this is common, job seekers and employers who are well connected prefer informal recruitment, regarding it as cheap and efficient. But a full understanding of matching requires also an assessment of when formal procedures have an advantage, and when we may expect to find them. This is an important subject about which we know very little.

Formal mechanisms that are purely impersonal—in which a formal intermediary has no prior knowledge of either job seekers or job opportunities, but acts only as an impartial broker attempting to make the best match from information provided by both sides—seem rarely to succeed. The prototype of such a mechanism is a public employment service, hereafter ES, though such services have different names in different countries. It is typically seen by both sides of the market as an undesirable last resort, though some recent revisionism should be taken into account. Osberg (1993) shows, for example, for his Canadian data, that in sufficiently deep recession the ES serves a useful function, in part because it then draws job seekers who would ordinarily shun it (366–369). He points out, moreover, that although average search duration through the employment service is typically longer than through other means (see, for example, Wielgosz and Carpenter's data from the NLSY; 1987:159), it does not follow that no useful function is being served, since ES users are not a random sample but are likely drawn disproportionately from among those with poor contact networks; thus, duration of search may actually be reduced for this particular group of people (1993:354). And Thomas (1994) reports from British data that part of the longer search spells reported by those who find their jobs through the ES results from the fact that they have used other methods first, unsuccessfully. For the United States, Ports reports a substantial decrease between 1970 and 1992 in the proportion of unemployed job seekers who report using the ES, from 30.2% to 22.6%.

She speculates that this results in part from the decline in manufacturing employment, and also from the decline in the proportion of unemployed receiving benefits, since benefit seekers must register with the ES. By contrast, there has been a steady increase in the proportion using newspaper and other advertisements, from 23.4% in 1970 to 41.7% in 1992, perhaps reflecting the heavier use of advertising by service industries and expanding white-collar occupations (1993:65). Bishop suggests that the reputation of the ES has significantly declined in the past twenty years and that its budget has been cut substantially (1993:381).

In general one might expect an important role for formal matching in situations and populations where there is no easy way for job seekers and recruiters to assess one another's qualities. This may happen, for example, as students emerge from school, with no previous work experience and therefore no network of contacts from previous jobs. Systems of apprenticeships or of school placements might then play a serious role in the labor market, but it is quite variable whether they do. Brinton and Kariya (1994) suggest that where educational institutions have evolved in such a way that their reputation rests on ability to place students in good jobs, they will play this role, as in Japan.

Rosenbaum et al. (1990) describe differences in the transition from high school to work among several countries. In Japan, particular firms have long-term ties with particular high schools, and the schools send the students with the best grades to be interviewed for the best jobs. The firms feel constrained to hire, and the schools to recommend based on merit—as measured by grades—in order to maintain the relationship. In high schools whose graduates are not college-bound, employers hire over 80% of those whom the school recommends (Rosenbaum and Kariya 1989). In Germany, linkages between schools and employers are more indirect, mediated by a system of apprenticeships managed by trade unions and firms, into which many students are channeled through the public employment service. About two-thirds of the German work force complete an apprenticeship of two- to three-and-a-half years (see Harhoff and Kane 1994). In this setup, the ES is not a purely impersonal intermediary, but rather part of a network of relations with firms, unions, and schools that would repay further study.

In the United States, no system has clearly taken hold since the decline of apprenticeship in the mid to late nineteenth century; instead, a mixture of private and public vocational education and schools run directly by corporations has ebbed and flowed over the last hundred years, without settling into any definite pattern (see Nelson-Rowe 1988, 1991; Licht 1992: Chap. 4). Ironically, because in Japan ties between particular firms and high schools are strong, there are less clear-cut ties between particular teachers and counterparts in the firm than in the U.S.; here, where there are few institutionalized relationships at the organizational level, ties from schools to firms usually rest on personal links forged between employers and particular teachers, and the flow of students rests on these particular links (Rosenbaum and Binder 1994. Similarly, Watanabe [personal communication], drawing on his detailed interviews with job changers and managers, reports personal links between employers and school officials in Japan, at the college level, where formal placement is less certain). On the whole, most American high-school students are on their own upon graduation or earlier school-leaving, and thus shop around, moving from job to job with much higher frequency than in most other countries. Bishop, drawing on OECD data, indicates that for workers with less than a year on the job, the probability of a separation in the next twelve months is 59% in the United States compared to 24% in Japan. American job tenures are also lower than for Belgium, Canada, France, Germany, Italy, and England (1993: 339). Similar sharp differences can be found between mobility rates of American workers compared to those in Japan, Germany, or France (Hakusho 1988).

It is unclear whether these contrasting systems differ dramatically in efficiency. One line of argument in labor economics is that it is efficient for young workers to "job shop," finding out about the labor market and how their skills will best match available jobs; then by their mid-thirties they will settle into jobs that nicely match their tastes and abilities. This literature equates length of a job tenure with quality of a match. Hall comments that most workers "do wind up in lifetime work. . . . Multiple tries eventually succeed" (1982:720–721).[9] Bishop, on the other hand, sees job hopping rather than job shopping, and considers it the costly result of poor initial matches that could be improved by a freer flow of information, including that on grades from high schools (1993:340). Rosenbaum et al. (1990) concur, and note that American high schools are extremely lax in providing information such as transcripts even upon explicit request. But they also note that most American employers doubt the connection between high-school grades and skills. Although they provide evidence that there is some relation, there are few studies; some older literature raises doubts about the linkage between years of education and occupational performance, but without specific evidence on the role of grades (Berg 1971; Squires 1979).

Rosenbaum et al. also point out that students in American high schools

---

[9] For a detailed discussion and critique of these job-matching arguments, see my 1988 paper, esp. pp. 189–197 and 207–210.

have little incentive to work for good grades, since they have no obvious economic payoff, in contrast to the Japanese system where they are directly linked to good jobs. But given this incentive structure, it may follow that the correlation between grades and skills is in fact low, since there is little incentive for achieving good grades, and students with good academic skills may have other ways to deploy their time and energy. Employers' beliefs may then be correct, and the situation would not change unless a system was introduced in which grades really did count; but without employer demand this is unlikely to happen. A similar conundrum involves turnover. American employers are reluctant to invest in hiring workers right out of high school because of fears that they will soon quit. Comparative data show that this fear is well-founded. Thus, without the longer tenures that may result in part from systematic connection of firms to schools, such connection may be difficult to establish—especially in a large, decentralized economy like that of the United States. Linkages between firms and institutions of higher education have been studied much less. Although recruiters from particular corporations are well known in the U.S. to have long-standing links to particular schools where they interview, the research literature is not sufficiently well developed to give us much sense of how important such links are in placement.

One situation that has received attention is where large numbers of individuals enter a national labor market at one time for more or less similar jobs. Examples are medical interns or residents, law clerks, beginning professional athletes, newly minted Ph.D.'s looking for academic jobs, or MBA's scouting corporations for managerial slots. Interest has centered especially on the evolution of centralized matching systems to replace whatever combination previously existed of informal matching and a specific institution's (such as a particular university) recruitment activity. The most comprehensive account is offered by Roth and Xing (1994).

They point out that in some markets, where many transactions are to be made, participants may sometimes gain by "jumping the gun" and transacting earlier than competitors. If some of the best positions are filled early, then participants on both sides who waited will be relatively disadvantaged. There can then be an unraveling process in which positions are filled earlier and earlier; in some cases positions have been filled as much as two years before employment would begin. This is problematic because hiring takes place without knowledge of future needs or of the quality of those hired when they finish their training two years hence. Generally a first attempt at remedy is to establish a uniform date before which offers should not be made, an earlier one before which interviews should not be conducted, and a later date before which candidates should not have to respond (1994:5). Such a remedy is typically unstable, breaking down into the earlier unraveling or moving forward to centralized matching.[10]

Roth and Xing suggest that markets will not be subject to unraveling if the "uncertainty associated with hiring early is relatively large compared to the possible benefits" (1994:60). Thus, with new Ph.D.'s looking for positions at research universities, a successful dissertation is typically considered to dwarf any other evidence of how likely a scholar is to be creative and productive; hence few are hired before a substantial part of the dissertation is completed. By contrast, making law review or performance in clinical rotations are considered good indicators of the likely quality of lawyers or doctors.

What role do contact networks play in such entry level professional markets? Because new entrants have not yet worked, they do not have a highly developed contact network that could relay detailed information about their skills and personality to prospective employers. But to the extent contact networks are in place, rather than solving the unraveling problem they appear to exacerbate it. It may be, for example, that before centralized systems were in place, those who could jump the gun most effectively were those whose advisers or teachers were well connected to networks of those controlling openings for internships or clerkships. To hire early without hard information about skills will be less dangerous if candidates are certified by known and trusted referees. Roth and Xing report that an attempt in the 1970's to establish firm dates for recruiting graduates of Japanese universities was thwarted in part by underground recruiting, "arranged informally, through the 'old boy' network of alumni from a given university" (1994:29). When those who abide by guidelines are likely to lose out to those who do not, there is a strong incentive to jump the gun; what makes this possible is "de facto recruiting through informal channels" (1994:30). Much more study is required to know what kind of contact networks lead to this result; Brinton and Kariya (1994)

---

[10] In *GAJ* I discussed a different kind of centralized matching, implemented by the Rabbinical Assembly, the central administrative body of the Conservative Jewish movement, for the placement of rabbis (1974:21–22). This situation is different from those described by Roth and Xing in two important ways: 1) The placement procedure applies to all vacancies, none of which are explicitly defined as "entry level," and thus the distribution over time of vacancies is not sharply spiked, as it would be for new medical interns, but spread out in some stochastic way; and 2), closely related to 1), rabbis at all career stages, not just entry level, may be interested in new positions. The reason here for centralized control is not, therefore, that of unraveling because of jumping the gun, but rather that the previous system, in which rabbis used their personal contacts with, for example, boards of trustees, and competed with other rabbis in "lineups" of interviews for desirable positions, was considered undignified. Thus centralized matching may be set up for mainly ideological rather than economic reasons.

report that for the six elite universities they studied, young alumni were assigned by their companies to recruit at their universities. It appears that jumping the gun does not occur if relations between schools and firms are stable and decisive for recruitment, as for Japanese high schools (Rosenbaum et al. 1990).

Even when centralized matching systems are in place, there can be problems. Medical students may take "audition electives" at other institutions, which makes them more likely to be a high choice when the actual matching takes place. Law students in Canada serve summer internships that are a kind of extended interview before the formal matching procedure is activated. This is a form of unraveling because the actual selection is, in effect, being pushed back before the formal process (Roth and Xing 1994:39–43). It would be of interest to know the extent to which this unraveling is facilitated by contact networks, and how such networks are formed by students without previous work experience.

Roth and Xing comment that "one of the larger themes of this paper is that markets may require a good deal of organization. This runs counter to the view implicit in much of the economic literature, which is that markets are largely self-organizing" (1994:2). To this I would add that, ironically, the timing problems in the markets they study arise because there are so many positions and so many candidates in play at more or less the same time—that is, because the situation actually resembles that of a competitive market. In the situation of most job seekers, there are few positions they look at seriously, and few applicants are seriously considered for any given position. Barron et al. report that in a national employer survey, about 90% of jobs were filled with a single job offer (1985:50). In such fragmented markets, the usual mechanisms of direct application, contact networks, and some formal means operate to fill positions without unraveling.

At the outset of this section I noted that formal intermediaries that are purely impersonal rarely succeed. Scattered evidence suggests that successful operation of formal intermediaries may result from their taking a hybrid form, in which formal procedures are supplemented by or operate through informal networks. For example, though there have been no systematic studies of "headhunters" who provide prospective employees to corporations, it is common to hear that such companies were formed by people previously in a particular industry whose success depends on their former occupational networks. Similarly, social service agencies place retrained disabled workers much better if placement personnel know the retrained clients well and also have long-standing relationships with local employers. Such relationships, however, are discouraged by the clinical psychology orientation of many rehabilitation professionals, who consider the task of learning the local labor market to be unrelated to or beneath their skills (see Granovetter 1979).

An interesting piece of evidence on the mixture of the formal and the informal comes from Grieco's account of how Scottish workers were recruited to industrial employment in England. Public employment exchanges in Scotland, nominally an impersonal and formal source of job leads, actually served to reinforce the kinship networks that coordinated this migration. When English employers listed jobs in Scotland, the exchanges screened prospects so that all interested parties did not have equal access to the listings. But if you were not on the approved list and your relatives were, you could protest, and the exchange might well add your name. One employment exchange officer said that "if somebody was borderline and we'd listed his father or his brother, nine times out of ten, we'd list him as well if he pushed it. More likely to stay if they went with somebody!" (1987:120). Thus the formal and informal routes to jobs, which we keep distinct in our statistics, get blurred in actual daily practice.

On a larger scale, Brinton and Kariya (1994) report what they refer to as "semi-institutional networks" mediating employment between elite universities and corporations in Japan. After World War II, Japanese universities played an important role in linking their graduates to employment, and linkages were so strong that employers sent job applications only to their preferred institutions. But this led to harsh criticism in the 1970's, since those who did not attend the top universities were completely shut out of jobs with the most prestigious companies. This criticism ended the strong explicit relationship, and in the 1980's, according to survey data, far fewer graduates than before reported that their school had channeled them into a position, and any student could apply for any job. But in fact, Brinton and Kariya suggest, universities and firms were unwilling to completely give up what had been a satisfactory arrangement for them. Firms therefore use recent alumni (a young "old boy" network) as unofficial recruiters who informally contact potential recruits; this mixture of formal and informal methods, they argue, constitutes an attempt to restore the old system. Universities collude in this effort by keeping records of recent alumni and their whereabouts for graduates to consult. Since these consultations often take place ahead of the official dates specified as the earliest permissible contacts, it appears that one possibly unintentional by-product of the attempt to retain preferential recruiting has been further unraveling of attempts to monitor agreed-upon dates for recruitment.

CONTACT NETWORKS AND EQUALITY OF OPPORTUNITY

Few dispute that equal opportunity in most economies has not been achieved. There remains substantial inequality by race, gender, and ethnicity. In this concluding section I will assess how this inequality is related to the social structure of placement.

I begin with gender. Studies vary in whether women use contacts to find jobs more than men, but certain patterns recur in the types of contacts women use. McPherson and Smith-Lovin (1982) studied the sizes and types of voluntary organizations populated by men and women, finding that on the average women belonged to much smaller organizations than men, and ones oriented not to economic activity but to local, domestically related issues. They concluded that this makes women far less likely to be exposed to the kind of weak ties apt to carry information about job opportunities. Though it does not directly assess the finding of jobs by women, Callender's study in Wales gives a comparable account, in which women laid off from a clothing factory used job-finding networks that were overwhelmingly kin and community based, consisting of strong ties leading them to jobs segregated by gender—"women's work." She observes that especially given their household responsibilities, they had been less likely than men to develop outside ties with fellow workers, whereas men had "access to the public realm of clubs and pubs" (1987:36). Virtually all the women who were reemployed found their new work through personal contacts, and Callender comments that this "strategy clearly does not give all workers access to similar jobs. Women's disadvantage in the labor market is compounded by jobs found through informal social networks" (1987:42).

In their comparative study of men and women in Worcester, Massachusetts, Hanson and Pratt reach similar conclusions, stressing the geographic concentration produced by women's patterns of contacts; neighborhood contacts typically lead women to local jobs, "reflecting the more localized activity patterns—including the more localized work experience—of these female contacts" (1991:242). They found that women holding jobs in typically women's occupations were more likely than other women to have learned about them from women in the neighborhood and that 60% of women's contacts, compared to 32% of men's, were from family or community (1991: 240).

On the other hand, strong ties may, under certain circumstances, provide a route to upward mobility for women. In *GAJ*, (pp. 48–50) I noted that social or kinship ties were especially likely to be the ones used when people made a major change of occupation, since most work acquaintances connect you to jobs similar to the ones you have already had. Hanson and Pratt note that for their sample, women in male-dominated occupations are much more likely than those in other occupations to have found their jobs through personal contacts, and that in such cases the contacts were often male family members with the authority to hire. They conclude that "networking" is crucial for "expanding women's opportunities in male-dominated occupations" (1991:240).[11]

The other side of the labor market, employers, also must be analyzed in any discussion of inequality. Discussion of their role typically focuses on the issue of "discrimination," as in the long-running dispute between Gary Becker (1971) and his critics on whether any employer "taste" for discrimination could persist in reasonably competitive markets. But it is too narrow to focus on this negative motive, since employers favor as well as disfavor certain groups. Preferences among groups must be relative to the entire available pool; thus, groups disfavored in one setting may be thought the best available in another, and changes in the proportions of different groups, even when the rank-ordering of groups does not change, may affect the quality of jobs available to any particular group (see Lieberson on "occupational queues," 1980:376–381). Simon and Warner define "favoritism" as a preference for some workers "for reasons that are unrelated to productivity" (1992:307). So defined, it is the other side of discrimination. Although employers often have clear preferences among groups, their comments rarely convey information about favoritism or discrimination since they virtually always explain preferences by asserting differences in productivity by group. Neither is it econometrically simple to sort this out. Having shown that referred workers earn significantly higher salaries than those hired through advertisements or the ES, Simon and Warner note that this finding is consistent with an argument that referral yields better matches of persons to jobs, but that favoritism could not be ruled out, and that devising a test that "distinguishes between favoritism and job-matching provides a fruitful area for further research" (1992:328).

Employer preferences among groups, and their tendency to tap these groups through network hiring, may play havoc with what otherwise appear to be reasonable inferences about the role of "spatial mismatch" in creating inequality. William J. Wilson (1987) and others (see the excellent review in Fernandez 1992) have suggested that inner-city blacks are in desperate straits because the manufacturing jobs of yesteryear, which used to provide an upward mobility ladder for ethnic groups low in the status hierarchy, have moved away from the central city locations they

[11] To establish an exact comparison to the point made in *GAJ* we would need to know whether women taking jobs in such occupations were changing from female-dominated or gender-neutral occupations.

previously occupied, or have been replaced by service-sector jobs that also are located far from this workforce. Manufacturing jobs have indeed become much more scarce in the inner city. But to the extent that entrée to jobs comes through networks rather than geographic contiguity, the implicit assumption that nearby jobs are thereby automatically available to residents is false. Thus, Kasinitz and Rosenberg studied the Red Hook section of Brooklyn (New York City), an inner-city community of about 13,500. This mainly black and Hispanic area had about 3,600 private sector jobs, but "local residents in general and black public housing residents in particular rarely hold jobs" (1994:8). Interviews with employers made it clear why. Especially for unskilled jobs, employers want reliability and believe that it can be best gotten by personal referral. But this "reliance on referrals and the reluctance to hire from newspaper ads 'off the streets' often amounts to reliance on ethnic networks" (1994:13), and there is positive discrimination in favor of certain ethnic groups such as Irish, Polish, Mexican, or Spanish immigrants, but not blacks or Puerto Ricans. Employers do not voice explicit antiblack discrimination, but rather a preference to hire outside the neighborhood, as local people are viewed as dangerous and unreliable. One "large contractor reports that over half of his workers are immigrants from Spain and travel to Red Hook each day from Jersey City and Newark, NJ (a journey of over an hour by car and longer by public transportation)" (1994:13). Mier and Giloth (1985) found that the Mexican Americans in the Pilsen neighborhood of Chicago had virtually no access to the many local employment opportunities; instead, both their networks and local public agencies led them outside the neighborhood to larger employers, constrained by affirmative action stipulations, such as hospitals, public agencies, construction firms, and large national manufacturers (1985:305). Meanwhile, local firms recruited by word of mouth, which, for historical reasons, led them outside the area. One Mexican American in a large Pilsen factory explained that when a job opens, "word is passed on to sons and nephews, most of whom are now living in the suburbs. [The neighborhood was previously home mainly to Eastern European immigrants.] I'm one of the few Latin workers here, only because my father broke in during World War II" (1985:305).

The clear implication is that spatial matching of jobs to prospective workers is only a necessary but not a sufficient condition for employment and community revitalization. Careful attention must also be paid to how local residents can be linked to whatever new jobs are developed in the inner city through programs such as "enterprise zones" or other incentives. Conversely, existing jobs that are closed to local residents because of historically determined patterns of recruitment need to be identified and targeted for reconnection to the local population.

Employers do not always, of course, operate through loyalty systems that dictate hiring through solidary networks. Tilly and I (1988:201–207) discuss some of the conditions that lead to this strategy. Manwaring (1984) points out that recruitment of this kind can lead to more solidarity than management wants among its workers, and so can be expected to occur only when management already is in a favorable position of strength vis-à-vis the workforce (169). He further argues that *local* recruitment will lead to workplace solidarity only in communities which themselves have high social stability and solidarity, since otherwise the recruited residents would not generate a cohesive group at work. Thus, what he calls the "extended internal labor market"—recruitment limited to current employees and to only those outsiders connected to insiders—will be found especially in stable communities where people have lengthy residence, such as Birmingham (England), but not less stable areas such as West London. He notes that in West London, the only such recruitment in his study was for ethnic minorities such as Asians. At one firm where the workers were, by design, 90% Asian, the employer observed that "we're not looking for morons, but placid people.... Asians? They're magic" (1984:182). These considerations may help identify conditions under which spatial mismatch would occur—namely, in communities where local recruitment would not produce the cohesive work groups many employers prefer. But this then implies that it is precisely in the unstable and unsolidary communities where people are least able to help one another, that even having jobs nearby may not solve the preeminent problem of employment.

Exclusive focus on employee or employer motives and actions obscures how groups maneuver to structure the preferences and opportunities that employers display. Kinship groups often lay exclusive claim to labor market niches. For example, in Grieco's 1977 survey of fish processing in Aberdeen she found that for small and large firms alike, the strong preference was to hire through existing employees. One employer noted that "most of our girls come from families which have been in the fish for years" (1987:13). Employers who might try to branch out beyond dominant families would be penalized. One explained why he preferred to hire among families and friends: "There are lots of tricks of the trade that could never be included in a training manual; you have to be shown by somebody who knows exactly what they are doing. The girls train one another, but they won't train just anybody. They'll train their own but ask them to train a stranger, and you run up against a brick wall fast enough. Of course, they go through the motions but that is it" (1987:13). This comment nicely demonstrates why it is a mistake to regard all potential workers as well-defined bundles of human capital attributes, whose productivity is predictable independent of their position in the social structure of the workplace.

These families as well as larger groups are attempting what Max Weber called the "closure" of economic relationships:

> One frequent economic determinant is the competition for a livelihood—offices, clients and other remunerative opportunities. When the number of competitors increases in relation to the profit span, the participants become interested in curbing competition. Usually one group of competitors takes some externally identifiable characteristic of another group of (actual or potential) competitors—race, language, religion, local or social origin, descent, residence, etc.—as a pretext for attempting their exclusion. It does not matter which characteristic is chosen in the individual case: whatever suggests itself most easily is seized upon. (Weber 1968/1921:342)

Manwaring points to the "extended internal labor market" as one important way that "particular groups organize to exclude others from material gain" (1984:162n). Closure is thorough in that one is excluded from jobs unless one knows someone in the firm. During the typical two-week posting period in which jobs are advertised internally, those outsiders in touch with plant workers are also in the running. Manwaring suggests that the frequent occurrence of jobs being filled by those who were not even job seekers, and for jobs that were never even vacancies, signals still more closure (1984:166). The evidence cited above, that blacks may be disadvantaged by the low level of access to jobs in their contact networks, and the related evidence in the literature on "social resources" must be taken as more than mere descriptive facts: they are also the end result of particular groups doing whatever is necessary to close off opportunities to outsiders. Their motive is probably that of conserving opportunities for those within; but the aggregated result of such action is little different than if exclusion had been the principal intent.

One understudied arena where ethnic closure is common is that of public employment, where patronage systems, typically curbed only in part by civil service reforms, allocate large numbers of jobs. Licht shows historically for Philadelphia that in each period, those ethnic groups well connected politically were the ones that dominated city employment (1992: Chap. 6). Waldinger's (1992c) detailed historical reconstruction of ethnicity in the New York City government discloses a more complex picture, in which political connection must be coupled with the distribution of labor supply by group to explain outcomes. Thus, before the 1970's, the situation was a classic "extended internal labor market" in that the "population of persons with ties to municipal workers virtually became the applicant pool" (1992c:15). But this situation changed dramatically when large-scale loss of employees through attrition and declining interest in civil service jobs on the part of white workers led to substantial increases in minority representation (1992c:19–20). Exceptions are such units as the Fire Department, which, in 1990, remained 93% white, down only from 96% in 1963. This is so because unlike other departments, it continues to attract a large white applicant pool, "with informed sources suggesting that one-third to one-half of firefighters have family members" in the City or suburban departments (1992c:28). In other departments where blacks had achieved a foothold, their networks operated to exclude other groups; thus, although the city has equal black and Hispanic populations, the latter hold only one-third as many municipal jobs as do blacks. In all these circumstances, outcomes resulted from some combination of the political mobilization capacity of particular groups, the city's fiscal situation—whether it was hiring or downsizing—and whether competing groups were interested in city jobs, which depended on the attractiveness of those jobs relative to opportunities elsewhere. As new immigrant groups have arrived, and established footholds in the city's bureaucracy, they, like groups before them, have brought in their fellow countrymen to form ethnic enclaves, such as a group of Egyptian accountants living in Brooklyn and Jersey City (Waldinger 1992a).[12] Immigrants find the city bureaucracy comparatively hospitable in that there is less discrimination and more tolerance for language and religious practices than in the private sector.

Ironically, because all vacancies must be internally posted, the social networks of current employees that reach outside the agency are given free rein, and groups with effective networks are at great advantage. This raises an extremely important question that lies largely unexamined: do ethnic or other groups differ in the efficacy of their referral networks? Although a torrent of evidence makes clear that ethnic networks dominate hiring in many situations, we have virtually no systematic attempts to establish the detailed characteristics and differences among such networks. But there are hints in the literature that such differences may matter.

Waldinger cites one New York City information services manager as noting that the "Indian connection is amazing, that's a phenomenon. They network like crazy, they look out for each other like unreal." An executive in a city engineering agency noted that "once we had a recruitment for managers and engineers by invitation only. And there was somebody who flew in from India that day" (Waldinger 1992a:22). Fragmentary accounts suggest, by contrast, that African American referral networks function

---

[12] That a particular group gets a foothold in a particular department is often a matter of chance. The first Egyptian accountant hired by New York City's Department of Finance told Waldinger: "I went to the New York State Employment office and said I want a government job. And the person called up and sent me over and I had an interview with a Jewish person who said '—, that's a Hungarian name', and they hired me right away as a provisional" (1992a: 11n).

less well. One Los Angeles hotel manager complained to Waldinger that black employees "don't produce referrals" (1993a:18), and a comparison of black, Korean, and white contractors suggests that black employers have more difficulty filling their positions with co-ethnics than do other groups (Waldinger 1993c:29–31). Waters (1992) documents a case where the mostly black personnel of a large food services operation was replaced over a twenty-year period with immigrants, predominantly Caribbean. Employers explain this as resulting from the better work attitudes of black immigrants as compared to natives. But it is also the case that the numerical dominance of the immigrants is sustained by extremely effective hiring through their own referral networks. It could be that the previously dominant black workers were less effective on this dimension.

Light (1972) explained the superior entrepreneurial results of Asian Americans compared to African Americans by noting that the former but not the latter made use of rotating credit associations—systems in which money was pooled by participants through periodic contributions from each, which results in a large "pot" going successively to each one. This forced savings regime could work because unlike American blacks, Chinese and Japanese immigrants strongly identified themselves with a particular village or region of their homeland, and this solidarity provided a framework within which regular contributions could be monitored and assured. American blacks had no such home areas in the South which structured their everyday lives.[13] A similar logic may govern the efficacy of immigrant referral networks. The motivation and the capacity to make good referrals may be enhanced by membership in a solidary group that is identified with some particular, bounded set of people, marked off by some geographic or other well-defined boundary. The more open and free-floating social structure of the African American community—if it is so— might be less conducive to this activity. But in the virtual complete absence of research on questions like this, these comments are purely speculative.

Another factor that may operate is that to the extent that groups are insulated from one another, for whatever reasons, ethnic domination of certain niches becomes more probable, as the groups will find it easier to think of themselves as having distinct identities and interests.[14] This cuts both ways, however, since groups that are quite isolated from others may

[13] For a more detailed account see Granovetter 1994.

[14] This is supported also in a general way by Montgomery's mathematical model of the equilibrium outcomes of various configurations of weak and strong ties in the labor market, in which he shows that under all parameter conditions, the greater use of weak ties for information about employment decreases inequality (1994). We can assume that ethnic closure implies a reduction of weak ties, since most intergroup connections can

find mobilization easier, but may themselves also then be more visible and obvious targets for exclusion, as with black Americans (see Massey and Denton 1993).

Once groups are ensconced in a work setting, however this may have occurred, they can also exclude others—perhaps also with varying degrees of effectiveness. Grieco's account, cited above, of how families exclude others from training in the Scottish fish-processing industry, reflects a common phenomenon. Waldinger documents for the garment industry before 1950 how the substantial numbers of blacks were confined to lower-level jobs because to rise required training from other workers, and this was unavailable from the Jews and Italians who dominated higher-level work (Waldinger 1993a:5–12; for a general account of how "skill" is a product of group action, see Granovetter and Tilly 1988:207–213). The combination of effective referral networks and the domination of informal training that can be mobilized against newcomers from the wrong kinship, ethnic, or friendship group may be extremely effective in closing off whole segments of the labor market to groups that have no foothold there. Complaints by employers that members of certain groups are ineffective employees (see, for example, Kirschenmann and Neckerman 1991) may result in part from cases where such individuals were inserted into otherwise homogeneous ethnic networks, and were indeed unable to function effectively.

From the perspective of social equity and social policy these considerations raise perplexing problems. Group solidarity at work may be conducive to higher productivity while simultaneously perpetuating systematic inequalities among groups. In Chapter 10 of *GAJ,* I discussed how one might equalize opportunities with various schemes for inserting disfavored groups into employment settings previously closed to them, and noted the tradeoff between solidarity if a cohesive set of new employees was chosen, and outreach if the set was more weakly tied internally. I also raised the question of how one might construct referral networks artificially; something of this kind has in fact been accomplished in so-called "micro-lending" programs, which simulate the natural solidarities that sustain rotating credit associations (see, for instance, Holloway and Wallich 1992). Although this already too long Afterword shows what an out-

be expected to be through such ties. This may read too much into Montgomery's particular model, which is based on interaction in dyads, rather than larger groups of the sort that one might characterize as an "ethnic" group. But the point is that models of this kind may shed light on the precise determinants of inequality in labor market outcomes. Further insight would depend on the extent to which Montgomery's results depended on size of clique, and what extensions would be necessary to draw comparable conclusions about inequality for social configurations closer to what one might observe in an actual market.

pouring of research has occurred in the past twenty years on the dynamics of labor recruitment, understanding the complex network processes by which inequities are produced and reproduced, and how such reproduction can be discouraged, has not had comparable priority on the research agendas of labor scholars; consequently, we know little more about my speculations on this subject in *GAJ* than we did then. In my view, this is the single research gap most in need of being filled.

REFERENCES

Abegglen, James. 1958. *The Japanese Factory.* Glencoe, Ill.: The Free Press.

Baron, John, and John Bishop. 1985. "Extensive Search, Intensive Search and Hiring Costs: New Evidence on Employer Hiring Activity." *Economic Inquiry* 23 (July):363–382.

Barron, John M., John Bishop, and William C. Dunkelberg. 1985. "Employer Search: The Interviewing and Hiring of New Employees." *Review of Economics and Statistics* 67 (February):43–52.

Becker, Gary. 1971. *The Economics of Discrimination.* Chicago: University of Chicago Press.

Berg, Ivar. 1971. *Education and Jobs: The Great Training Robbery.* Boston: Beacon Press.

Bian, Yanjie. 1994. "Bringing Close Friends Back In: Interpersonal Trust, Bridging Strong Ties, and Status Attainment." Manuscript, Department of Sociology, University of Minnesota.

Bishop, John. 1993. "Improving Job Matches in the U.S. Labor Market." Pp. 335–400 in *Brookings Papers in Economic Activity,* vol. 1, edited by Martin N. Baily, Peter C. Reiss and Clifford Winston. Washington, D.C.: The Brookings Institution.

Blau, David M. 1992. "An Empirical Analysis of Employed and Unemployed Job Search Behavior." *Industrial and Labor Relations Review* 45, no. 4 (July): 738–752.

Blau, David M., and Philip K. Robins. 1990. "Job Search Outcomes for the Employed and Unemployed." *Journal of Political Economy* 98, no. 3: 637–55.

Bortnick, Steven, and Ports, Michelle. 1992. "Job Search Methods and Results: Tracking the Unemployed, 1991." *Monthly Labor Review* (December): 29–35.

Bott, Elizabeth. 1957. *Family and Social Network.* London: Tavistock.

Boxman, Ed, Paul De Graaf, and Hendrik Flap. 1991. "The Impact of Social and Human Capital on the Income Attainment of Dutch Managers." *Social Networks* 13: 51–73.

Braddock, Jomills, and James McPartland. 1987. "How Minorities Continue to Be Excluded from Equal Employment Opportunities: Research on Labor Market and Institutional Barriers." *Journal of Social Issues* 43, no. 1: 5–39.

Bradshaw, Thomas F. 1973. "Jobseeking Methods Used by Unemployed Workers." *Monthly Labor Review* (February): 35–40.

Bridges, William, and Wayne Villemez. 1986. "Informal Hiring and Income in the Labor Market." *American Sociological Review* 51 (August): 574–582.

Brinton, Mary, and Takehiko Kariya. 1994. "Institutional and Semi-Institutional Networks in the Japanese Labor Market." Manuscript, Department of Sociology, University of Chicago.

Burdett, Kenneth, and Randall Wright. 1994. "Two Sided Search." Manuscript, Department of Economics, University of Essex.

Burt, Ronald. 1992. *Structural Holes: The Social Structure of Competition.* Cambridge, Mass.: Harvard University Press.

Callender, Claire. 1987. "Women Seeking Work." Pp. 22–45 in *Unemployment: Personal and Social Consequences.* Edited by Stephen Fineman. London: Tavistock.

Campbell, Karen, and Rachel Rosenfeld. 1985. "Job Search and Job Mobility: Sex and Race Differences." *Research in the Sociology of Work* 3: 147–174.

Carson, Edgar. 1992. "Social Networks in the Labor Market: Job Acquisition by Retrenched Workers in South Australia." Unpublished Ph.D. dissertation, Faculty of Social Sciences, Department of Sociology, Flinders University of South Australia.

Cole, Robert. 1979. *Mobility and Participation: A Comparative Study of American and Japanese Industry.* Berkeley: University of California Press.

Corcoran, Mary, Linda Datcher, and Greg Duncan. 1980. "Information and Influence Networks in Labor Markets." Pp. 1–37 in *Five Thousand American Families: Patterns of Economic Progress,* vol. VIII. Edited by Greg Duncan and James Morgan. Ann Arbor, Mich.: Institute for Social Research.

———. 1980. "Most Workers Find Jobs through Word of Mouth." *Monthly Labor Review* (August): 33–35.

Coverdill, James. 1994. "Personal Contacts and Post-Hire Job Outcomes." Manuscript, Department of Sociology, University of Georgia.

Devine, Theresa, and Nicholas Kiefer. 1991. *Empirical Labor Economics: The Search Approach.* New York: Oxford University Press.

DiPrete, Thomas. 1989. *The Bureaucratic Labor Market: The Case of the Federal Civil Service.* New York: Plenum Press.

Ericksen, Eugene, and William Yancey. 1980. "The Locus of Strong Ties." Manuscript, Department of Sociology, Temple University, Philadelphia.

Farber, Henry S. 1993. "The Analysis of Inter-Firm Worker Mobility." National Bureau of Economic Research Working Paper No. 1462. Cambridge, Mass.: NBER.

Fernandez, Roberto. 1992. "Race, Space and Job Accessibility: Evidence from a Plant Relocation." Manuscript, Graduate School of Business, Stanford University.

Fevre, Ralph. 1989. "Informal Practices, Flexible Firms and Private Labour Markets." *Sociology* 23, no. 1 (February): 91–109.

Granovetter, Mark. 1973. "The Strength of Weak Ties." *American Journal of Sociology* 78 (May): 1360–1380.

———. 1979. "Placement as Brokerage: Information Problems in the Labor Market for Rehabilitated Workers." Pp. 83–101 in *Placement in Rehabilitation: A Career Development Perspective.* Edited by D. Vandergoot and J. Worrall. Baltimore: University Park Press.

———. 1981. "Toward a Sociological Theory of Income Differences." Pp. 11–47 in *Sociological Perspectives on Labor Markets.* Edited by Ivar Berg. New York: Academic Press.

———. 1983. "The Strength of Weak Ties: A Network Theory Revisited." *Sociological Theory* 1: 201–233.

———. 1984. "Small Is Bountiful: Labor Markets and Establishment Size." *American Sociological Review* 49 (June): 323–334.

———. 1986. "Japanese Firm Size: A Small Note." *Sociology and Social Research* 71 (October): 27–28.

———. 1988. "The Sociological and Economic Approach to Labor Markets: A Social Structural View." Pp. 187–216 in *Industries, Firms and Job: Sociological and Economic Approaches.* Edited by George Farkas and Paula England. New York: Plenum Press.

———. 1994. "The Economic Sociology of Firms and Entrepreneurs." In *The Economic Sociology of Immigration.* Edited by Alejandro Portes. New York and Princeton, N.J.: Russell Sage Foundation and Princeton University Press.

Granovetter, Mark, and Charles Tilly. 1988. "Inequality and Labor Processes." Pp. 175–

221 in *Handbook of Sociology*. Edited by Neil Smelser. Newbury Park, Calif.: Sage Publications.

Grieco, Margaret. 1987. *Keeping It in the Family: Social Networks and Employment Chance*. London: Tavistock.

Hagan, John. 1993. "The Social Embeddedness of Crime and Unemployment." *Criminology* 31, no. 4: 465–491.

Hakusho, Rodo. 1988. "Labor White Paper." Tokyo: Japan Ministry of Labor.

Halaby, Charles. 1988. "Action and Information in the Job Mobility Process: The Search Decision." *American Sociological Review* 53 (February): 9–25.

Hall, Robert. 1982. "The Importance of Lifetime Jobs in the U.S. Economy." *American Economic Review* 72: 716–724.

Hanson, Susan, and Geraldine Pratt. 1991. "Job Search and the Occupational Segregation of Women." *Annals of the Association of American Geographers* 81, no. 2: 229–253.

———. 1992. "Dynamic Dependencies: A Geographic Investigation of Local Labor Markets." *Economic Geography* 68, no. 2: 373–405.

Harhoff, Dietmar, and Thomas Kane. 1994. "Financing Apprenticeship Training: Evidence from Germany." National Bureau of Economic Research Working Paper No. 4557. Cambridge, Mass.: NBER.

Harris, C. C. 1987. "Redundancy and Social Transition." Chapter 11 (pp. 218–231) in Chris C. Harris, P. Brown, R. Fevre, G. G. Leaver, R. M. Lee, and L. D. Morris. *Redundancy and Recession in South Wales*. Oxford: Basil Blackwell.

Harris, C. C., and P. Brown. 1987. "The Determinants of Labour Market Experience." Chapter 10 (pp. 195–217) in Chris C. Harris, P. Brown, R. Fevre, G. G. Leaver, R. M. Lee, and L. D. Morris. *Redundancy and Recession in South Wales*. Oxford: Basil Blackwell.

Harris, C. C., R. M. Lee, and P. Brown. 1987. "The Fate of the Redundant in the Market." Chapter 9 (pp. 177–194) in Chris C. Harris, P. Brown, R. Fevre, G. G. Leaver, R. M. Lee, and L. D. Morris. *Redundancy and Recession in South Wales*. Oxford: Basil Blackwell.

Harris, Chris C., P. Brown, R. Fevre, G. G. Leaver, R. M. Lee, and L. D. Morris. 1987. *Redundancy and Recession in South Wales*. Oxford: Basil Blackwell.

Holloway, Marguerite, and Paul Wallich. 1992. "A Risk Worth Taking." *Scientific American* 267, no. 5 (November): 126.

Holzer, Harry J. 1987. "Informal Job Search and Black Youth Unemployment." *American Economic Review* 77, no. 3: 446–452.

———. 1987. "Job Search by Employed and Unemployed Youth." *Industrial and Labor Relations Review* 40, no. 4 (July): 601–611.

———. 1988. "Search Method Use by Unemployed Youth." *Journal of Labor Economics*, no. 1: 1–20.

Jenkins, Richard, Alan Bryman, Janet Ford, Teresa Keil, and Alan Beardsworth. 1983. "Information in the Labour Market: The Impact of Recession." *Sociology* 17, no. 2 (May): 260–267.

Kasinitz, Philip, and Jan Rosenberg. 1994. "Missing the Connection: Social Isolation and Employment on the Brooklyn Waterfront." Working paper, the Michael Harrington Center, Queens College, City University of New York.

Kirschenmann, Joleen, and Kathryn Neckerman. 1991. " 'We'd Love to Hire Them, But . . .': The Meaning of Race for Employers." Pp. 203–232 in *The Urban Underclass*. Edited by Christopher Jencks and Paul Peterson. Washington, D.C.: The Brookings Institution.

Korenman, Sanders, and Susan Turner. 1994. "On Employment Contacts and Differences in Wages between Minority and White Youths." Manuscript, Humphrey Institute of Public Affairs, University of Minnesota.

Lai, Gina, Shu-Yin Leung, and Nan Lin. 1994. "Network Resources, Contact Resources and Status Attainment." Manuscript, Department of Sociology, Duke University.

Lee, Jung-Kyu. 1993. "Organizational Constraints, Network Matching, and the Reemployment of Displaced Workers." Ph.D. dissertation, Department of Sociology, State University of New York, Stony Brook.

Lee, R. M. 1987. "Looking for Work." Chapter 5 (pp. 109–126) in *Redundancy and Recession in South Wales*. Edited by Chris C. Harris, P. Brown, R. Fevre, G. G. Leaver, R. M. Lee, and L. D. Morris. Oxford: Basil Blackwell.

Licht, Walter. 1992. *Getting Work: Philadelphia, 1840–1950*. Cambridge, Mass.: Harvard University Press.

Lieberson, Stanley, 1980. *A Piece of the Pie: Blacks and White Immigrants since 1880*. Berkeley: University of California Press.

Light, Ivan. 1972. *Ethnic Enterprise in America: Business and Welfare among Chinese, Japanese and Blacks*. Berkeley: University of California Press.

Lin, Nan. 1990. "Social Resources and Social Mobility: A Structural Theory of Status Attainment." Pp. 247–271 in *Social Mobility and Social Structure*. Edited by Ronald Breiger. New York: Cambridge University Press.

Lin, Nan, and Yanjie Bian. 1991. "Getting Ahead in Urban China." *American Journal of Sociology* 97, no. 3: 657–688.

Lin, Nan, Walter Ensel, and John Vaughn. 1981. "Social Resources and Strength of Ties: Structural Factors in Occupational Status Attainment." *American Sociological Review* 46: 393–405.

Manwaring, Tony. 1984. "The Extended Internal Labor Market." *Cambridge Journal of Economics* 8: 161–187.

Marsden, Peter, and Karen Campbell. 1984. "Measuring Tie Strength." *Social Forces* 63, no. 2: 482–501.

———. 1990. "Recruitment and Selection Processes: The Organization Side of Job Searches." Pp. 59–79 in *Social Mobility and Social Structure*. Edited by Ronald Breiger. New York: Cambridge University Press.

Marsden, Peter, and Jeanne Hurlbert. 1988. "Social Resources and Mobility Outcomes: A Replication and Extension." *Social Forces* 66, no. 4 (June): 1038–1059.

Marx, Jonathan, and Kevin Leicht. 1992. "Formality of Recruitment to 229 Jobs: Variations by Race, Sex and Job Characteristics. *Sociology and Social Research* 76, no. 4 (July): 190–196.

Massey, Douglas, and Nancy Denton. 1993. *American Apartheid: Segregation and the Making of the Underclass*. Cambridge, Mass.: Harvard University Press.

McPherson, J. M., and Lynn Smith-Lovin. 1982. "Women and Weak Ties: Differences by Sex in the Size of Voluntary Organizations." *American Journal of Sociology* 87, no. 4: 883–904.

Menon, Ramdas. 1989. "The Impact of Social Networks on the Duration of Post-Migration Job Searches." *Journal of Asian and African Studies* 24, nos. 3, 4: 252–259.

Mier, Robert, and Robert Giloth. 1985. "Hispanic Employment Opportunities: A Case of Internal Labor Markets and Weak-Tied Social Networks." *Social Science Quarterly* 66: 296–309.

Montgomery, James. 1991. "Social Networks and Labor-Market Outcomes: Toward an Economic Analysis." *American Economic Review* 81, no. 5: 1408–1418.

———. 1992. "Job Search and Network Composition: Implications of the Strength-of-Weak-Ties Hypothesis." *American Sociological Review* 57, no. 5: 586–596.

———. 1994. "Weak Ties, Employment, and Inequality: An Equilibrium Analysis." *American Journal of Sociology* 99, no. 5: 1212–1236.

Morris, Lydia. 1984. "Patterns of Social Activity and Post-Redundancy Labour-Market Experience." *Sociology* 18, no. 3: 339–352.

Morris, Lydia D. 1987. "The Household and the Labour Market." Chapter 6 (pp. 127–140) in *Redundancy and Recession in South Wales*. Edited by Chris C. Harris, P. Brown, R. Fevre, G. G. Leaver, R. M. Lee, and L. D. Morris. Oxford: Basil Blackwell.

Mortensen, Dale. 1986. "Job Search and Labor Market Analysis." Chapter 15 (pp. 849–

919) in *Handbook of Labor Economics,* vol. II. Edited by O. Ashenfelter and R. Layard. Amsterdam: Elsevier.

Mostacci-Calzavara, Liviana. 1982. "Social Networks and Access to Job Opportunities." Unpublished Ph.D. dissertation, Department of Sociology, University of Toronto.

Nadel, S. F. 1957. *The Theory of Social Structure.* Melbourne: Melbourne University Press.

Nelson-Rowe, Shan. 1988. "Markets, Politics and Professions: The Rise of Vocationalism in American Education." Ph.D. dissertation, Department of Sociology, State University of New York, Stony Brook.

———. 1991. "Corporation Schooling and the Labor Market at General Electric." *History of Education Quarterly* 31, no. 1: 27–46.

Osberg, Lars. 1993. "Fishing in Different Pools: Job-Search Strategies and Job-Finding Success in Canada in the Early 1980's." *Journal of Labor Economics* 11, no. 2: 348–385.

Pattison, Philippa. 1993. *Algebraic Models for Social Networks.* New York: Cambridge University Press.

Pfeffer, Jeffrey, and James Baron. 1988. "Taking the Workers Back Out: Recent Trends in the Structuring of Employment." Pp. 257–303 in *Research in Organizational Behavior.* Edited by B. Shaw and L. Cummings. Greenwich, Conn.: JAI Press.

Ports, Michelle Harrison. 1993. "Trends in Job Search Methods, 1970–1992." *Monthly Labor Review* (October): 63–67.

Powell, Walter, and Laurel Smith-Doerr. 1994. "Networks and Economic Life." Pp. 368–402 in *Handbook of Economic Sociology.* Edited by N. Smelser and R. Swedberg. New York: Russell Sage Foundation and Princeton University Press.

Rogers, Everett, and Lawrence Kincaid. 1981. *Communication Networks: Toward a New Paradigm for Research.* New York: Free Press.

Rosenbaum, James. 1984. *Career Mobility in a Corporate Hierarchy.* New York: Academic Press.

Rosenbaum, James, and Amy Binder. 1994. "Do Employers Really Need More Educated Youth?" Manuscript, School of Education and Social Policy, Northwestern University.

Rosenbaum, James, and Takehiko Kariya. 1989. "From High School to Work: Market and Institutional Mechanisms in Japan." *American Journal of Sociology* 94: 1334–1365.

Rosenbaum, James, Takehiko Kariya, Rick Settersten, and Tony Maier. 1990. "Market and Network Theories of the Transition from High School to Work: Their Application to Industrialized Societies." *Annual Review of Sociology* 16: 263–299.

Roth, Alvin, and Xiaolin Xing. 1994. "Jumping the Gun: Imperfections and Institutions Related to the Timing of Market Transactions." *American Economic Review,* forthcoming.

Sabel, Charles. 1991. "Moebius-Strip Organizations and Open Labor Markets: Some Consequences of the Reintegration of Conception and Execution in a Volatile Economy." Pp. 23–54 in *Social Theory for a Changing Society.* Edited by P. Bourdieu and J. Coleman. Boulder: Colo.: Westview Press.

Saxenian, AnnaLee. 1994. *Regional Advantage: Culture and Competition in Silicon Valley and Route 128.* Cambridge, Mass.: Harvard University Press.

Simon, Curtis J., and John T. Warner. 1992. "Matchmaker, Matchmaker: The Effect of Old-Boy Networks on Job Match Quality, Earnings and Tenure." *Journal of Labor Economics* 10, no. 3: 306–329.

Spilerman, Seymour. 1977. "Careers, Labor Market Structure, and Socioeconomic Achievement." *American Journal of Sociology* 83, no. 3: 551–593.

Squires, G. D. 1979. *Education and Jobs.* New Brunswick, N.J.: Transaction Books.

Staiger, Doug. 1990. "The Effects of Connections on the Wages and Mobility of Young Workers." Manuscript, Kennedy School of Public Policy, Harvard University.

Thomas, Jonathan. 1994. "Public Employment Agencies and Unemployment Spells: Exploring the Relationship." Manuscript, Center for Urban Affairs and Policy Research, Northwestern University.

U.S. Department of Labor. 1975. "Jobseeking Methods Used by American Workers." Bureau of Labor Statistics Bulletin No. 1886.

Waldinger, Roger. 1992a. "The Making of An Immigrant Niche." Manuscript, Department of Sociology, University of California, Los Angeles, February.

————. 1992b. "Taking Care of the Guests: The Impact of Immigrants on Services— an Industry Case Study." *International Journal of Urban and Regional Research* 16, no. 1: 97–113.

————. 1992c. "The Ethnic Politics of Municipal Jobs." Manuscript, Department of Sociology, University of California, Los Angeles. December.

————. 1993a. "Who Makes the Beds? Who Washes the Dishes? Black/Immigrant Competition Reassessed." Institute of Industrial Relations Working Paper 246, April. University of California, Los Angeles.

————. 1993b. "Who Gets the Lousy Jobs? New Immigrants and African Americans in New York, 1940–1990." Manuscript, Department of Sociology, University of California, Los Angeles, October.

————. 1993c. "The 'Other Side' of Embeddedness: A Case Study of the Interplay of Economy and Ethnicity." Manuscript, Department of Sociology, University of California, Los Angeles. December.

Wanous, John P. 1980. *Organizational Entry: Recruitment, Selection, and Socialization of Newcomers.* Reading, Mass.: Addison-Wesley.

Wasserman, Stanley, and Katherine Faust. 1994. *Social Network Analysis: Methods and Applications.* New York: Cambridge University Press.

Watanabe, Shin. 1987. "Job-Searching: A Comparative Study of Male Employment Relations in the United States and Japan." Unpublished Ph.D. dissertation, Department of Sociology, University of California, Los Angeles. UMI Dissertation Information Service Order No. 8727817.

Waters, Mary. 1992. "Hiring Practices and Racial and Ethnic Dynamics at American Food Services." Unpublished manuscript, Harvard University, Department of Sociology. Forthcoming in *Black Like Who?*, University of California Press.

Weber, Max. 1968/1921. *Economy and Society.* Totowa, N.J.: Bedminster Press.

Wegener, Bernd. 1991. "Job Mobility and Social Ties: Social Resources, Prior Job and Status Attainment." *American Sociological Review* 56 (February): 60–71.

White, Harrison C. 1992. *Identity and Control: A Structural Theory of Social Action.* Princeton, N.J.: Princeton University Press.

White, Harrison, Scott Boorman, and Ronald Breiger. 1976. "Social Structure from Multiple Networks: I. Blockmodels of Roles and Positions." *American Journal of Sociology* 81: 730–780.

Wial, Howard. 1991. "Getting a Good Job: Mobility in a Segmented Labor Market." *Industrial Relations* 30, no. 3 (Fall): 396–415.

Wielgosz, John, and Susan Carpenter. 1987. "The Effectiveness of Alternative Methods of Searching for Jobs and Finding Them: An Exploratory Analysis of the Data Bearing upon the Ways of Coping with Joblessness." *American Journal of Economics and Sociology* 46, no. 2 (April): 151–164.

Wilson, William. 1987. *The Truly Disadvantaged.* Chicago: University of Chicago Press.

Windolf, Paul. 1986. "Recruitment, Selection, and Internal Labour Markets in Britain and Germany." *Organization Studies* 7, no. 3: 235–254.

Wood, Stephen. 1985. "Recruitment Systems and the Recession." *British Journal of Industrial Relations* 23, no. 3 (November): 103–120.

Appendix

Design and Conduct of the Study

It is perhaps worth pointing out that, for better or worse, a study like the present one can be conducted on a relatively small budget. The main expense was computer time for producing the crosstabulations used in the text, as well as for others not shown. Other expenses were those of the 1968 and 1969 Newton city directories ($90.00), automobile maintenance for my 75-some-odd trips between Cambridge and Newton, minor telephone and duplication expenses, and the typing of the manuscript. While I do not have detailed figures, it is certain that the total is under $900. It is obvious how this is possible: I did all of the interviewing, coding, mailing, calling back, and analysis myself. I have to say that I thought of this, at the time, as being, mainly, the cross that an aspiring graduate student must bear. Consequently, it would not have occurred to me to make a virtue of this necessity. My editor at the Harvard University Press points out to me, however, that at a time of shrinking research funding, low-budget research must come to have general relevance as a methodological theme. Another reader of the manuscript urged me to emphasize the "likely higher quality and greater reliability of the results" stemming from the fact that all the field work and analysis was done by me alone. The trouble is that, being *in* this position, I am all too aware of the limitations and ambiguity of the data I have collected and, so, feel reluctant to trumpet their high quality. Some specific problems are spelled out below.

Having said this, I can also express surprise at how little many principal investigators actually know about the meaning of their data. To this extent, I am sympathetic with ethnomethodological critiques of sociological data. Many not only never see their respondents (or their locale) but never even see those who *elicit* the survey results from them. Some research is well suited to straightforward, closed-ended survey work, and in such cases that design may be appropriate. But where the subject matter is deeply ambiguous, as I feel it to be in the case of this study, and where the intent is exploratory, as here also, the hired-survey design is not only expensive, but misleading. Where the interviewing is at all open-ended, first of all, even one interviewer introduces a systematic bias. That bias is at least consistent, and if the interviewer is the researcher, or in close contact with him, an account can be given of it. Multiple interviewers introduce multiple biases. This source of variation is difficult enough for the investigator to sense even when in contact with the interviewers. If, in addition, however, one or more coders is hired to reduce the open-ended questions to specified codes (or worse, scales) then the investigator is unlikely to have any sense whatever of the ambiguities that arose in the collection of the data, or of how ambiguous findings are to be interpreted.

The structure of the academic profession makes it unlikely that the one-man research model will be widely adopted. It is all very well for graduate students or NORC to be out interviewing respondents—but as one moves up the hierarchy a presumption develops that such mucking around is for underlings. I find myself wondering if I would go through such a detailed project again, unassisted. Clerical help, at a minimum, would relieve some of the burden. As one adds other layers of help, the low-cost aspect of the research fades, as does one's closeness to the data. But an increase in the scale of the project becomes possible. One-man research is, clearly, best-suited for well-defined problems of limited scope and scale. No single investigator could hope, for instance, to offer a comprehensive study of a complex metropolitan community. Nevertheless, I believe that enough problems do allow of a sufficiently narrow formulation to make some of the considerations outlined here of interest.

Traditionally, the issues I refer to arise in discussion of participant-observation or anthropological methods, as opposed to survey or sociological ones. Sociologists have developed an unstated assumption that a well-conducted survey is a large-scale enterprise, and that small projects must constitute "soft" analysis. Proponents of participant-observation and anthropological methods, rather than fighting this assumption, tend to defend the virtues of soft analysis.

The dichotomy strikes me as wrong headed. We know that, statistically, a carefully drawn sample with high response rate, *even if rather small*, is nicely representative of its population. The main handicaps of small samples are: 1) difficulty in constructing multivariate analyses, and 2) unreliability of inferences from small *sub*samples to the corresponding *sub*populations. But in our eagerness to deploy impressive statistical techniques, we forget that "mere" marginals and zero or first-order relationships can be quite revealing and suggestive—hence, ideal for exploratory research. The advantage of economy is thus joined to the increased openness to unexpected findings of an anthropological style, without sacrificing careful sampling design. Such, at least, has been my aim. The reader

can judge my success better from the following detailed account
of my methods.

Sampling

The method of selecting respondents is an adaptation of that
reported by Reynolds (1951). The key is the existence of commercial city directories which list, annually, the name, address, occupation, and employer of each resident. Having purchased copies of
the 1968 and 1969 directories for Newton, Massachusetts from
their publisher, R.L. Polk and Company, Boston,[1] I underlined,
on every other page of the 1969 directory, the name of each PTM
worker, as defined by U.S. Census categories (1960). Individuals
who were self-employed or who worked for firms owned by a
member of the family were not included, on the grounds that it
made no sense in such cases to ask how one found out about the
job. Thus, the effective population was a systematic 50 percent
random sample of all non-self-employed (or family-employed)
PTM workers living in Newton in 1969.[2]

Each name was then checked against its previous year's listing
to see whether the employer listed in 1969 was different from that
in 1968, or if the name was listed for the first time in 1969. In
either case, the name was checked and entered on an index card.
Five hundred and fifteen names were selected in this way, of whom
it was my intention to use 300 in the study. (The 515 names
represented 15.3 percent of all the names that had been underlined.) Those listed as having changed employer entered the sample
automatically. When a name was listed in 1969 for the first time,
it was subsequently eliminated if the person proved not to have
changed employers within a five-year period. At first glance, the
five-year criterion may appear to yield a subsample of new residents
with less recent job changes than those who had remained in
Newton while changing jobs. Actually, however, because of lags
in data collection for these directories, respondents who supposedly
had last changed jobs within a year had the actual time of job
change distributed over a five-year period. It therefore seemed
expedient to allow the same range for new residents. In principle,
then, my sample is a random one of all those who changed employers within the last five years. This cannot be quite true because
comparisons of successive *earlier* directories (for example, 1967

1. Actually, the publisher had no copies of the 1968 directory, but did
release to me a list of purchasers. In a short time I was able to find one who
sold me his (by that time obsolete) copy.
2. Note that leaving out those employed by relatives introduces an under-
estimation of the use of personal contacts, even if a small one.

and 1968) would also reveal some such individuals; job changes found by this comparison would, however, be distributed over periods reaching back longer than 1964, so that no clear definition of sample could be achieved by that method except by an unfeasible amount of sifting potential respondents derived from several exhaustive directory checks. Even then, I would not catch those who moved to Newton after the 1969 directory had been compiled. Methods beyond my scope in time and cost could have made the sample definition more precise, but it seemed unlikely that the effort would be worth the cost.

After I had collected all my data, I did attempt to determine whether the year in which a job was found *had* any influence on the labor-market behavior of the respondents. I divided the sample into three groups: those who began their job within one year prior to interview (or mail survey) ($N = 94$); between one and two years ($N = 92$) and those who had begun their current job 3–5 years before responding ($N = 96$). These three groups showed no systematic differences in occupation, search behavior, methods of finding their current job, or degree of job satisfaction.

I had decided, after a pilot study (of 15 personal interviews), that for greater efficiency in interviewing, some geographical clustering of the sample was desirable. With clusters as the units sampled, rather than individuals, I would lose less time on account of a particular respondent not being home—others would live nearby. For similar reasons, Reynolds (1951) used city blocks as his primary sampling units (PSU's); in suburban Newton, laid out in nothing like a rectangular grid, this did not seem feasible. I therefore divided the map of Newton into small squares, and located every potential respondent in one square. In cluster sampling, it is of some importance to have roughly equal-sized PSU's, in terms of number of respondents included (cf. Hansen et al., 1953: 244–246, 337). Therefore, I broke up PSU's which were much larger than average, and combined some which were much smaller, and contiguous. There were finally 140 PSU's, each containing an average of 3.7 respondents; none had less than 1 or more than 8. These PSU's were numbered sequentially from 1–140. Using a random number table from Fisher & Yates' *Statistical Tables* (1963: 134–139), I drew PSU's at random, including in my sample everyone in a PSU drawn. The first of the 125 PSU's drawn were included in my interview sample; those drawn subsequently were included in the mail sample. Ultimately, 457 of the 515 names originally drawn were included in one of the initial survey lists.

Interview Survey

Those chosen for the interview sample were sent a copy of the first letter shown in Appendix C. I had decided that, in view of the relatively small sample, high response rate was important; pilot study results showed that people were less likely to refuse an interview to a student already on their doorstep than to a more or less anonymous voice over the telephone, requesting an appointment. Eighty-nine of the 100 interviews were completed between June and August of 1969, the rest in September and October. On each evening except Saturday, I arrived in Newton around 7:30 P.M. and proceeded to the home of a potential respondent, who had received my letter within one or two weeks. If the respondent was not at home, I went to some other person in the same PSU (when possible). If the respondent was home I asked if it would be convenient to conduct the interview at that time. In about three-fourths of these cases, I was able to carry out the interview immediately. (Since respondents were home with probability about one-half, this accounts for a little more than a third of all cases.) I attempted to arrange an appointment if that evening was not convenient. Those who were not home I visited a second time; 26 interviews were completed on this second visit. I contacted by telephone any respondents who were not home twice, and attempted to arrange an appointment in this way. Of the 109 people whom I contacted, eventually, only 9 refused to be interviewed. About 10 more indicated that they would have probably refused except that I was already there. The method was not *grossly* inefficient; only once or twice during the summer did I return without an interview; on some nights I was able to carry out two and even three. There is, however, wasted time and frustration inherent in this style; I began to understand what it must feel like to be a travelling salesman. When resources permit the drawing of a larger sample, making 85–90 percent response less crucial, I would, in the future, follow the initial letter by a telephoned request for appointment. This would also make the sample easier to draw by eliminating the need for geographic clustering.

My pilot study had suggested that people moving away from Newton could present difficulties in sampling. I adopted two expedients to deal with this. 1) I began compiling my list just a few days after the 1969 directory was released by the publisher; 2) in cases where people had, nevertheless moved away before I could reach them ($N = 22$), I tried to determine a forwarding address from present occupants of the home, or from neighbors. I succeeded in 14 cases. In 5 of the cases, the new address was in geographical range of Cambridge (3 in Newton, 2 in Brighton), so I arranged interviews at the new addresses. In 9 cases the new addresses were not in feasible interviewing range; these were added to the mail survey, and all responded. Eight individuals could not be traced; in addition, 38 potential respondents whom I contacted personally turned out to be ineligible; they did not meet the sample criterion of holding a full-time PTM job, non self-employed, begun within five years.

Response rate for the interview survey thus comes to 85.5 percent; the 14.5 percent non-response is made up of the 9 refusals and the 8 who could not be contacted. As with the figure given later for mail survey non-response, this estimate is conservative, since it assumes that all those not able to be contacted would have been eligible for the survey; this is unlikely since about 25 percent of those who *were* contacted were found ineligible.

My interviews were carried out using the first schedule shown in Appendix C as a skeleton; I asked all the questions listed there, but not necessarily in that order or with the precise wording indicated in every case. Rather, I used an open-ended style which I had found, in a pilot study, necessary to elicit the various semi-obscure details I wanted about times, places, and circumstances of meetings and conversations. Much of the anecdotal material and many fresh insights were obtained via this open-endedness. The average length of interviews was 44 minutes and ranged from 20 to 90. Though some respondents were reluctant to begin the interview, almost all were extremely cooperative once they had begun to discuss the questions.

In the interest of replicability, I should add a comment about interviewing procedures. While the anecdotal material in the text may seem straightforward, it is not at all easy to extract. Many respondents cannot imagine that the interviewer is interested in "trivial" details, and so, answer questions about the circumstances under which job information was passed in a way too vague for the kind of analysis I have done here. The complexity of social life being what it is, one may occasionally miss crucial details; in a few cases I felt that I had a clear picture of how a particular job had been found, until some detail, mentioned later—almost in passing— cast a different light on the situation. Sometimes this related to respondents' defenses, but more often to their conceptions of what is important and what is not. In many cases, the full picture was not obtained from the initial question about how a job was found but only through persistent, open-ended questioning. Respondents were being asked to recall detailed sequences of events, sometimes several years old, which they had not necessarily classified as significant. This meant not that they could not do so—in most cases recall seemed definite and clear—but that their recall was not always immediate. As they answered various related questions, relevant details filtered from memory into their awareness. These details were, in a few cases, scattered through an entire interview, though more often they cropped up near the relevant questions.

The point is not that a fairly complete picture cannot be reconstructed, but rather that it would be difficult to do so in a mechanical way. This runs counter to considerations of efficiency and intersubjective application of the interviewing instrument. Other researchers would be well-advised to revise the interview guide of Appendix C with this in mind, trying to add whatever detailed considerations they are interested in, and spacing memory prods as best they can. The instrument as presented here must be thought of as exploratory.

The difficulty encountered here raises an interesting point about the value of open-ended procedures. Respondents who were intelligent in general and often perceptive about their own situations rarely understood why I wanted the kind of details I did. A closed-ended survey would have elicited from them the standard picture most of them (and many sociologists) have of an orderly career progression determined by level of education and other "demographic" variables.

In a pilot study, I asked respondents how they thought other people in their *own* line of work were generally recruited; blank stares resulted. The details given in anecdotes of previous chapters are apparently almost certain to be unknown to anyone except the person centrally involved. The point is that although everyone knows his own case perfectly well, most lack perspective on it. A frequent response to my question of how one heard of one's present job was: "that's a really funny story"; yet the story that followed was often quite typical.

Exactly because respondents had no *general* information about such phenomena, they had no intellectual framework in which to respond to my probes, and thus tried to fit their experience into received cultural wisdom about career patterns. No one can pretend that open-ended questioning is not liable to lead a respondent down the interviewer's particular garden path—but this is well known. The point that needs more stress is that answers to highly *structured* questions are not at all "objective," but are liable, instead, to elicit answers nicely confirming what we already "know."

Mail Survey

The main purpose of the mail survey was to add statistical backbone to interview results. Categories for the survey form (shown in Appendix C) were derived from my experience in pilot interviews. Each respondent was sent the second letter shown in Appendix C along with a copy of the survey. The respondent's address on the form enabled me to keep track of who had returned it. After four weeks, those who had not responded were sent a copy of the third letter shown in Appendix C, along with another copy of the survey. After four more weeks, those respondents who had still not replied were contacted by telephone; in some cases I was able to elicit answers to the questions on the form during the phone call. In others, the respondent promised to send it back, and usually did. Of the 302 mail surveys sent out, 72 were returned and found not eligible for this study. Of the valid forms, 109 were returned after the first letter, 38 were returned after the follow-up letter, and 17 were returned after the follow-up phone call. Eighteen forms were filled out by answers given to me over the telephone; 2 individuals refused by mail, and 14 in response to my phone call. Five promised to send the form back, but did not. In 27 cases, the respondent did not return the form and could not be reached by telephone. Response rate comes to 79.1 percent for the mail survey.

Though response rate was high, it seemed desirable to explore the nature of bias, if any, caused by non-response. For this purpose, I divided the mail sample into three groups: those who responded after the first mailing ($N = 109$), after the second mailing ($N = 37$), and those from whom data was obtained only after a follow-up phone call. (No comparable division was feasible for the interview survey.) I assume that each successive group is more similar than the previous one to those who did not respond at all; thus, any systematic trends should indicate the direction of response bias.

No significant difference appears among the three groups in income or occupation.[3] Earlier responders *were* more likely to hold Ph.D. or law degrees, to have attained B.A. degrees at more prestigious colleges, to be younger, married, have fathers in PTM occupations, and to be Protestant rather than Catholic. Of these relationships, only the last reaches significance ($P = 0.06$).

There is little systematic difference in job and occupational matters. All three groups began their current jobs around the same time, and have similar proportions of P, T, and M workers. The earlier the response, the more likely the respondent to have searched for his job, *not* to have used personal contacts in finding it, and to be "very satisfied" with it. None of these trends is significant, though the job-finding relation is close ($p = 0.12$); 45 percent of those responding to the first letter, but 60 percent of those answering the second mailing or the phone call, found out about their job through contacts. Non-response, then, may introduce *under*-estimation of the use of contacts. Generally, though, no important bias appears related to non-response.

Were I to rewrite the instrument, I would make certain changes. In Question 7, the response "I once worked with him" is too vague, as is "I once worked under him." The former fails to specify whether one's colleague was in the same company (cf. discussion on interorganizational relations, in Chapter 8) while the latter does not distinguish between supervisors and employers. Question 10 was not particularly useful. It should be replaced by one dealing with frequency of contact at the time job-information was given. In

addition, a question about the perceived closeness of the relationship would be useful.

Question 14, about job satisfaction, was adapted from Nancy
Morse's *White Collar Job Satisfaction*. I have mixed feelings about
it. On the one hand, it produced little variance, with only about
5 percent admitting any dissatisfaction, and another 8 percent
indicating neither satisfaction or dissatisfaction. Perhaps more
degrees of satisfaction would be more illuminating. On the other
hand, many tables based on dichotomizing at categories 1–2 vs.
3–4–5 were of interest. Also, of course, when the question is asked
in this way, it is more comparable to that of other studies.

Comparability of Mail and Interview Surveys

Since for many questions, I have pooled mail and interview
answers in the text, it is necessary to show that there is no substantial difference between the samples. Of the 457 individuals sent
letters for either survey, 24.1 percent were found to be ineligible.
Percentage of ineligibility is essentially the same between the two
subsamples: 24.5 percent for the interview sample and 23.8 percent
for the mail sample.

Systematic comparison of the two subsamples on data collected
in the study failed to reveal any significant differences, though
some differences are nearly so.[3] Occupational distribution is
nearly identical, as is job satisfaction. Those in the interview sample
were somewhat more likely to search for their job (76 percent)
than those in the mail group (68 percent $p = 0.17$). Although the
overall pattern of how jobs were found is not significantly different
between samples, ($p = 0.13$), there is a clear tendency for those in
the interview sample to cite the use of contacts (66 percent) more
often than those in the mail sample (51 percent). This is likely
to be, in part, due to intensive questioning in interviews, disclosing
the use of contacts when the same respondent might have checked
"direct application" on the survey form.[4]

Given the cluster method of sampling, there was some likelihood
that demographic differences related to the spatial organization of
Newton would create differences between two subsamples. The
interview sample respondents are likely to be: of somewhat lower
education ($p = 0.20$), lower prestige of college granting the B.S.
($p = 0.14$), Jewish rather than Protestant ($p = 0.25$), and natives of
Massachusetts ($p = 0.101$). Most of these small differences stem
from oversampling in the interview study of relatively poor areas in
the north of Newton, and of heavily Jewish ones in the south.

3. X^2 test, where "significant" means $p \leqslant 0.10$, a conservative criterion in
this context.
4. See the further discussion of this point in Appendix B.

Distributions of age, income, and size of town in which respondent grew up are nearly identical in the two subsamples. On the whole, differences between the two sources of data seem sufficiently small to justify pooling of the subsamples in cases where both present data on the same variable.

Newton: A Representative Case?

Assuming that findings of this study are indeed representative of Newton, Mass., it is natural to wonder in what measure such findings might be generalizable to larger (American) populations of PTM workers. Those familiar with the Boston area view Newton as "atypical" of suburbia, in being a predominantly Jewish, professionally oriented area. This idea is based on the identification of one or two prominent sections with the whole city. I found Newton to be extremely heterogeneous, consisting of (in addition to the expected Jewish, higher-status areas) clearly delimited wealthy "WASP" sections as well as small and large pockets of rural and urban poverty, and lower middle-class ethnic enclaves. One section presented difficulties because my inability to speak Italian made it impractical to ask directions of passersby. Perhaps as in most cities, in reality, startling contrasts could be found between one block and the next.

The religious background of the Newton sample is: 37.2 percent Jewish, 31.2 percent Roman Catholic, 29.3 percent Protestant, and 2.3 percent None. Jews, while the largest group, are barely more than a third. It is hard to know what national figures to compare this with; we have no census data giving the religious composition of occupational groups. In may not be radically different from proportions of PTM workers in many large, non-Southern, coastal metropolitan areas, though numerous coastal-Southern and inland cities can readily be imagined among whose PTM workers Jews and Catholics would be far less prominently represented.

Some national comparisons are possible on occupation and mobility. According to Table No. 330, 1967 Statistical Abstract of the U.S., about 60 percent of the male PTM group (non-self-employed) in 1960 were P and T. The figure for my sample is 71.3 percent. Partly, the discrepancy is due to the secular trend, 1960–69 for the PT group to become an increasing proportion of the PTM segment (cf. Table No. 327); partly it reflects the large number of universities in the Boston area. Whereas college professors were 2 percent of the national PTM group in 1960 (Table No. 330), they are about 20 percent of my sample. It should be kept in mind, however, that my sample is not a general one, but one of those who are recently mobile; thus comparisons are difficult.

It is important to point out that, in the Introduction I analyzed the labor-market behavior of various demographic subgroups. The interested reader can determine from this analysis what difference it *would* make if the Newton sample did overrepresent this or that category of individual. In particular, it is of interest that few significant differences were found in the labor-market behavior of various religious and ethnic groups. In a larger sense, I am not primarily concerned with this issue. A one-location sample is bound not to be entirely representative of the possible total sampling universe. I have hoped mainly to suggest relationships to be tested and further investigated and elaborated in studies which are larger and conducted in different contexts.

Appendix

Coding Rules and Problems

The more information one has, the more difficult coding is. The best solution is to impose relatively arbitrary rules consistently, and try to explain their logic.

Job-Finding Classifications

Three ways of finding out about a job are distinguished in the Introduction: personal contact, formal means, and direct application. Brief definitions of each category are given there. The main coding difficulty is that some cases involving formal means or direct application also involve personal contacts. A coding rule for such cases could require a substantive decision about how to judge, in general, which element is more significant in making it possible for the individual to take a given job. But since my *emphasis* is on the use of personal contacts, I have tried to develop coding rules which are conservative in this respect—that is, which avoid coding ambiguous cases as uses of contacts.

The following cases show ways in which formal means may be mixed with personal contacts:

Case #23: Frederick Y. was out of college and doing only part-time work. To pacify his family, he agreed to have lunch one day with his brother and his brother's friend, who ran an employment agency. The friend took Mr. Y. back to his office and called a Boston newspaper which needed an assistant credit manager. After a brief interview he was offered the job and accepted. (It had been helpful that those interviewing him recognized the family name—Mr. Y.'s father had owned a newspaper.)

Case #24: Earl W. is now a purchasing agent for a large industrial firm. In his previous job, he was approached by an acquaintance, A, in his personnel department; A said that a friend of his, B, part-owner of an employment agency, was trying to fill a job that Mr. W. might be interested in. B knew A because he had previously worked in that same personnel department; he knew of the opening because he had placed the man who was doing the hiring. Mr. W. subsequently took this job.

Case #25: John W., 19 years old, was an unemployed technician. A close friend, also unemployed, saw a newspaper ad, which they then both answered. Both were hired.

Case #26: Kenneth D. was an executive with a Chicago firm which was on the verge of bankruptcy. He went to personnel consultants in hope of lining up something new. An opening in a Boston firm seemed promising, and a representative of that firm flew to Chicago to interview him. This representative turned out to be someone who had grown up in the same neighborhood as Mr. D., in Maine, whom he had not seen for about thirty years. They had been only acquaintances then, but had had many mutual friends; they spent the first hour comparing notes. Eventually an offer was made and accepted. Mr. D. believes that the personal contact was of considerable importance.

In all four cases, personal contacts played an important role, but since it is debatable whether that role is more significant than that of the formal intermediary, "formal means" is the classification. The coding rule is to classify "formal means" where there is *any* formal intermediary in the information chain between respondent and employer.

The category "direct application" is ambiguous because it leaves open the question of how one *knew* to apply at a particular place. If this knowledge is derived from a newspaper ad, then "formal means" have been used, and the case is so classified; the same is true if an employment agency supplied the information. If a friend has influenced one to apply, coding is ambiguous. I have coded "personal contact" only if the friend knew of a *specific opening*, *or* if he knew of the *specific person* who ultimately hired the respondent, *and* put in a good word with that person.

Cases which do represent direct application fall roughly into three categories: 1) respondent applied to a firm with nearly no knowledge about it or its hiring situation. The only knowledge in such cases was what the firm did; this could be gotten from standard lists of firms. Some teachers send out many letters of inquiry to school systems or colleges around the country (the "buckshot approach"). In one case, a restaurant bookkeeper working in Providence, who wanted to return to the Boston area, acquired a copy of the Boston Yellow Pages, and called every restaurant listed until he found a job. 2) The respondent applied to a company only because he had heard of it, knew it by reputation as a firm which might have the proper opening or be good to work for. Such knowledge of reputations may come from the newspaper, from friends or may simply derive from an industry's being dominated by a few firms, well-known for the excellence (or at least the ubiquity) of their products. An illustration is:

Case #27: Antonio Z. took a master's degree in Portugese, and started teaching the subject in a high school. He read in the newspaper that a new college was opening nearby. When it opened, he called the dean and argued that the college should offer Portugese. The dean interviewed him and hired him on a part-time basis; after three years, enrollment in Portugese courses had increased substantially, and his position was made full-time.

3) The respondent heard from one or more people that a certain company was "hiring," and was perhaps given other information about working conditions there, but was not told of a specific opening, and was not recommended personally to a specific company official.

These three instances represent varying degrees of knowledge of the respondent of the situation into which he is thrusting himself, but all have in common that the initiative is taken by him with less specific knowledge than in most cases classified as "contacts."

Those filling out survey forms in other studies often construe "applied directly to the firm" more widely than here. They check this category even if they have found out about the job for which they apply from a friend, ad or agency; the act of applying seems most salient to them (De Schweinetz, 1932:90; Sheppard and Belitsky, 1966:187; Wilcock and Sobel, 1958:98–99). If the rationale of my coding is accepted, it would follow that studies using mail-surveys or closed-ended interviews are likely to overestimate this category.

My coding rule is conservative also in the sense that personal contact may be important *after* direct application, as in

Case #28: Issac E. applied to a large, new electronics firm which everyone in the field knew was opening a branch in the Boston area. He had a friend working in another branch of the company who knew of his application. While visiting the Boston branch, the friend told a friend of *his*, in a high position, that Mr. E. was well-qualified and should be sought out. This friend of Mr. E.'s friend retrieved the application from the personnel office and became his employer.

In a small number of cases, it is clear that neither "direct application" nor "formal means" is appropriate, but the "personal contact" involved is so tenuous as to make one hesitate to use this classification. Two such cases arose in the interview sample:

Case #29: Robert B. was a personnel-relations manager working for a large electronics firm. A colleague of his was slated to give a talk at a college of business administration, but couldn't go; Mr.

B. agreed to take his place. After the talk, he was offered a part-time teaching job, which later became the full-time position he now holds.

Case #30: Kevin C. was a midwestern magazine editor who came to the Boston area on a "busman's holiday," to have a look at the operations or various magazines he knew by reputation. On one such tour, he fell into a long discussion with a magazine editor; their philosophies were congruent and a job was offered to him. Though he had not come looking for a new job, the offer was attractive and he eventually accepted it.

In neither case was the "personal contact" known before the (more-or-less accidental) circumstance which led to an offer; yet even the impression received by personal contact of a few hours is qualitatively different from the knowledge one can cull from an application or even a brief job-interview. For this reason, and because any other category is clearly inappropriate, the "personal contact" classification is adopted here.

Much as I would like to construct an exhaustive classification, I must confess that I can imagine cases not covered by the three categories given. The difficulty arises when a job is offered to someone who does not apply for it, and no personal contact or formal intermediary is involved. This could occur, for instance, if someone were well-known in his field and were offered a job by a stranger purely on the basis of reputation. Such offers occur but are rarely accepted, since well-known people usually have their pick of jobs and prefer to take ones offered by people they know. No such cases, therefore, arose in my sample.

One respondent sent his resumé to a firm which did not hire him; a female employee saw the resumé and showed it to her husband who worked in a different firm. He then called the respondent and offered him a job. One could stretch this into "direct application," since there usually is the formality of making out an application—but this is really inaccurate since the respondent had not actually applied to this firm. This case was classified, therefore, as "other."

In practice, unclassifiable cases are rare and ambiguous ones like those presented in this appendix are few compared to the large majority which fit straightforwardly into the three designated categories.

Contact Chain Length

In Chapter 3 I develop the concept of "chain length" for cases where people found out about a job through personal contacts. The most straightforward instance is where the respondent hears of a job through A who heard from B who heard from C, etc., who heard from the employer. In this case, A, B, and C are the three intermediaries and define a chain length of three.

Ambiguities arise because initiative may flow from either end of the chain or from intermediaries, and also because it is not always clear whom to count in the chain. At a minimum, one is counted as an intermediary *only* if he is personally acquainted with those on either side, but this is not enough. Consider

Case #31: Peter J. was teaching philosophy at a college in New York. A, whom he had known briefly as a colleague there, was assisting his chairman in recruiting someone for his department in the Boston area university to which he had moved. Before contacting Mr. J., however, A got in touch with a mutual friend who knew him better than he did, to be sure he was the right man for the job. Then he contacted Mr. J. who was interviewed by the chairman and hired.

The mutual friend meets the minimum condition for inclusion but is not counted because A already *knew* Peter J., and contacted him directly. A similar case is that of Franklin B. (discussed in Chapter 1) whose friend's suggestion that they have lunch with the president of a brokerage firm resulted in a job offer. Mr. B. already knew the president, so the mutual friend is not counted. Peter J.'s case is coded as a chain of length one, Franklin B.'s as length zero. In both cases the mutual friends were crucial *catalysts*—but a coding rule should not require difficult causal judgments about what *activated* a chain. Once we begin to make such judgments there is no end, since nearly any pair of people have been connected in the past by mutual friends, who therefore made their present conjunction more probable. The relevant question must be, instead, whether omitting someone actually *breaks* a chain of personal contacts, in a descriptive rather than a causal sense. If, for example, A had learned of Peter J.'s *existence* only through their mutual friend, or Franklin B. of the president's, then the friends would have to appear in the chain or it would not *be* a chain of contacts. Similarly, if X is an employer and asks A to recommend someone to fill a job, and A asks his friend B, who recommends Y, and X contacts Y, whom he did not previously know, I count a chain of length two (note the case of Lawrence F. in Chapter 3); but if X *had* previously known Y, a chain of zero would be coded. If A had previously known Y, chain-length would be one.

It must be admitted that this rule builds in a bias toward short chains since what is coded is the minimal observed chain. The bias has a substantive rationale, explained in Chapter 3, relating chain-length to social distance and information pools.

Some cases are hard to classify. A respondent may hear of a job from a friend working in a place where it was general knowledge that a vacancy had opened up. While some argument could be made for coding a chain-length of one, in terms of the "social distance" between the respondent and employer, I have not coded such cases at all; there were very few. Cases which did not arise, but would be uncodeable, can be imagined. Suppose that an employer writes to someone he knows only by reputation, who recommends a friend for a job. If the friend takes the job, he has used personal contacts, but no *chain* of contacts has linked him to the employer. As with the problem of how jobs were found, very few cases are unclassifiable, and most are relatively unambiguous.

Appendix

C

Letters and Interview Schedules

1. Letter sent to those in interview subsample

HARVARD UNIVERSITY
DEPARTMENT OF SOCIAL RELATIONS

William James Hall
Cambridge, Massachusetts 02138

    The mobility patterns of Americans are of great interest to us in the social sciences. I am now conducting a study, at Harvard University, of individuals in professional, technical and managerial occupations who have recently changed their address and/or job.

    A sample of such individuals has been selected at random from among residents of Newton, Mass., in which your name is included. We hope that your ideas and experiences can become part of this study.

    Within the next week or two, I will come by to conduct an interview which should take no more than about 30 minutes. As in all such research, your replies will be considered strictly confidential and will be reported only without the use of names, either of persons or firms.

    I look forward to discussing these matters with you. Thank you very much for your cooperation.

Sincerely yours,

MSG:cbh   Mark S. Granovetter

2. Interview Guide

I. *JOB-FINDING AND CAREER PATTERNS*

1. (Verify that present job is that listed in Directory. If R has subsequently changed, ask about the most recent job.) How long have you had this job? (If R has just moved to Newton): Were you changing jobs at the time you moved to Newton? Is that why you moved?

2. Was there a point in your previous job when you *decided* to look for a new one—or did something just "come along"? Was there a period of time when you weren't working at all?

3. How did you find the job you hold now?
   (Ascertain also:
   1. If R searched, did some search methods fail to turn up offers?
   2. Were offers made and rejected in roughly the same period as the accepted one? How did they arise?)

4. (If personal contact(s) cited in 3., ask for each such contact:)
   1. Did this person put in a good word for you as well as telling you about the job?
   2. How did you happen to know him? (I.e., relative, former work-mate, etc.)
   3. What was his job—where did he work then?
   4. How did *he* know about the opening he mentioned to you?
   5. How did you happen to find out about it from him?
   6. (If contact took the initiative:) Why do you suppose he let you know about this job—what made him do that?
   7. How often and in what way(s) were you in contact with him at the time he told you about the new job? (Home visits, casual street meetings, church, phone, Xmas cards, etc.)
   8. Where was he living then?
   9. (If follow-up might be interesting): What is his name? Where does he live now?

5. When you took your job, do you know whether you replaced anyone in particular? (If not, probe to determine exactly how the new job was created.)

6. Do you know whether any particular person replaced *you* in your old job? (If not, probe to determine what happened to the old job.)

7. The job you held before your present one—do you remember how you found that? (Trace complete work history backwards like this, to the first full-time job *if feasible*. If too many jobs, find out about *first* full-time job and one or two of longest duration; estimate total number.)

8. Which of these categories best describes how satisfied you are with your present job? (Hand card to R).

9. Have you recently thought about looking for another job? (If yes:) Have you actually done anything along these lines?

10. (If answer to 9 is no:) if you wanted to look for a new job, how would you go about it?

11. Now think about your friends in the same occupation as you are in. How have they found *their* jobs? Is that typical of this occupation?

12. About how many people work for the company you now work for?

13. Have you recently told anyone you know about a job opening? (If yes:) Did he take that job? How did you know about this job? How did you happen to pass the information along? What made you do that?

II. *BACKGROUND QUESTIONS*

1. What was your father's occupation while you were growing up?
2. How far did you go in school? (if college, which one?)
3. What is your age?
4. What is your marital status?
5. Where did you spend most of your time while you were growing up? (Name of city or town)
6. Where did you move to Newton from?
7. How long have you lived in this house? Newton?
8. How many times have you moved since you started working?
9. Do you have a religious preference? (If no, ascertain religious background)
10. What country would you say *most* of your ancestors are from?
11. Which of these groups best describes your yearly income in your present job? Tell me the letter. (Hand card to R)
[12. Some people make a strong distinction between work friends and social friends. Would you say you make this distinction?]

3. Letter sent to those in mail survey subsample

HARVARD UNIVERSITY
DEPARTMENT OF SOCIAL RELATIONS

William James Hall
Cambridge, Massachusetts 02138

The mobility patterns of those in professional,
technical and managerial occupations are of great
interest to us in the social sciences. I am now
conducting a study, at Harvard University, of
individuals in this category who have recently
changed their address and/or job; your name is
included in a sample of such individuals selected at
random from among residents of Newton, Mass. We hope
that your experiences can now become part of this study.

The enclosed survey will take you only ten or
fifteen minutes to fill out. I have included a stamped,
addressed envelope in which it may be returned. If
you would like to receive a summary of the findings
of this study, please write in the letter "S" at the
top of the first page of the survey.

As in all such research, your replies will be
considered strictly confidential, and will be reported
only without the names of persons, places or firms.

I will be looking forward to your reply. Thank
you very much for your cooperation.

Sincerely yours,

MSG:cbh   Mark S. Granovetter

4. Follow-up letter sent to those in mail survey subsample

HARVARD UNIVERSITY
DEPARTMENT OF SOCIAL RELATIONS

William James Hall
Cambridge, Massachusetts 02138

     A few weeks ago, I sent you a questionnaire on the subject of job mobility, as part of a survey I am carrying out for my Ph.D. thesis. If your schedule is as hectic as mine, it is easy to neglect or misplace this sort of thing. I am enclosing another copy, and hope that you will take ten minutes or so to fill it out and return it in the envelope I am also sending.

     In surveys of this kind, even a few instances of non-response cast significant doubt on the accuracy of results. Thus, I will be especially looking forward to hearing from you.

     Thank you for your cooperation.

               Sincerely yours,

               Mark S. Granovetter

5. Letter sent to those in interview subsample who had moved out of Newton

HARVARD UNIVERSITY
DEPARTMENT OF SOCIAL RELATIONS

William James Hall
Cambridge, Massachusetts 02138

The mobility patterns of those in professional, technical and managerial occupations are of great interest to us in the social sciences. I am now conducting a study, at Harvard University, of individuals in this category who have recently changed their address and/or job.

Your name appeared in a sample of such individuals, drawn at random from among residents of Newton, Mass. When I arrived at your Newton address, however, hoping to arrange an interview, I found that you had moved to your current address.

Since I am unable to visit the various towns to which people in this sample have moved, I have put my questions in the form of a mail survey which I have included with this letter. This survey will take only ten or fifteen minutes to fill out, and can be returned in the stamped, addressed envelope I have also sent. If you would like to receive a summary of the findings of this study, please write in the letter "S" at the top of the first page.

As in all such research, your replies will be considered strictly confidential and will be reported only without the names of persons, places or firms.

I will be looking forward to your reply. Thank you very much for your cooperation.

Sincerely yours,

MSG: cbh   Mark S. Granovetter

6. Mail Survey.

Job Mobility Survey

INSTRUCTIONS: FOR EACH QUESTION, CHECK ONE *OR MORE* ANSWERS, OR FILL IN ANSWERS IN THE BLANK SPACE PROVIDED.

SECTION I: JOB-FINDING

1. When you first moved to
   were you changing jobs at the same time?
   a. Yes_____
   b. No_____

2. When was the last time you started in a new job—roughly what month and year?

   _____

3. What was the job you held *before* this change?
   Job Title:_____
   Company:_____
   City: _____

4. What was the job you held *after* this change? (Your present job)
   Job Title: _____
   Company: _____
   City: _____

5. Was there a period of time when you were actively *searching* for a new job, before you found the job listed in #4?
   a. Yes _____
   b. No _____

6. How exactly did you *find out* about the new job listed in #4?
   a. I saw an advertisement in a newspaper (or magazine, or trade or technical journal). _____
   b. I found out through an employment agency (or personnel consultants, "head-hunters", etc.). _____
   c. I asked a friend, who told me about the job. _____
   d. A friend who knew I was looking for something new contacted me. _____
   e. A friend who didn't know whether I wanted a new job contacted me. _____
   f. Someone I didn't know contacted me and said I had been recommended for the job. _____
   g. I applied directly to the company. _____
   h. I became self-employed. _____
   i. Other (please explain):

IF YOU FOUND OUT ABOUT THE JOB LISTED IN #4.
THROUGH A FRIEND, PLEASE ANSWER QUESTIONS 7–10.
OTHERWISE, SKIP TO #11.

7. How did you happen to know this friend?
    a. We went to college together. _____
    b. We went to high school together. _____
    c. We grew up in the same neighborhood. _____
    d. I once worked with him. _____
    e. I once worked under him. _____
    f. Other (please explain):

8. Did your friend put in a good word for you as well as telling you about the job?
    a. Yes _____
    b. No _____
    c. Don't Know _____

9. How did this friend know about the job?
    a. He worked in the same place where the job opened up. _____
    b. He was a business friend of the employer. _____
    c. He was a social friend of the employer. _____
    d. He was the employer. _____
    e. Other (please explain):

10. At the time when your friend told you about this job, how did you know how to get in touch with each other?
    a. We saw each other pretty often then. _____
    b. We saw each other occasionally then. _____
    c. We spoke to each other on the phone pretty often then. _____
    d. We spoke to each other on the phone occasionally then. _____
    e. We were exchanging letters then. _____
    f. We were exchanging Christmas (or other holiday) cards then. _____
    g. We hadn't been in contact recently, but mutual friends put us in touch. _____
    h. Other (please explain):

11. Was there a period of time between the jobs listed in #3. and #4. when you weren't working at all?
    a. Yes _____
    b. No _____

12. Which of the following best describes the new job listed in #4.?
    a. There were several jobs of the same type, and I replaced someone who held one of these. _____
    b. There was only one job of this type, and I replaced the man who held it. _____

    c. I was the first man to hold this particular job. _____
    d. There were several jobs of the same type, and my job was
       added on to these. _____
    e. Other (please explain):

13. About how many people work for the company listed in #4.?

    _____

14. About how satisfied would you say you are with your present job?
    a. Very satisfied _____
    b. Fairly satisfied _____
    c. Neither satisfied nor dissatisfied _____
    d. Fairly dissatisfied _____
    e. Very dissatisfied _____

15. Which of the following best describes your *old* job, the one you left to take the job listed in #4.?
    a. I know the name of the man who replaced me. _____
    b. I'm not sure who replaced me, but I know that someone
       did. _____
    c. I don't know whether I was replaced or not. _____
    d. They are still looking for a replacement. _____
    e. They decided not to fill the job at that time. _____
    f. The particular job that I held doesn't exist any more. _____
    g. Other (please explain):

SECTION II: BACKGROUND QUESTIONS

1. What was your father's occupation while you were growing up?

    _____

2. How far did you go in school? (If college, which one?)

    _____

3. What is your age? _____

4. Do you have a religious preference?
    a. Protestant _____
    b. Catholic _____
    c. Jewish _____
    d. Other _____
    e. None _____ (If "none", please circle parents' preference.)

5. What is your marital status?
    a. Married _____
    b. Divorced or separated _____
    c. Single _____

6. How long have you lived in Newton? _____

7. Where did you move to Newton from? _____

8. Where did you spend most of your time while you were growing up? (Name of city or town)

_____

9. How many times have you moved since you took your first full-time job?

_____

10. Which of the following letters best describes your personal income (before taxes) per year in your present job? _____
    a. Under $5,000.
    b. $5,000. to 7,500.
    c. $7,500. to 10,000.
    d. $10,000. to 15,000.
    e. $15,000. to 25,000.
    f. $25,000. to 40,000.
    g. More than $40,000.

THANK YOU VERY MUCH FOR YOUR COOPERATION.

Appendix D

Economic Action and Social Structure: The Problem of Embeddedness[1]

How behavior and institutions are affected by social relations is one of the classic questions of social theory. This paper concerns the extent to which economic action is embedded in structures of social relations, in modern industrial society. Although the usual neoclassical accounts provide an "undersocialized" or atomized-actor explanation of such action, reformist economists who attempt to bring social structure back in do so in the "oversocialized" way criticized by Dennis Wrong. Under- and oversocialized accounts are paradoxically similar in their neglect of ongoing structures of social relations, and a sophisticated account of economic action must consider its embeddedness in such structures. The argument is illustrated by a critique of Oliver Williamson's "markets and hierarchies" research program.

INTRODUCTION: THE PROBLEM OF EMBEDDEDNESS

How behavior and institutions are affected by social relations is one of the classic questions of social theory. Since such relations are always present, the situation that would arise in their absence can be imagined only through a thought experiment like Thomas Hobbes's "state of nature" or John Rawls's "original position." Much of the utilitarian tradition, including classical and neoclassical economics, assumes rational, self-interested behavior affected minimally by social relations, thus invoking an idealized state not far from that of these thought experiments. At the other extreme lies what I call the argument of "embeddedness": the argu-

[1] Earlier drafts of this paper were written in sabbatical facilities kindly provided by the Institute for Advanced Study and Harvard University. Financial support was provided in part by the institute, by a John Simon Guggenheim Memorial Foundation fellowship, and by NSF Science Faculty Professional Development grant SPI 81-65055. Among those who have helped clarify the arguments are Wayne Baker, Michael Bernstein, Albert Hirschman, Ron Jepperson, Eric Leifer, Don McCloskey, Charles Perrow, James Rule, Michael Schwartz, Theda Skocpol, and Harrison White.

Reprinted from: *AJS* Volume 91 Number 3 (November 1985): 481–510

ment that the behavior and institutions to be analyzed are so constrained by ongoing social relations that to construe them as independent is a grievous misunderstanding.

This article concerns the embeddedness of economic behavior. It has long been the majority view among sociologists, anthropologists, political scientists, and historians that such behavior was heavily embedded in social relations in premarket societies but became much more autonomous with modernization. This view sees the economy as an increasingly separate, differentiated sphere in modern society, with economic transactions defined no longer by the social or kinship obligations of those transacting but by rational calculations of individual gain. It is sometimes further argued that the traditional situation is reversed: instead of economic life being submerged in social relations, these relations become an epiphenomenon of the market. The embeddedness position is associated with the "substantivist" school in anthropology, identified especially with Karl Polanyi (1944; Polanyi, Arensberg, and Pearson 1957) and with the idea of "moral economy" in history and political science (Thompson 1971; Scott 1976). It has also some obvious relation to Marxist thought.

Few economists, however, have accepted this conception of a break in embeddedness with modernization; most of them assert instead that embeddedness in earlier societies was not substantially greater than the low level found in modern markets. The tone was set by Adam Smith, who postulated a "certain propensity in human nature . . . to truck, barter and exchange one thing for another" ([1776] 1979, book 1, chap. 2) and assumed that since labor was the only factor of production in primitive society, goods must have exchanged in proportion to their labor costs—as in the general classical theory of exchange ([1776] 1979, book 1, chap. 6). From the 1920s on, certain anthropologists took a similar position, which came to be called the "formalist" one: even in tribal societies, economic behavior was sufficiently independent of social relations for standard neoclassical analysis to be useful (Schneider 1974). This position has recently received a new infusion as economists and fellow travelers in history and political science have developed a new interest in the economic analysis of social institutions—much of which falls into what is called the "new institutional economics"—and have argued that behavior and institutions previously interpreted as embedded in earlier societies, as well as in our own, can be better understood as resulting from the pursuit of self-interest by rational, more or less atomized individuals (e.g., North and Thomas 1973; Williamson 1975; Popkin 1979).

My own view diverges from both schools of thought. I assert that the level of embeddedness of economic behavior is lower in nonmarket societies than is claimed by substantivists and development theorists, and it has changed less with "modernization" than they believe; but I argue also that this level has always been and continues to be more substantial than is allowed for by formalists and economists. I do not attempt here to treat the issues posed by nonmarket societies. I proceed instead by a theoretical elaboration of the concept of embeddedness, whose value is then illustrated with a problem from modern society, currently important in the new institutional economics: which transactions in modern capitalist society are carried out in the market, and which subsumed within hierarchically organized. firms? This question has been raised to prominence by the "markets and hierarchies" program of research initiated by Oliver Williamson (1975).

OVER- AND UNDERSOCIALIZED CONCEPTIONS OF HUMAN ACTION IN SOCIOLOGY AND ECONOMICS

I begin by recalling Dennis Wrong's 1961 complaint about an "oversocialized conception of man in modern sociology"—a conception of people as overwhelmingly sensitive to the opinions of others and hence obedient to the dictates of consensually developed systems of norms and values, internalized through socialization, so that obedience is not perceived as a burden. To the extent that such a conception was prominent in 1961, it resulted in large part from Talcott Parsons's recognition of the problem of order as posed by Hobbes and his own attempt to resolve it by transcending the atomized, *undersocialized* conception of man in the utilitarian tradition of which Hobbes was part (Parsons 1937, pp. 89–94). Wrong approved the break with atomized utilitarianism and the emphasis on actors' embeddedness in social context—the crucial factor absent from Hobbes's thinking—but warned of exaggerating the degree of this embeddedness and the extent to which it might eliminate conflict:

> It is frequently the task of the sociologist to call attention to the intensity with which men desire and strive for the good opinion of their immediate associates in a variety of situations, particularly those where received theories or ideologies have unduly emphasized other motives. . . . Thus sociologists have shown that factory workers are more sensitive to the attitudes of their fellow workers than to purely economic incentives. . . . It is certainly not my intention to criticize the findings of such studies. My objection is that . . . [a]lthough sociologists have criticized past efforts to single out one fundamental motive in human conduct, the desire to achieve a favorable self-image by winning approval from others frequently occupies such a position in their own thinking. [1961, pp. 188–89]

Classical and neoclassical economics operates, in contrast, with an atomized, *under*socialized conception of human action, continuing in the utilitarian tradition. The theoretical arguments disallow by hypothesis any impact of social structure and social relations on production, distribution, or consumption. In competitive markets, no producer or consumer noticeably influences aggregate supply or demand or, therefore, prices or other terms of trade. As Albert Hirschman has noted, such idealized markets, involving as they do "large numbers of price-taking anonymous buyers and sellers supplied with perfect information . . . function without any prolonged human or social contact between the parties. Under perfect competition there is no room for bargaining, negotiation, remonstration or mutual adjustment and the various operators that contract together need not enter into recurrent or continuing relationships as a result of which they would get to know each other well" (1982, p. 1473).

It has long been recognized that the idealized markets of perfect competition have survived intellectual attack in part because self-regulating economic structures are politically attractive to many. Another reason for this survival, less clearly understood, is that the elimination of social relations from economic analysis removes the problem of order from the intellectual agenda, at least in the economic sphere. In Hobbes's argument, disorder arises because conflict-free social and economic transactions depend on trust and the absence of malfeasance. But these are unlikely when individuals are conceived to have neither social relationships nor institutional context—as in the "state of nature." Hobbes contains the difficulty by superimposing a structure of autocratic authority. The solution of classical liberalism, and correspondingly of classical economics, is antithetical: repressive political structures are rendered unnecessary by competitive markets that make force or fraud unavailing. Competition determines the terms of trade in a way that individual traders cannot manipulate. If traders encounter complex or difficult relationships, characterized by mistrust or malfeasance, they can simply move on to the legion of other traders willing to do business on market terms; social relations and their details thus become frictional matters.

In classical and neoclassical economics, therefore, the fact that actors may have social relations with one another has been treated, if at all, as a frictional drag that impedes competitive markets. In a much-quoted line, Adam Smith complained that "people of the same trade seldom meet together, even for merriment and diversion, but the conversation ends in a conspiracy against the public, or in some contrivance to raise prices." His laissez-faire politics allowed few solutions to this problem, but he did suggest repeal of regulations requiring all those in the same trade to sign a public register; the public existence of such information "connects individuals who might never otherwise be known to one another and gives every man of the trade a direction where to find every other man of it." Noteworthy here is not the rather lame policy prescription but the recognition that *social atomization is prerequisite to perfect competition* (Smith [1776] 1979, pp. 232–33).

More recent comments by economists on "social influences" construe these as processes in which actors acquire customs, habits, or norms that are followed mechanically and automatically, irrespective of their bearing on rational choice. This view, close to Wrong's "oversocialized conception," is reflected in James Duesenberry's quip that "economics is all about how people make choices; sociology is all about how they don't have any choices to make" (1960, p. 233) and in E. H. Phelps Brown's description of the "sociologists' approach to pay determination" as deriving from the assumption that people act in "certain ways because to do so is customary, or an obligation, or the 'natural thing to do,' or right and proper, or just and fair" (1977, p. 17).

But despite the apparent contrast between under- and oversocialized views, we should note an irony of great theoretical importance: both have in common a conception of action and decision carried out by atomized actors. In the undersocialized account, atomization results from narrow utilitarian pursuit of self-interest; in the oversocialized one, from the fact that behavioral patterns have been internalized and ongoing social relations thus have only peripheral effects on behavior. That the internalized rules of behavior are social in origin does not differentiate this argument decisively from a utilitarian one, in which the source of utility functions is left open, leaving room for behavior guided entirely by consensually determined norms and values—as in the oversocialized view. Under- and oversocialized resolutions of the problem of order thus merge in their atomization of actors from immediate social context. This ironic merger is already visible in Hobbes's *Leviathan,* in which the unfortunate denizens of the state of nature, overwhelmed by the disorder consequent to their atomization, cheerfully surrender all their rights to an authoritarian power and subsequently behave in a docile and honorable manner; by the artifice of a social contract, they lurch directly from an undersocialized to an oversocialized state.

When modern economists do attempt to take account of social influences, they typically represent them in the oversocialized manner represented in the quotations above. In so doing, they reverse the judgment that social influences are frictional but sustain the conception of how such influences operate. In the theory of segmented labor markets, for example, Michael Piore has argued that members of each labor market segment are characterized by different styles of decision making and that the making of decisions by rational choice, custom, or command in upper-primary, lower-primary, and secondary labor markets respectively corresponds to the origins of workers in middle-, working-, and lower-class subcultures (Piore 1975). Similarly, Samuel Bowles and Herbert Gintis, in their account of the consequences of American education, argue that different social classes display different cognitive processes because of differences in the education provided to each. Those destined for lower-level jobs are trained to be dependable followers of rules, while those who will be channeled into elite positions attend "elite four-year colleges" that "emphasize social relationships conformable with the higher levels in the production hierarchy. . . . As they 'master' one type of behavioral regulation they are either allowed to progress to the next or are channeled into the corresponding level in the hierarchy of production" (Bowles and Gintis 1975, p. 132).

But these oversocialized conceptions of how society influences individual behavior are rather mechanical: once we know the individual's social class or labor market sector, everything else in behavior is automatic, since they are so well socialized. Social influence here is an external force that, like the deists' God, sets things in motion and has no further effects—a force that insinuates itself into the minds and bodies of individuals (as in the movie *Invasion of the Body Snatchers*), altering their way of making decisions. Once we know in just what way an individual has been affected, ongoing social relations and structures are irrelevant. Social influences are all contained inside an individual's head, so, in actual decision situations, he or she can be atomized as any *Homo economicus,* though perhaps with different rules for decisions. More sophisticated (and thus less oversocialized) analyses of cultural influences (e.g., Fine and Kleinman 1979; Cole 1979, chap. 1) make it clear that culture is not a once-for-all influence but an ongoing process, continuously constructed and reconstructed during interaction. It not only shapes its members but also is shaped by them, in part for their own strategic reasons.

Even when economists do take social relationships seriously, as do such diverse figures as Harvey Leibenstein (1976) and Gary Becker (1976), they invariably abstract away from the history of relations and their position with respect to other relations—what might be called the historical and structural embeddedness of relations. The interpersonal ties described in their arguments are extremely stylized, average, "typical"— devoid of specific content, history, or structural location. Actors' behavior results from their named role positions and role sets; thus we have arguments on how workers and supervisors, husbands and wives, or criminals and law enforcers will interact with one another, but these relations are not assumed to have individualized content beyond that given by the named roles. This procedure is exactly what structural sociologists have criticized in Parsonian sociology—the relegation of the specifics of individual relations to a minor role in the overall conceptual scheme, epiphenomenal in comparison with enduring structures of normative role prescriptions deriving from ultimate value orientations. In economic models, this treatment of social relations has the paradoxical effect of preserving atomized decision making even when decisions are seen to involve more than one individual. Because the analyzed set of individuals—usually dyads, occasionally larger groups—is abstracted out of social context, it is atomized in its behavior from that of other groups and from the history of its own relations. Atomization has not been eliminated, merely transferred to the dyadic or higher level of analysis. Note the use of an oversocialized conception—that of actors behaving exclusively in accord with their prescribed roles—to implement an atomized, undersocialized view.

A fruitful analysis of human action requires us to avoid the atomization implicit in the theoretical extremes of under- and oversocialized conceptions. Actors do not behave or decide as atoms outside a social context, nor do they adhere slavishly to a script written for them by the particular intersection of social categories that they happen to occupy. Their attempts at purposive action are instead embedded in concrete, ongoing systems of social relations. In the remainder of this article I illustrate how this view of embeddedness alters our theoretical and empirical approach to the study of economic behavior. I first narrow the focus to the question of trust and malfeasance in economic life and then use the "markets and hierarchies" problem to illustrate the use of embeddedness ideas in analyzing this question.[2]

EMBEDDEDNESS, TRUST, AND MALFEASANCE IN ECONOMIC LIFE

Since about 1970, there has been a flurry of interest among economists in the previously neglected issues of trust and malfeasance. Oliver Williamson has noted that real economic actors engage not merely in the pursuit of self-interest but also in "opportunism"—"self-interest seeking with guile; agents who are skilled at dissembling realize transactional advantages.[3] Economic man . . . is thus a more subtle and devious creature than the usual self-interest seeking assumption reveals" (1975, p. 255).

[2] There are many parallels between what are referred to here as the "undersocialized" and "oversocialized" views of action and what Burt (1982, chap. 9) calls the "atomistic" and "normative" approaches. Similarly, the embeddedness approach proposed here as a middle ground between under- and oversocialized views has an obvious family resemblance to Burt's "structural" approach to action. My distinctions and approach also differ from Burt's in many ways that cannot be quickly summarized; these can be best appreciated by comparison of this article with his useful summary (1982, chap. 9) and with the formal models that implement his conception (1982, 1983). Another approach that resembles mine in its emphasis on how social connections affect purposive action is Marsden's extension of James Coleman's theories of collective action and decision to situations where such connections modify results that would occur in a purely atomistic situation (Marsden 1981, 1983).

[3] Students of the sociology of sport will note that this proposition had been put forward previously, in slightly different form, by Leo Durocher.

But this points out a peculiar assumption of modern economic theory, that one's economic interest is pursued only by comparatively gentlemanly means. The Hobbesian question—how it can be that those who pursue their own interest do not do so mainly by force and fraud—is finessed by this conception. Yet, as Hobbes saw so clearly, there is nothing in the intrinsic meaning of "self-interest" that excludes force or fraud.

In part, this assumption persisted because competitive forces, in a self-regulating market, could be imagined to suppress force and fraud. But the idea is also embedded in the intellectual history of the discipline. In *The Passions and the Interests,* Albert Hirschman (1977) shows that an important strand of intellectual history from the time of *Leviathan* to that of *The Wealth of Nations* consisted of the watering down of Hobbes's problem of order by arguing that certain human motivations kept others under control and that, in particular, the pursuit of economic self-interest was typically not an uncontrollable "passion" but a civilized, gentle activity. The wide though implicit acceptance of such an idea is a powerful example of how under- and oversocialized conceptions complement one another: atomized actors in competitive markets so thoroughly internalize these normative standards of behavior as to guarantee orderly transactions.[4]

What has eroded this confidence in recent years has been increased attention to the micro-level details of imperfectly competitive markets, characterized by small numbers of participants with sunk costs and "specific human capital" investments. In such situations, the alleged discipline of competitive markets cannot be called on to mitigate deceit, so the classical problem of how it can be that daily economic life is not riddled with mistrust and malfeasance has resurfaced.

In the economic literature, I see two fundamental answers to this problem and argue that one is linked to an undersocialized, and the other to an oversocialized, conception of human action. The undersocialized account is found mainly in the new institutional economics—a loosely defined confederation of economists with an interest in explaining social institutions from a neoclassical viewpoint. (See, e.g., Furubotn and Pejovich 1972; Alchian and Demsetz 1973; Lazear 1979; Rosen 1982; Williamson 1975, 1979, 1981; Williamson and Ouchi 1981.) The general story told by members of this school is that social institutions and arrangements previously thought to be the adventitious result of legal, historical, social, or political forces are better viewed as the efficient solution to certain economic problems. The tone is similar to that of structural-functional sociology of the 1940s to the 1960s, and much of the argumentation fails the elementary tests of a sound functional explanation laid down by

---

[4] I am indebted to an anonymous referee for pointing this out.

Robert Merton in 1947. Consider, for example, Schotter's view that to understand any observed economic institution requires only that we "infer the evolutionary problem that must have existed for the institution as we see it to have developed. Every evolutionary economic problem requires a social institution to solve it" (1981, p. 2).

Malfeasance is here seen to be averted because clever institutional arrangements make it too costly to engage in, and these arrangements—many previously interpreted as serving no economic function—are now seen as having evolved to discourage malfeasance. Note, however, that they do not produce trust but instead are a functional substitute for it. The main such arrangements are elaborate explicit and implicit contracts (Okun 1981), including deferred compensation plans and mandatory retirement—seen to reduce the incentives for "shirking" on the job or absconding with proprietary secrets (Lazear 1979; Pakes and Nitzan 1982)—and authority structures that deflect opportunism by making potentially divisive decisions by fiat (Williamson 1975). These conceptions are undersocialized in that they do not allow for the extent to which concrete personal relations and the obligations inherent in them discourage malfeasance, quite apart from institutional arrangements. *Substituting* these arrangements for trust results actually in a Hobbesian situation, in which any rational individual would be motivated to develop clever ways to evade them; it is then hard to imagine that everyday economic life would not be poisoned by ever more ingenious attempts at deceit.

Other economists have recognized that some degree of trust *must* be assumed to operate, since institutional arrangements alone could not entirely stem force or fraud. But it remains to explain the source of this trust, and appeal is sometimes made to the existence of a "generalized morality." Kenneth Arrow, for example, suggests that societies, "in their evolution have developed implicit agreements to certain kinds of regard for others, agreements which are essential to the survival of the society or at least contribute greatly to the efficiency of its working" (1974, p. 26; see also Akerlof [1983] on the origins of "honesty").

Now one can hardly doubt the existence of some such generalized morality; without it, you would be afraid to give the gas station attendant a 20-dollar bill when you had bought only five dollars' worth of gas. But this conception has the oversocialized characteristic of calling on a generalized and automatic response, even though moral action in economic life is hardly automatic or universal (as is well known at gas stations that demand exact change after dark).

Consider a case where generalized morality does indeed seem to be at work: the legendary (I hesitate to say apocryphal) economist who, against all economic rationality, leaves a tip in a roadside restaurant far from home. Note that this transaction has three characteristics that make it somewhat unusual: (1) the transactors are previously unacquainted, (2) they are unlikely to transact again, and (3) information about the activities of either is unlikely to reach others with whom they might transact in the future. I argue that it is only in situations of this kind that the absence of force and fraud can mainly be explained by generalized morality. Even there, one might wonder how effective this morality would be if large costs were incurred.

The embeddedness argument stresses instead the role of concrete personal relations and structures (or "networks") of such relations in generating trust and discouraging malfeasance. The widespread preference for transacting with individuals of known reputation implies that few are actually content to rely on either generalized morality *or* institutional arrangements to guard against trouble. Economists *have* pointed out that one incentive not to cheat is the cost of damage to one's reputation; but this is an undersocialized conception of reputation as a generalized commodity, a ratio of cheating to opportunities for doing so. In practice, we settle for such generalized information when nothing better is available, but ordinarily we seek better information. Better than the statement that someone is known to be reliable is information from a trusted informant that he has dealt with that individual and found him so. Even better is information from one's own past dealings with that person. This is better information for four reasons: (1) it is cheap; (2) one trusts one's own information best—it is richer, more detailed, and known to be accurate; (3) individuals with whom one has a continuing relation have an economic motivation to be trustworthy, so as not to discourage future transactions; and (4) departing from pure economic motives, continuing economic relations often become overlaid with social content that carries strong expectations of trust and abstention from opportunism.

It would never occur to us to doubt this last point in more intimate relations, which make behavior more predictable and thus close off some of the fears that create difficulties among strangers. Consider, for example, why individuals in a burning theater panic and stampede to the door, leading to desperate results. Analysts of collective behavior long considered this to be prototypically irrational behavior, but Roger Brown (1965, chap. 14) points out that the situation is essentially an *n*-person Prisoner's Dilemma: each stampeder is actually being quite rational given the absence of a guarantee that anyone else will walk out calmly, even though all would be better off if everyone did so. Note, however, that in the case of the burning houses featured on the 11:00 P.M. news, we never hear that everyone stampeded out and that family members trampled one another. In the family, there is no Prisoner's Dilemma because each is confident that the others can be counted on.

In business relations the degree of confidence must be more variable, but Prisoner's Dilemmas are nevertheless often obviated by the strength of personal relations, and this strength is a property not of the transactors but of their concrete relations. Standard economic analysis neglects the identity and past relations of individual transactors, but rational individuals know better, relying on their knowledge of these relations. They are less interested in *general* reputations than in whether a particular other may be expected to deal honestly with *them*—mainly a function of whether they or their own contacts have had satisfactory past dealings with the other. One sees this pattern even in situations that appear, at first glance, to approximate the classic higgling of a competitive market, as in the Moroccan bazaar analyzed by Geertz (1979).

Up to this point, I have argued that social relations, rather than institutional arrangements or generalized morality, are mainly responsible for the production of trust in economic life. But I then risk rejecting one kind of optimistic functionalism for another, in which networks of relations, rather than morality or arrangements, are the structure that fulfills the function of sustaining order. There are two ways to reduce this risk. One is to recognize that as a solution to the problem of order, the embeddedness position is less sweeping than either alternative argument, since networks of social relations penetrate irregularly and in differing degrees in different sectors of economic life, thus allowing for what we already know: distrust, opportunism, and disorder are by no means absent.

The second is to insist that while social relations may indeed often be a necessary condition for trust and trustworthy behavior, they are not sufficient to guarantee these and may even provide occasion and means for malfeasance and conflict on a scale larger than in their absence. There are three reasons for this.

1. The trust engendered by personal relations presents, by its very existence, enhanced opportunity for malfeasance. In personal relations it is common knowledge that "you always hurt the one you love"; that person's trust in you results in a position far more vulnerable than that of a stranger. (In the Prisoner's Dilemma, knowledge that one's coconspirator is certain to deny the crime is all the more rational motive to confess, and personal relations that abrogate this dilemma may be less symmetrical than is believed by the party to be deceived.) This elementary fact of social life is the bread and butter of "confidence" rackets that simulate certain relationships, sometimes for long periods, for concealed purposes. In the business world, certain crimes, such as embezzling, are simply impossible for those who have not built up relationships of trust that permit the opportunity to manipulate accounts. The more complete the trust, the greater the potential gain from malfeasance. That such

instances are statistically infrequent is a tribute to the force of personal relations and reputation; that they do occur with regularity, however infrequently, shows the limits of this force.

2. Force and fraud are most efficiently pursued by teams, and the structure of these teams requires a level of internal trust—"honor among thieves"—that usually follows preexisting lines of relationship. Elaborate schemes for kickbacks and bid rigging, for example, can hardly be executed by individuals working alone, and when such activity is exposed it is often remarkable that it could have been kept secret given the large numbers involved. Law-enforcement efforts consist of finding an entry point to the network of malfeasance—an individual whose confession implicates others who will, in snowball-sample fashion, "finger" still others until the entire picture is fitted together.

Both enormous trust and enormous malfeasance, then, may follow from personal relations. Yoram Ben-Porath, in the functionalist style of the new institutional economics, emphasizes the positive side, noting that "continuity of relationships can generate behavior on the part of shrewd, self-seeking, or even unscrupulous individuals that could otherwise be interpreted as foolish or purely altruistic. Valuable diamonds change hands on the diamond exchange, and the deals are sealed by a hand-shake" (1980, p. 6). I might add, continuing in this positive vein, that this transaction is possible in part because it is not atomized from other transactions but embedded in a close-knit community of diamond merchants who monitor one another's behavior closely. Like other densely knit networks of actors, they generate clearly defined standards of behavior easily policed by the quick spread of information about instances of malfeasance. But the temptations posed by this level of trust are considerable, and the diamond trade has also been the scene of numerous well-publicized "insider job" thefts and of the notorious "CBS murders" of April 1982. In this case, the owner of a diamond company was defrauding a factoring concern by submitting invoices from fictitious sales. The scheme required cooperation from his accounting personnel, one of whom was approached by investigators and turned state's evidence. The owner then contracted for the murder of the disloyal employee and her assistant; three CBS technicians who came to their aid were also gunned down (Shenon 1984).

3. The extent of disorder resulting from force and fraud depends very much on how the network of social relations is structured. Hobbes exaggerated the extent of disorder likely in his atomized state of nature where, in the absence of sustained social relations, one could expect only desultory dyadic conflicts. More extended and large-scale disorder results from coalitions of combatants, impossible without prior relations. We do not generally speak of "war" unless actors have arranged themselves into two

sides, as the end result of various coalitions. This occurs only if there are insufficient crosscutting ties, held by actors with enough links to both main potential combatants to have a strong interest in forestalling conflict. The same is true in the business world, where conflicts are relatively tame unless each side can escalate by calling on substantial numbers of allies in other firms, as sometimes happens in attempts to implement or forestall takeovers.

Disorder and malfeasance do of course occur also when social relations are absent. This possibility is already entailed in my earlier claim that the presence of such relations inhibits malfeasance. But the *level* of malfeasance available in a truly atomized social situation is fairly low; instances can only be episodic, unconnected, small scale. The Hobbesian problem is truly a problem, but in transcending it by the smoothing effect of social structure, we also introduce the possibility of disruptions on a larger scale than those available in the "state of nature."

The embeddedness approach to the problem of trust and order in economic life, then, threads its way between the oversocialized approach of generalized morality and the undersocialized one of impersonal, institutional arrangements by following and analyzing concrete patterns of social relations. Unlike either alternative, or the Hobbesian position, it makes no sweeping (and thus unlikely) predictions of universal order or disorder but rather assumes that the details of social structure will determine which is found.

THE PROBLEM OF MARKETS AND HIERARCHIES

As a concrete application of the embeddedness approach to economic life, I offer a critique of the influential argument of Oliver Williamson in *Markets and Hierarchies* (1975) and later articles (1979, 1981; Williamson and Ouchi 1981). Williamson asked under what circumstances economic functions are performed within the boundaries of hierarchical firms rather than by market processes that cross these boundaries. His answer, consistent with the general emphasis of the new institutional economics, is that the organizational form observed in any situation is that which deals most efficiently with the cost of economic transactions. Those that are uncertain in outcome, recur frequently, and require substantial "transaction-specific investments"—for example, money, time, or energy that cannot be easily transferred to interaction with others on different matters—are more likely to take place within hierarchically organized firms. Those that are straightforward, nonrepetitive, and require no transaction-specific investment—such as the one-time purchase of standard equipment—will more likely take place between firms, that is, across a market interface.

In this account, the former set of transactions is internalized within hierarchies for two reasons. The first is "bounded rationality," the inability of economic actors to anticipate properly the complex chain of contingencies that might be relevant to long-term contracts. When transactions are internalized, it is unnecessary to anticipate all such contingencies; they can be handled within the firm's "governance structure" instead of leading to complex negotiations. The second reason is "opportunism," the rational pursuit by economic actors of their own advantage, with all means at their command, including guile and deceit. Opportunism is mitigated and constrained by authority relations and by the greater identification with transaction partners that one allegedly has when both are contained within one corporate entity than when they face one another across the chasm of a market boundary.

The appeal to authority relations in order to tame opportunism constitutes a rediscovery of Hobbesian analysis, though confined here to the economic sphere. The Hobbesian flavor of Williamson's argument is suggested by such statements as the following: "Internal organization is not beset with the same kinds of difficulties that autonomous contracting [among independent firms] experiences when disputes arise between the parties. Although interfirm disputes are often settled out of court . . . this resolution is sometimes difficult and interfirm relations are often strained. Costly litigation is sometimes unavoidable. Internal organization, by contrast . . . is able to settle many such disputes by appeal to fiat—an enormously efficient way to settle instrumental differences" (1975, p. 30). He notes that complex, recurring transactions require long-term relations between identified individuals but that opportunism jeopardizes these relations. The adaptations to changing market circumstances required over the course of a relationship are too complex and unpredictable to be encompassed in some initial contact, and promises of good faith are unenforceable in the absence of an overarching authority:

> A general clause . . . that "I will behave responsibly rather than seek individual advantage when an occasion to adapt arises," would, in the absence of opportunism, suffice. Given, however, the unenforceability of general clauses and the proclivity of human agents to make false and misleading (self-disbelieved) statements, . . . both buyer and seller are strategically situated to bargain over the disposition of any incremental gain whenever a proposal to adapt is made by the other party. . . . Efficient adaptations which would otherwise be made thus result in costly haggling or even go unmentioned, lest the gains be dissipated by costly subgoal pursuit. *Governance structures* which attenuate opportunism and otherwise infuse confidence are evidently needed. [1979, pp. 241–42, emphasis mine]

This analysis entails the same mixture of under- and oversocialized assumptions found in *Leviathan*. The efficacy of hierarchical power within the firm is overplayed, as with Hobbes's oversocialized sovereign state.[5] The "market" resembles Hobbes's state of nature. It is the atomized and anonymous market of classical political economy, minus the discipline brought by fully competitive conditions—an undersocialized conception that neglects the role of social relations among individuals in different firms in bringing order to economic life. Williamson does acknowledge that this picture of the market is not always appropriate: "Norms of trustworthy behavior sometimes extend to markets and are enforced, in some degree, by group pressures. . . . Repeated personal contacts across organizational boundaries support some minimum level of courtesy and consideration between the parties. . . . In addition, expectations of repeat business discourage efforts to seek a narrow advantage in any particular transaction. . . . Individual aggressiveness is curbed by the prospect of ostracism among peers, in both trade and social circumstances. The reputation of a firm for fairness is also a business asset not to be dissipated" (1975, pp. 106–8).

A wedge is opened here for analysis of social structural influences on market behavior. But Williamson treats these examples as exceptions and also fails to appreciate the extent to which the dyadic relations he describes are themselves embedded in broader systems of social relations. I argue that the anonymous market of neoclassical models is virtually nonexistent in economic life and that transactions of all kinds are rife with the social connections described. This is not necessarily more the case in transactions between firms than within—it seems plausible, on the contrary, that the network of social relations within the firm might be more dense and long-lasting on the average than that existing between—but all I need show here is that there is sufficient social overlay in economic transactions across firms (in the "market," to use the term as in Williamson's dichotomy) to render dubious the assertion that complex market transactions approximate a Hobbesian state of nature that can only be resolved by internalization within a hierarchical structure.

In a general way, there is evidence all around us of the extent to which business relations are mixed up with social ones. The trade associations deplored by Adam Smith remain of great importance. It is well known that many firms, small and large, are linked by interlocking directorates so that relationships among directors of firms are many and densely knit. That business relations spill over into sociability and vice versa, espe-

---

[5] Williamson's confidence in the efficacy of hierarchy leads him, in discussing Chester Barnard's "zone of indifference"—that realm within which employees obey orders simply because they are indifferent about whether or not they do what is ordered—to speak instead of a "zone of acceptance" (1975, p. 77), thus undercutting Barnard's emphasis on the problematic nature of obedience. This transformation of Barnard's usage appears to have originated with Herbert Simon, who does not justify it, noting only that he "prefer[s] the term 'acceptance' " (Simon 1957, p. 12).

cially among business elites, is one of the best-documented facts in the sociological study of business (e.g., Domhoff 1971; Useem 1979). In his study of the extent to which litigation was used to settle disputes between firms, Macaulay notes that disputes are "frequently settled without reference to the contract or potential or actual legal sanctions. There is a hesitancy to speak of legal rights or to threaten to sue in these negotiations. . . . Or as one businessman put it, 'You can settle any dispute if you keep the lawyers and accountants out of it. They just do not understand the give-and-take needed in business.' . . . Law suits for breach of contract appear to be rare" (1963, p. 61). He goes on to explain that the

> top executives of the two firms may know each other. They may sit together on government or trade committees. They may know each other socially and even belong to the same country club. . . . Even where agreement can be reached at the negotiation stage, carefully planned arrangements may create undesirable exchange relationships between business units. Some businessmen object that in such a carefully worked out relationship one gets performance only to the letter of the contract. Such planning indicates a lack of trust and blunts the demands of friendship, turning a cooperative venture into an antagonistic horse trade. . . . Threatening to turn matters over to an attorney may cost no more money than postage or a telephone call; yet few are so skilled in making such a threat that it will not cost some deterioration of the relationship between the firms. [Pp. 63–64]

It is not only at top levels that firms are connected by networks of personal relations, but at all levels where transactions must take place. It is, for example, a commonplace in the literature on industrial purchasing that buying and selling relationships rarely approximate the spot-market model of classical theory. One source indicates that the "evidence consistently suggests that it takes some kind of 'shock' to jolt the organizational buying out of a pattern of placing repeat orders with a favored supplier or to extend the constrained set of feasible suppliers. A moment's reflection will suggest several reasons for this behavior, including the costs associated with searching for new suppliers and establishing new relationships, the fact that users are likely to prefer sources, the relatively low risk involved in dealing with known vendors, and the likelihood that the buyer has established personal relationships that he values with representatives of the supplying firm" (Webster and Wind 1972, p. 15).

In a similar vein, Macaulay notes that salesmen "often know purchasing agents well. The same two individuals may have dealt with each other from five to 25 years. Each has something to give the other. Salesmen have gossip about competitors, shortages and price increases to give purchasing agents who treat them well" (1963, p. 63). Sellers who do not satisfy their customers "become the subject of discussion in the gossip exchanged by purchasing agents and salesmen, at meetings of purchasing agents' associations and trade associations or even at country clubs or social gatherings . . ." (p. 64). Settlement of disputes is eased by this embeddedness of business in social relations: "Even where the parties have a detailed and carefully planned agreement which indicates what is to happen if, say, the seller fails to deliver on time, often they will never refer to the agreement but will negotiate a solution when the problem arises as if there never had been any original contract. One purchasing agent expressed a common business attitude when he said, 'If something comes up, you get the other man on the telephone and deal with the problem. You don't read legalistic contract clauses at each other if you ever want to do business again. One doesn't run to lawyers if he wants to stay in business because one must behave decently'" (Macaulay 1963, p. 61).

Such patterns may be more easily noted in other countries, where they are supposedly explained by "cultural" peculiarities. Thus, one journalist recently asserted,

> Friendships and longstanding personal connections affect business connections everywhere. But that seems to be especially true in Japan. . . . The after-hours sessions in the bars and nightclubs are where the vital personal contacts are established and nurtured slowly. Once these ties are set, they are not easily undone. . . . The resulting tight-knit nature of Japanese business society has long been a source of frustration to foreign companies trying to sell products in Japan. . . . Chalmers Johnson, a professor at . . . Berkeley, believes that . . . the exclusive dealing within the Japanese industrial groups, buying and selling to and from each other based on decades-old relationships rather than economic competitiveness . . . is . . . a real nontariff barrier [to trade between the United States and Japan]. [Lohr 1982]

The extensive use of subcontracting in many industries also presents opportunities for sustained relationships among firms that are not organized hierarchically within one corporate unit. For example, Eccles cites evidence from many countries that in construction, when projects "are not subject to institutional regulations which require competitive bidding . . . relations between the general contractor and his subcontractors are stable and continuous over fairly long periods of time and only infrequently established through competitive bidding. This type of 'quasi-integration' results in what I call the 'quasifirm.' It is a preferred mode to either pure market transactions or formal vertical integration" (1981, pp. 339–40). Eccles describes this "quasifirm" arrangement of extensive and long-term relationships among contractors and subcontractors as an organizational form logically intermediate between the pure market and the vertically integrated firm. I would argue, however, that it is not *empirically* intermediate, since the former situation is so rare. The case of construction is closer to vertical integration than some other situations where firms interact, such as buying and selling relations, since subcontractors are physically located on the same site as the contractor and are under his general supervision. Furthermore, under the usual fixed-price contracts, there are "obvious incentives for shirking performance requirements" (Eccles 1981, p. 340).

Yet a hierarchical structure associated with the vertically integrated firm does not arise to meet this "problem." I argue this is because the long-term relations of contractors and subcontractors, as well as the embeddedness of those relations in a community of construction personnel, generate standards of expected behavior that not only obviate the need for but are superior to pure authority relations in discouraging malfeasance. Eccles's own empirical study of residential construction in Massachusetts shows not only that subcontracting relationships are long term in nature but also that it is very rare for a general contractor to employ more than two or three subcontractors in a given trade, whatever number of projects is handled in the course of a year (1981, pp. 349–51). This is true despite the availability of large numbers of alternative subcontractors. This phenomenon can be explained in part in investment terms—through a "continuing association both parties can benefit from the somewhat idiosyncratic investment of learning to work together" (Eccles 1981, p. 340)—but also must be related to the desire of individuals to derive pleasure from the social interaction that accompanies their daily work, a pleasure that would be considerably blunted by spot-market procedures requiring entirely new and strange work partners each day. As in other parts of economic life, the overlay of social relations on what may begin in purely economic transactions plays a crucial role.

Some comments on labor markets are also relevant here. One advantage that Williamson asserts for hierarchically structured firms over market transactions is the ability to transmit accurate information about employees. "The principal impediment to effective interfirm experience-rating," he argues, "is one of communication. By comparison with the firm, markets lack a rich and common rating language. The language problem is particularly severe where the judgments to be made are highly subjective. The advantages of hierarchy in these circumstances are especially great if those persons who are most familiar with a worker's characteristics, usually his immediate supervisor, also do the experience-rating" (1975, p. 78). But the notion that good information about the characteristics of an employee can be transmitted only within firms and not between can be sustained only by neglecting the widely variegated social network of interaction that spans firms. Information about employees travels among firms not only because personal relations exist between those in each firm who do business with each other but also, as I have shown in detail (Granovetter 1974), because the relatively high levels of interfirm mobility in the United States guarantee that many workers will be reasonably well known to employees of numerous other firms that might require and solicit their services. Furthermore, the idea that internal information is necessarily accurate and acted on dispassionately by promotion procedures keyed to it seems naive. To say, as Williamson does, that reliance "on internal promotion has affirmative incentive properties because workers can anticipate that differential talent and degrees of cooperativeness will be rewarded" (1975, p. 78) invokes an ideal type of promotion as reward-for-achievement that can readily be shown to have only limited correspondence to existing internal labor markets (see Granovetter 1983, pp. 40–51, for an extended analysis).

The other side of my critique is to argue that Williamson vastly overestimates the efficacy of hierarchical power ("fiat," in his terminology) within organizations. He asserts, for example, that internal organizations have a great auditing advantage: "An external auditor is typically constrained to review written records. . . . An internal auditor, by contrast, has greater freedom of action. . . . Whereas an internal auditor is not a partisan but regards himself and is regarded by others in mainly instrumental terms, the external auditor is associated with the 'other side' and his motives are regarded suspiciously. The degree of cooperation received by the auditor from the audited party varies accordingly. The external auditor can expect to receive only perfunctory cooperation" (1975, pp. 29–30). The literature on intrafirm audits is sparse, but one thorough account is that of Dalton, in *Men Who Manage,* for a large chemical plant. Audits of parts by the central office were supposed to be conducted on a surprise basis, but warning was typically surreptitiously given. The high level of cooperation shown in these internal audits is suggested by the following account: "Notice that a count of parts was to begin provoked a flurry among the executives to hide certain parts and equipment . . . materials *not* to be counted were moved to: 1) little-known and inaccessible spots; 2) basements and pits that were dirty and therefore unlikely to be examined; 3) departments that had already been inspected and that could be approached circuitously while the counters were en route between official storage areas and 4) places where materials and supplies might be used as a camouflage for parts. . . . As the practice developed, cooperation among the [department] chiefs to use each other's storage areas and available pits became well organized and smoothly functioning" (Dalton 1959, pp. 48–49).

Dalton's work shows brilliantly that cost accounting of all kinds is a highly arbitrary and therefore easily politicized process rather than a technical procedure decided on grounds of efficiency. He details this especially for the relationship between the maintenance department and various production departments in the chemical plant; the department to which maintenance work was charged had less to do with any strict time accounting than with the relative political and social standing of department executives in their relation to maintenance personnel. Furthermore, the more aggressive department heads expedited their maintenance work "by the use of friendships, by bullying and implied threats. As all the heads had the same formal rank, one could say that an inverse relation existed between a given officer's personal influence and his volume of uncompleted repairs" (1959, p. 34). Questioned about how such practices could escape the attention of auditors, one informant told Dalton, "If Auditing got to snooping around, what the hell could they find out? And if they did find anything, they'd know a damn sight better than to say anything about it. . . . All those guys [department heads] have got lines through Cost Accounting. That's a lot of bunk about Auditing being independent" (p. 32).

Accounts as detailed and perceptive as Dalton's are sadly lacking for a representative sample of firms and so are open to the argument that they are exceptional. But similar points can be made for the problem of transfer pricing—the determination of prices for products traded between divisions of a single firm. Here Williamson argues that though the trading divisions "may have profit-center standing, this is apt to be exercised in a restrained way. . . . Cost-plus pricing rules, and variants thereof, preclude supplier divisions from seeking the monopolistic prices [to] which their sole source supply position might otherwise entitle them. In addition, the managements of the trading divisions are more susceptible to appeals for cooperation" (1975, p. 29). But in an intensive empirical study of transfer-pricing practices, Eccles, having interviewed nearly 150 managers in 13 companies, concluded that no cost-based methods could be carried out in a technically neutral way, since there is "no universal criterion for what is cost. . . . Problems often exist with cost-based methods when the buying division does not have access to the information by which the costs are generated. . . . Market prices are especially difficult to determine when internal purchasing is mandated and no external purchases are made of the intermediate good. . . . There is no obvious answer to what is a markup for profit . . ." (1982, p. 21). The political element in transfer-pricing conflicts strongly affects whose definition of "cost" is accepted: "In general, when transfer pricing practices are seen to enhance one's power and status they will be viewed favorably. When they do not, a countless number of strategic and other sound business reasons will be found to argue for their inadequacy" (1982, p. 21; see also Eccles 1983, esp. pp. 26–32). Eccles notes the "somewhat ironic fact that many managers consider internal transactions to be more difficult than external ones, even though vertical integration is pursued for presumed advantages" (1983, p. 28).

Thus, the oversocialized view that orders within a hierarchy elicit easy obedience and that employees internalize the interests of the firm, suppressing any conflict with their own, cannot stand scrutiny against these empirical studies (or, for that matter, against the experience of many of us in actual organizations). Note further that, as shown especially well in Dalton's detailed ethnographic study, resistance to the encroachment of organizational interests on personal or divisional ones requires an extensive network of coalitions. From the viewpoint of management, these coalitions represent malfeasance generated by teams; it could not be managed at all by atomized individuals. Indeed, Dalton asserted that the level of cooperation achieved by divisional chiefs in evading central audits involved joint action "of a kind rarely, if ever, shown in carrying on official activities . . ." (1959, p. 49).

In addition, the generally lower turnover of personnel characteristic of large hierarchical firms, with their well-defined internal labor markets and elaborate promotion ladders, may make such cooperative evasion more likely. When many employees have long tenures, the conditions are met for a dense and stable network of relations, shared understandings, and political coalitions to be constructed. (See Homans 1950, 1974, for the relevant social psychological discussions; and Pfeffer 1983, for a treatment of the "demography of organizations.") James Lincoln notes, in this connection, that in the ideal-typical Weberian bureaucracy, organizations are "designed to function independently of the collective actions which can be mobilized through [internal] interpersonal networks. Bureaucracy prescribes fixed relationships among positions through which incumbents flow, without, in theory, affecting organizational operations" (1982, p. 26). He goes on to summarize studies showing, however, that "when turnover is low, relations take on additional contents of an expressive and personal sort which may ultimately transform the network and change the directions of the organization" (p. 26).

To this point I have argued that social relations between firms are more important, and authority within firms less so, in bringing order to economic life than is supposed in the markets and hierarchies line of thought. A balanced and symmetrical argument requires attention to power in "market" relations and social connections within firms. Attention to power relations is needed lest my emphasis on the smoothing role of social relations in the market lead me to neglect the role of these relations in the conduct of conflict. Conflict is an obvious reality, ranging from well-publicized litigation between firms to the occasional cases of "cutthroat competition" gleefully reported by the business press. Since the effective exercise of power between firms will prevent bloody public battles, we can assume that such battles represent only a small proportion of actual conflicts of interest. Conflicts probably become public only when the two sides are fairly equally matched; recall that this rough equality was precisely one of Hobbes's arguments for a probable "war of all against all" in the "state of nature." But when the power position of one firm is obviously dominant, the other is apt to capitulate early so as to cut its losses. Such capitulation may require not even explicit confrontation but only a clear understanding of what the other side requires (as in the recent Marxist literature on "hegemony" in business life; see, e.g., Mintz and Schwartz 1985).

Though the exact extent to which firms dominate other firms can be debated, the voluminous literature on interlocking directorates, on the role of financial institutions vis-à-vis industrial corporations, and on dual economy surely provides enough evidence to conclude that power relations cannot be neglected. This provides still another reason to doubt that the complexities that arise when formally equal agents negotiate with one another can be resolved only by the subsumption of all parties under a single hierarchy; in fact, many of these complexities are resolved by implicit or explicit power relations *among* firms.

Finally, a brief comment is in order on the webs of social relations that are well known from industrial and organizational sociology to be important within firms. The distinction between the "formal" and the "informal" organization of the firm is one of the oldest in the literature, and it hardly needs repeating that observers who assume firms to be structured in fact by the official organization chart are sociological babes in the woods. The connection of this to the present discussion is that insofar as internalization within firms does result in a better handling of complex and idiosyncratic transactions, it is by no means apparent that hierarchical organization is the best explanation. It may be, instead, that the effect of internalization is to provide a focus (see Feld 1981) for an even denser web of social relations than had occurred between previously independent market entities. Perhaps this web of interaction is mainly what explains the level of efficiency, be it high or low, of the new organizational form.

It is now useful to summarize the differences in explanation and prediction between Williamson's markets and hierarchies approach and the embeddedness view offered here. Williamson explains the inhibition of "opportunism" or malfeasance in economic life and the general existence of cooperation and order by the subsumption of complex economic activity in hierarchically integrated firms. The empirical evidence that I cite shows, rather, that even with complex transactions, a high level of order can often be found in the "market"—that is, across firm boundaries—and a correspondingly high level of disorder within the firm. Whether these occur, instead of what Williamson expects, depends on the nature of personal relations and networks of relations between and within firms. I claim that both order *and* disorder, honesty *and* malfeasance have more to do with structures of such relations than they do with organizational form.

Certain implications follow for the conditions under which one may expect to see vertical integration rather than transactions between firms in a market. Other things being equal, for example, we should expect pressures toward vertical integration in a market where transacting firms lack a network of personal relations that connects them or where such a network eventuates in conflict, disorder, opportunism, or malfeasance. On the other hand, where a stable network of relations mediates complex transactions and generates standards of behavior between firms, such pressures should be absent.

I use the word "pressures" rather than predict that vertical integration will always follow the pattern described in order to avoid the functionalism implicit in Williamson's assumption that whatever organizational form is most efficient will be the one observed. Before we can make this assumption, two further conditions must be satisfied: (i) well-defined and powerful selection pressures toward efficiency must be operating, and (ii) some actors must have the ability and resources to "solve" the efficiency problem by constructing a vertically integrated firm.

The selection pressures that guarantee efficient organization of transactions are nowhere clearly described by Williamson. As in much of the new institutional economics, the need to make such matters explicit is obviated by an implicit Darwinian argument that efficient solutions, however they may originate, have a staying power akin to that enforced by natural selection in the biological world. Thus it is granted that not all business executives "accurately perceive their business opportunities and faultlessly respond. Over time, however, those [vertical] integration moves that have better rationality properties (in transaction cost and scale-economy terms) tend to have better survival properties" (Williamson and Ouchi 1981, p. 389; see also Williamson 1981, pp. 573–74). But Darwinian arguments, invoked in this cavalier fashion, career toward a Panglossian view of whatever institution is analyzed. The operation of alleged selection pressures is here neither an object of study nor even a falsifiable proposition but rather an article of faith.

Even if one could document selection pressures that made survival of certain organizational forms more likely, it would remain to show how such forms could be implemented. To treat them implicitly as mutations, by analogy to biological evolution, merely evades the issue. As in other functionalist explanations, it cannot be automatically assumed that the solution to some problem is feasible. Among the resources required to implement vertical integration might be some measure of market power, access to capital through retained earnings or capital markets, and appropriate connections to legal or regulatory authorities.

Where selection pressures are weak (especially likely in the imperfect markets claimed by Williamson to produce vertical integration) and resources problematic, the social-structural configurations that I have outlined are still related to the efficiency of transaction costs, but no guarantee can be given that an efficient solution will occur. Motives for integration unrelated to efficiency, such as personal aggrandizement of CEOs in acquiring firms, may in such settings become important.

What the viewpoint proposed here requires is that future research on the markets-hierarchies question pay careful and systematic attention to the actual patterns of personal relations by which economic transactions are carried out. Such attention will not only better sort out the motives for vertical integration but also make it easier to comprehend the various complex intermediate forms between idealized atomized markets and completely integrated firms, such as the quasi firm discussed above for the construction industry. Intermediate forms of this kind are so intimately bound up with networks of personal relations that any perspective that considers these relations peripheral will fail to see clearly what "organizational form" has been effected. Existing empirical studies of industrial organization pay little attention to patterns of relations, in part because relevant data are harder to find than those on technology and market structure but also because the dominant economic framework remains one of atomized actors, so personal relations are perceived as frictional in effect.

DISCUSSION

In this article, I have argued that most behavior is closely embedded in networks of interpersonal relations and that such an argument avoids the extremes of under- and oversocialized views of human action. Though I believe this to be so for all behavior, I concentrate here on economic behavior for two reasons: (i) it is the type-case of behavior inadequately interpreted because those who study it professionally are so strongly committed to atomized theories of action; and (ii) with few exceptions, sociologists have refrained from serious study of any subject already claimed by neoclassical economics. They have implicitly accepted the presumption of economists that "market processes" are not suitable objects of sociological study because social relations play only a frictional and disruptive role, not a central one, in modern societies. (Recent exceptions are Baker 1983; Burt 1983; and White 1981.) In those instances in which sociologists study processes where markets are central, they usually still manage to avoid their analysis. Until recently, for example, the large sociological literature on wages was cast in terms of "income attainment," obscuring the labor market context in which wages are set and focusing instead on the background and attainment of individuals (see Granovetter 1981 for an extended critique). Or, as Stearns has pointed out, the literature on who controls corporations has implicitly assumed that analysis must be at the level of political relations and broad assumptions about the nature of capitalism. Even though it is widely admitted that how corporations acquire capital is a major determinant of control, most relevant research "since the turn of the century has eliminated that [capital] market as an objective of investigation" (1982, pp. 5–6). Even in organization theory, where considerable literature implements the limits placed on economic decisions by social structural complexity, little attempt has been made to demonstrate the implications of this for the neoclassical theory of the firm or for a general understanding of production or such macroeconomic outcomes as growth, inflation, and unemployment.

In trying to demonstrate that all market processes are amenable to sociological analysis and that such analysis reveals central, not peripheral, features of these processes, I have narrowed my focus to problems of trust and malfeasance. I have also used the "market and hierarchies" argument of Oliver Williamson as an illustration of how the embeddedness perspective generates different understandings and predictions from that implemented by economists. Williamson's perspective is itself "revisionist" within economics, diverging from the neglect of institutional and transactional considerations typical of neoclassical work. In this sense, it may appear to have more kinship to a sociological perspective than the usual economic arguments. But the main thrust of the "new institutional economists" is to deflect the analysis of institutions from sociological, historical, and legal argumentation and show instead that they arise as the efficient solution to economic problems. This mission and the pervasive functionalism it implies discourage the detailed analysis of social structure that I argue here is the key to understanding how existing institutions arrived at their present state.

Insofar as rational choice arguments are narrowly construed as referring to atomized individuals and economic goals, they are inconsistent with the embeddedness position presented here. In a broader formulation of rational choice, however, the two views have much in common. Much of the revisionist work by economists that I criticize above in my discussion of over- and undersocialized conceptions of action relies on a strategy that might be called "psychological revisionism"—an attempt to reform economic theory by abandoning an absolute assumption of rational decision making. This strategy has led to Leibenstein's "selective rationality" in his arguments on "X-inefficiency" (1976), for example, and to the claims of segmented labor-market theorists that workers in different market segments have different kinds of decision-making rules, rational choice being only for upper-primary (i.e., professional, managerial, technical) workers (Piore 1979).

I suggest, in contrast, that while the assumption of rational action must always be problematic, it is a good working hypothesis that should not easily be abandoned. What looks to the analyst like nonrational behavior may be quite sensible when situational constraints, especially those of embeddedness, are fully appreciated. When the social situation of those in nonprofessional labor markets is fully analyzed, their behavior looks less like the automatic application of "cultural" rules and more like a reasonable response to their present situation (as, e.g., in the discussion of Liebow 1966). Managers who evade audits and fight over transfer pricing are acting nonrationally in some strict economic sense, in terms of a firm's profit maximization; but when their position and ambitions in intrafirm networks and political coalitions are analyzed, the behavior is easily interpreted.

That such behavior is rational or instrumental is more readily seen, moreover, if we note that it aims not only at economic goals but also at sociability, approval, status, and power. Economists rarely see such goals as rational, in part on account of the arbitrary separation that arose historically, as Albert Hirschman (1977) points out, in the 17th and 18th centuries, between the "passions" and the "interests," the latter connoting economic motives only. This way of putting the matter has led economists to specialize in analysis of behavior motivated only by "interest" and to assume that other motives occur in separate and nonrationally organized spheres; hence Samuelson's much-quoted comment that "many economists would separate economics from sociology upon the basis of rational or irrational behavior" (1947, p. 90). The notion that rational choice is derailed by social influences has long discouraged detailed sociological analysis of economic life and led revisionist economists to reform economic theory by focusing on its naive psychology. My claim here is that however naive that psychology may be, this is not where the main difficulty lies—it is rather in the neglect of social structure.

Finally, I should add that the level of causal analysis adopted in the embeddedness argument is a rather proximate one. I have had little to say about what broad historical or macrostructural circumstances have led systems to display the social-structural characteristics they have, so I make no claims for this analysis to answer large-scale questions about the nature of modern society or the sources of economic and political change. But the focus on proximate causes is intentional, for these broader questions cannot be satisfactorily addressed without more detailed understanding of the mechanisms by which sweeping change has its effects. My claim is that one of the most important and least analyzed of such mechanisms is the impact of such change on the social relations in which economic life is embedded. If this is so, no adequate link between macro- and micro-level theories can be established without a much fuller understanding of these relations.

The use of embeddedness analysis in explicating proximate causes of patterns of macro-level interest is well illustrated by the markets and hierarchies question. The extent of vertical integration and the reasons for the persistence of small firms operating through the market are not only narrow concerns of industrial organization; they are of interest to all students of the institutions of advanced capitalism. Similar issues arise in the analysis of "dual economy," dependent development, and the nature of modern corporate elites. But whether small firms are indeed eclipsed by giant corporations is usually analyzed in broad and sweeping macropolitical or macroeconomic terms, with little appreciation of proximate social structural causes.

Analysts of dual economy have often suggested, for example, that the persistence of large numbers of small firms in the "periphery" is explained by large corporations' need to shift the risks of cyclical fluctuations in demand or of uncertain R & D activities; failures of these small units will not adversely affect the larger firms' earnings. I suggest here that small firms in a market setting may persist instead because a dense network of social relations is overlaid on the business relations connecting such firms and reduces pressures for integration. This does not rule out risk shifting as an explanation with a certain face validity. But the embeddedness account may be more useful in explaining the large number of small establishments not characterized by satellite or peripheral status. (For a discussion of the surprising extent of employment in small establishments, see Granovetter 1984.) This account is restricted to proximate causes: it logically leads to but does not answer the questions why, when, and in what sectors does the market display various types of social structure. But those questions, which link to a more macro level of analysis, would themselves not arise without a prior appreciation of the importance of social structure in the market.

The markets and hierarchies analysis, important as it may be, is presented here mainly as an illustration. I believe the embeddedness argument to have very general applicability and to demonstrate not only that there is a place for sociologists in the study of economic life but that their perspective is urgently required there. In avoiding the analysis of phenomena at the center of standard economic theory, sociologists have unnecessarily cut themselves off from a large and important aspect of social life and from the European tradition—stemming especially from Max Weber—in which economic action is seen only as a special, if important, category of social action. I hope to have shown here that this Weberian program is consistent with and furthered by some of the insights of modern structural sociology.

REFERENCES

Akerlof, George. 1983. "Loyalty Filters." *American Economic Review* 73 (1): 54–63.

Alchian, Armen, and Harold Demsetz. 1973. "The Property Rights Paradigm." *Journal of Economic History* 33 (March): 16–27.

Arrow, Kenneth. 1974. *The Limits of Organization*. New York: Norton.

Baker, Wayne. 1983. "Floor Trading and Crowd Dynamics." In *Social Dynamics of Financial Markets,* edited by Patricia Adler and Peter Adler. Greenwich, Conn.: JAI.

Becker, Gary. 1976. *The Economic Approach to Human Behavior.* Chicago: University of Chicago Press.

Ben-Porath, Yoram. 1980. "The F-Connection: Families, Friends and Firms in the Organization of Exchange." *Population and Development Review* 6 (1): 1–30.

Bowles, Samuel, and Herbert Gintis. 1975. *Schooling in Capitalist America.* New York: Basic.

Brown, Roger. 1965. *Social Psychology.* New York: Free Press.

Burt, Ronald. 1982. *Toward a Structural Theory of Action.* New York: Academic Press.

———. 1983. *Corporate Profits and Cooptation.* New York: Academic Press.

Cole, Robert. 1979. *Work, Mobility and Participation: A Comparative Study of American and Japanese Industry.* Berkeley and Los Angeles: University of California Press.

Dalton, Melville. 1959. *Men Who Manage.* New York: Wiley.

Doeringer, Peter, and Michael Piore. 1971. *Internal Labor Markets and Manpower Analysis.* Lexington, Mass.: Heath.

Domhoff, G. William. 1971. *The Higher Circles.* New York: Random House.

Duesenberry, James. 1960. Comment on "An Economic Analysis of Fertility." In *Demographic and Economic Change in Developed Countries,* edited by the Universities–National Bureau Committee for Economic Research. Princeton, N.J.: Princeton University Press.

Eccles, Robert. 1981. "The Quasifirm in the Construction Industry." *Journal of Economic Behavior and Organization* 2 (December): 335–57.

———. 1982. "A Synopsis of *Transfer Pricing: An Analysis and Action Plan.*" Mimeographed. Cambridge, Mass.: Harvard Business School.

———. 1983. "Transfer Pricing, Fairness and Control." Working Paper no. HBS 83-167. Cambridge, Mass.: Harvard Business School. Reprinted in *Harvard Business Review* (in press).

Feld, Scott. 1981. "The Focused Organization of Social Ties." *American Journal of Sociology* 86 (5): 1015–35.

Fine, Gary, and Sherryl Kleinman. 1979. "Rethinking Subculture: An Interactionist Analysis." *American Journal of Sociology* 85 (July): 1–20.

Furubotn, E., and S. Pejovich. 1972. "Property Rights and Economic Theory: A Survey of Recent Literature." *Journal of Economic Literature* 10 (3): 1137–62.

Geertz, Clifford. 1979. "Suq: The Bazaar Economy in Sefrou." Pp. 123–225 in *Meaning and Order in Moroccan Society,* edited by C. Geertz, H. Geertz, and L. Rosen. New York: Cambridge University Press.

Granovetter, Mark. 1974. *Getting a Job: A Study of Contacts and Careers.* Cambridge, Mass.: Harvard University Press.

———. 1981. "Toward a Sociological Theory of Income Differences." Pp. 11–47 in *Sociological Perspectives on Labor Markets,* edited by Ivar Berg. New York: Academic Press.

———. 1983. "Labor Mobility, Internal Markets and Job-Matching: A Comparison of the Sociological and Economic Approaches." Mimeographed.

———. 1984. "Small Is Bountiful: Labor Markets and Establishment Size." *American Sociological Review* 49 (3): 323–34.

Hirschman, Albert. 1977. *The Passions and the Interests*. Princeton, N.J.: Princeton University Press.

———. 1982. "Rival Interpretations of Market Society: Civilizing, Destructive or Feeble?" *Journal of Economic Literature* 20 (4): 1463–84.

Homans, George. 1950. *The Human Group*. New York: Harcourt Brace & Co.

———. 1974. *Social Behavior*. New York: Harcourt Brace Jovanovich.

Lazear, Edward. 1979. "Why Is There Mandatory Retirement?" *Journal of Political Economy* 87 (6): 1261–84.

Leibenstein, Harvey. 1976. *Beyond Economic Man*. Cambridge, Mass.: Harvard University Press.

Liebow, Elliot. 1966. *Tally's Corner*. Boston: Little, Brown.

Lincoln, James. 1982. "Intra- (and Inter-) Organizational Networks." Pp. 1–38 in *Research in the Sociology of Organizations*, vol. 1. Edited by S. Bacharach. Greenwich, Conn.: JAI.

Lohr, Steve. 1982. "When Money Doesn't Matter in Japan." *New York Times* (December 30).

Macaulay, Stewart. 1963. "Non-Contractual Relations in Business: A Preliminary Study." *American Sociological Review* 28 (1): 55–67.

Marsden, Peter. 1981. "Introducing Influence Processes into a System of Collective Decisions." *American Journal of Sociology* 86 (May): 1203–35.

———. 1983. "Restricted Access in Networks and Models of Power." *American Journal of Sociology* 88 (January): 686–17.

Merton, Robert. 1947. "Manifest and Latent Functions." Pp. 19–84 in *Social Theory and Social Structure*. New York: Free Press.

Mintz, Beth, and Michael Schwartz. 1985. *The Power Structure of American Business*. Chicago: University of Chicago Press.

North, D., and R. Thomas. 1973. *The Rise of the Western World*. Cambridge: Cambridge University Press.

Okun, Arthur. 1981. *Prices and Quantities*. Washington, D.C.: Brookings.

Pakes, Ariel, and S. Nitzan. 1982. "Optimum Contracts for Research Personnel, Research Employment and the Establishment of 'Rival' Enterprises." NBER Working Paper no. 871. Cambridge, Mass.: National Bureau of Economic Research.

Parsons, Talcott. 1937. *The Structure of Social Action*. New York: Macmillan.

Pfeffer, Jeffrey. 1983. "Organizational Demography." In *Research in Organizational Behavior*, vol. 5. Edited by L. L. Cummings and B. Staw. Greenwich, Conn.: JAI.

Phelps Brown, Ernest Henry. 1977. *The Inequality of Pay*. Berkeley: University of California Press.

Piore, Michael. 1975. "Notes for a Theory of Labor Market Stratification." Pp. 125–50 in *Labor Market Segmentation*, edited by R. Edwards, M. Reich, and D. Gordon. Lexington, Mass.: Heath.

———, ed. 1979. *Unemployment and Inflation*. White Plains, N.Y.: Sharpe.

Polanyi, Karl. 1944. *The Great Transformation*. New York: Holt, Rinehart.

Polanyi, Karl, C. Arensberg, and H. Pearson. 1957. *Trade and Market in the Early Empires*. New York: Free Press.

Popkin, Samuel. 1979. *The Rational Peasant*. Berkeley and Los Angeles: University of California Press.

Rosen, Sherwin. 1982. "Authority, Control and the Distribution of Earnings." *Bell Journal of Economics* 13 (2): 311–23.

Samuelson, Paul. 1947. *Foundations of Economic Analysis*. Cambridge, Mass.: Harvard University Press.

Schneider, Harold. 1974. *Economic Man: The Anthropology of Economics*. New York: Free Press.

Schotter, Andrew. 1981. *The Economic Theory of Social Institutions*. New York: Cambridge University Press.

Scott, James. 1976. *The Moral Economy of the Peasant*. New Haven, Conn.: Yale University Press.

Shenon, Philip. 1984. "Margolies Is Found Guilty of Murdering Two Women." *New York Times* (June 1).

Simon, Herbert. 1957. *Administrative Behavior*. Glencoe, Ill.: Free Press.

Smith, Adam. (1776) 1979. *The Wealth of Nations*. Edited by Andrew Skinner. Baltimore: Penguin.

Stearns, Linda. 1982. "Corporate Dependency and the Structure of the Capital Market: 1880–1980." Ph.D. dissertation, State University of New York at Stony Brook.

Thompson, E. P. 1971. "The Moral Economy of the English Crowd in the Eighteenth Century." *Past and Present* 50 (February): 76–136.

Useem, Michael. 1979. "The Social Organization of the American Business Elite and Participation of Corporation Directors in the Governance of American Institutions." *American Sociological Review* 44:553–72.

Webster, Frederick, and Yoram Wind. 1972. *Organizational Buying Behavior*. Englewood Cliffs, N.J.: Prentice-Hall.

White, Harrison C. 1981. "Where Do Markets Come From?" *American Journal of Sociology* 87 (November): 517–47.

Williamson, Oliver. 1975. *Markets and Hierarchies*. New York: Free Press.

———. 1979. "Transaction-Cost Economics: The Governance of Contractual Relations." *Journal of Law and Economics* 22 (2): 233–61.

———. 1981. "The Economics of Organization: The Transaction Cost Approach." *American Journal of Sociology* 87 (November): 548–77.

Williamson, Oliver, and William Ouchi. 1981. "The Markets and Hierarchies and Visible Hand Perspectives." Pp. 347–70 in *Perspectives on Organizational Design and Behavior*, edited by Andrew Van de Ven and William Joyce. New York: Wiley.

Wrong, Dennis. 1961. "The Oversocialized Conception of Man in Modern Sociology." *American Sociological Review* 26 (2): 183–93.

References to the 1974 Edition

Abegglen, James C. 1958. *The Japanese Factory*. Glencoe, Illinois: The Free Press.

Adams, Leonard P. 1969. *The Public Employment Service in Transition, 1933–1968*. Ithaca, N.Y.: New York State School of Industrial and Labor Relations, Cornell University.

Banfield, Edward C. 1969. "An Act of Corporate Citzenship." In *Programs to Employ the Disadvantaged*, edited by Peter Doeringer. Englewood Cliffs, N.J.: Prentice-Hall.

Bennett, John W., and Iwao Ishino. 1963. *Paternalism in the Japanese Economy*. Minneapolis: University of Minnesota Press.

Blau, Peter, and O. Dudley Duncan. 1967. *The American Occupational Structure*. New York: Wiley.

Bloom, Gordon F., and Herbert R. Northrup. 1969. *Economics of Labor Relations*. Sixth edition. Homewood, Illinois: Richard D. Irwin, Inc.

Blumen, I., M. Kogan, and P. McCarthy. *The Industrial Mobility of Labor as a Probability Process*. Ithaca, N.Y.: New York State School of Industrial and Labor Relations, Cornell University.

Broadbent, D. 1958. *Perception and Communication*. London: Pergamon.

Brown, David G. 1965a. *The Market for College Teachers*. Chapel Hill: University of North Carolina Press.

—— 1965b. *Academic Labor Markets*. Washington, D.C.: U.S. Dept. of Labor, Office of Manpower, Automation and Training.

—— 1967. *The Mobile Professors*. Washington, D.C.: American Council on Education.

Caplow, Theodore, and R. McGee. 1958. *The Academic Marketplace*. New York: Basic Books.

Carlsson, Gosta. 1958. *Social Mobility and Class Structure*. Lund, Sweden: Gleerup.

Chernick, Jack, and Georgina Smith. 1969. "Employing the Disadvantaged." In *Programs to Employ the Disadvantaged*, edited by Peter Doeringer. Englewood Cliffs, N.J.: Prentice-Hall.

Coleman, James S., Elihu Katz, and H. Menzel. 1957. "The Diffusion of Innovation among Physicians." *Sociometry* 20: 253–270

Crain, Robert L. 1970. "School Integration and Occupational Achievement of Negroes." *American Journal of Sociology* 75 (January, Part 2): 593–606.

Crozier, Michel. 1964. *The Bureaucratic Phenomenon*. Chicago: University of Chicago Press.

Dalton, Melville. 1959. *Men Who Manage*. New York: Wiley.

Davis, James A., and S. Leinhardt. 1972. "The Structure of Positive Interpersonal Relations in Small Groups." In J. Berger, et al., eds., *Sociological Theories in Progress*, vol. 2. Boston: Houghton Mifflin.

De Schweinetz, Dorothea. 1932. *How Workers Find Jobs*. Philadelphia: University of Pennsylvania Press.

Doeringer, Peter. 1969. "Programs to Employ the Disadvantaged: A Labor Market Perspective." In *Programs to Employ the Disadvantaged*, edited by Peter Doeringer. Englewood Cliffs, N.J.: Prentice-Hall.

Dunlop, John T. 1966. "Job Vacancy Measures and Economic Analysis." In *The Measurement and Interpretation of Job Vacancies*, edited by Robert Ferber. New York: Columbia University Press.

Edelman, Murray, et al. 1952. *Channels of Employment*. Urbana, Illinois: University of Illinois Press.

Evan, William. 1966. "The Organization Set: Toward a Theory of Interorganizational Relations." In *Approaches to Organizational Design*, edited by J. Thompson. Pittsburgh: University of Pittsburgh Press.

Feller, William. 1957. *An Introduction to Probability Theory and its Applications*, vol. 1, 2nd edition. New York: Wiley.

Ferber, R., and N. Ford. 1965. "The Collection of Job Vacancy Data." In *Employment Policy and the Labor Market*, edited by A.M. Ross. Berkeley: University of California Press.

Fisher, Lloyd H. 1953. *The Harvest Labor Market in California*. Cambridge, Mass.: Harvard University Press.

Gans, Herbert. 1962. *The Urban Villagers*. New York: The Free Press.

Granovetter, Mark S. 1973. "The Strength of Weak Ties." *American Journal of Sociology* 78 (May): 1360–1380.

Gurevitch, Michael. 1961. "The Social Structure of Acquaintanceship Networks." Ph.D. diss., Massachusetts Institute of Technology.

Hansen, M.H., W. Hurwitz, and W. Madow. 1953. *Sample Survey Methods and Theory*, vol. 1. New York: Wiley.

Hempel, Carl G. 1965. *Aspects of Scientific Explanation*. New York: The Free Press.

Holt, Charles C., and Martin H. David. 1966. "The Concept Of Job Vacancies in a Dynamic Theory of the Labor Market." In *The Measurement and Interpretation of Job Vacancies*, edited by Robert Ferber. New York: Columbia University Press.

Holt, Charles C., and George Huber. 1969. "A Computer Aided Approach to Employment Service Placement and Counseling." *Management Science* 15 (#11): 573–593.

Homans, George. 1950. *The Human Group*. New York: Harcourt, Brace & World.

Jensen, Vernon H. 1964. *The Hiring of Dock Workers*. Cambridge, Mass.: Harvard University Press.

—— 1967. "Computer Hiring of Dock Workers in the Port of New York." *Industrial and Labor Relations Review* 20 (April): 414–432.

Kahl, Joseph. 1953. *The American Class Structure*. New York: Rinehart.

Katz, Elihu. 1957, "The Two-Step Flow of Communication: An Up-to-date Report on an Hypothesis." *Public Opinion Quarterly* 21 (Spring): 61–78.

Katz, Fred E. 1958. "Occupational Contact Networks." *Social Forces* 37 (October): 252–258.

Kemeny, John G., and J. Laurie Snell. 1960. *Finite Markov Chains*. Princeton: Van Nostrand.

Kemeny, John G., J. Laurie Snell, and Gerald L. Thompson. 1956. *Introduction to Finite Mathematics*. Englewood Cliffs, N.J.: Prentice-Hall.

Kerr, Clark. 1954. "The Balkanization of Labor Markets." In *Labor Mobility and Economic Opportunity*, edited by E. Wight Bakke et al. New York: Wiley.

Laumann, Edward O. 1966. *Prestige and Association in an Urban Community*. Indianapolis: Bobbs-Merrill.

Laumann, Edward O., and Howard Schuman. 1967. "Open and Closed Structures." Unpublished paper prepared for the 1967 meeting of the American Sociological Association.

Lawrence, Paul R., and Jay W. Lorsch. 1967. *Organization and Environment*. Boston: Harvard Graduate School of Business Administration.

Lee, Nancy H. 1969. *The Search for an Abortionist*. Chicago: University of Chicago Press.

Lester, Richard A. 1954. *Hiring Practices and Labor Competition*. Princeton: Industrial Relations Section Report #88.

—— 1966a. Comment on Part I of *The Measurement and Interpretation of Job Vacancies*, edited by Robert Ferber. New York: Columbia University Press.

—— 1966b. *Manpower Planning in a Free Society*. Princeton: Princeton University Press.

Levine, Joel. 1972. "The Sphere of Influence." *American Sociological Review* 37 (February): 14–27.

Levine, Sol and Paul White. 1961. "Exchange as a Conceptual

Framework for the Study of Interorganizational Relationships." *Administrative Science Quarterly* 5 (March): 585–601.

Lévi-Strauss, Claude. 1949. *The Elementary Structures of Kinship.* Boston: Beacon.

Levy, Marion. 1966. *Modernization and the Structure of Societies,* vol. 1. Princeton: Princeton University Press.

Litwak, Eugene and L. Hylton. 1962. "Interorganizational Analysis: A Hypothesis on Coordinating Agencies." *Administrative Science Quarterly* 6 (March): 397–420.

Lurie, Melvin, and Elton Rayack. 1968. "Racial Differences in Migration and Job Search: A Case Study." In *Negroes and Jobs,* edited by L. Ferman, J. Kornbluth and J. Miller. Ann Arbor: University of Michigan Press.

MacDonald, John S., and Leatrice MacDonald. 1964. "Chain Migration, Ethnic Neighborhood Formation, and Social Networks." *Milbank Memorial Fund Quarterly* 42: 82–97.

Malinowski, Bronislaw. 1922. *Argonauts of the Western Pacific.* London: Dutton.

Malm, F. Theodore. 1954. "Recruiting Patterns and the Functioning of Labor Markets." *Industrial and Labor Relations Review* (July): 511–525.

March, J.G., and H. Simon. 1958. *Organizations.* New York: Wiley.

Marsh, R. and H. Mannari. 1971. "Lifetime Commitment in Japan: Roles, Norms and Values." *American Journal of Sociology* 76 (March): 795–812.

Mayhew, L. 1969. "Ascription in Modern Societies." *Sociological Inquiry* 38 (Spring): 105–120.

McCall, John J. 1965. "The Economics of Information and Optimal Stopping Rules." *Journal of Business* 38 (July): 300–317.

—— 1970. "Economics of Information and Job Search." *Quarterly Journal of Economics* 84 (February): 113–126.

McFarland, David D. 1970. "Intragenerational Social Mobility as a Markov Process." *American Sociological Review* 35 (June): 463–476.

McGinnis, Robert. 1968. "A Stochastic Model of Social Mobility." *American Sociological Review* 33 (October): 713–722.

Milgram, Stanley, 1967. "The Small-World Problem." *Psychology Today* 1 (May): 62–67.

Miller, George. 1956. "The Magical Number Seven, Plus or Minus Two: Some Limits on our Capacity for Processing Information." *Psychological Review* 63: 81–97.

Mund, Vernon A. 1948. *Open Markets.* New York: Harper.

Myers, Charles A., and W.R. Maclaurin. 1943. *The Movement of Factory Workers.* New York: Wiley.

Myers, Charles A., and George Shultz. 1951. *The Dynamics of a Labor Market.* New York: Prentice-Hall.

National Bureau of Economic Research. 1966. *The Measurement and Interpretation of Job Vacancies.* New York: Columbia University Press.

Ozga, S.A. 1960. "Imperfect Markets Through Lack of Information." *Quarterly Journal of Economics* 74 (February): 29–52.

Palmer, Gladys L. 1954. *Labor Mobility in Six Cities.* New York: Social Science Research Council.

Parnes, Herbert. 1954. *Research on Labor Mobility.* New York: Social Science Research Council.

Parnes, Herbert, R. Miljus, and R. Spitz. 1970. *Career Thresholds,* vol. 1. (Manpower Research Monograph #16). Washington, D.C.: U.S. Dept. of Labor, Manpower Administration.

Parsons, T. 1961. "Some Considerations on the Theory of Social Change." *Rural Sociology* 26: 219–239.

Pool, Ithiel, and M. Kochen. 1958. "Contact Nets." M.I.T.: unpublished paper.

Rapoport, Anatol. 1963. "Mathematical Models of Social Interaction." In R. Luce et al., eds., *Handbook of Mathematical Psychology,* vol. 2. New York: Wiley.

Rapoport, Anatol, and William Horvath. 1961. "A Study of a Large Sociogram." *Behavioral Science* 6 (October): 279–291.

Rees, Albert. 1966. "Information Networks in Labor Markets." *American Economic Review* (May): 559–566.

Rees, Albert, and George Shultz. 1970. *Workers and Wages in an Urban Labor Market.* Chicago: University of Chicago Press.

Reynolds, Lloyd. 1951. *The Structure of Labor Markets.* New York: Harper.

Rice, Berkeley. 1970. "Down and Out Along Route 128." *New York Times Magazine* (November 1).

Selznick, P. 1949. *T.V.A. and the Grass Roots.* Berkeley: University of California Press.

Shapero, A.R., Richard Howell, and J. Tombaugh. 1965. *The Structure and Dynamics of the Defense R. and D. Industry: The Los Angeles and Boston Complexes.* Menlo Park, Cal.: Stanford Research Institute.

Sheppard, Harold L., and A. Harvey Belitsky. 1966. *The Job Hunt: Job-Seeking Behavior of Unemployed Workers in a Local Economy.* Baltimore: The Johns Hopkins Press.

Shubik, Martin. 1959. *Strategy and Market Structure.* New York: Wiley.

Sjoberg, Gideon, 1960. *The Preindustrial City.* New York: The Free Press.

Somers, Gerald, and Masumi Tsuda. 1966. "Job Vacancies and Structural Change in Japanese Labor Markets." In *The Measurement and Interpretation of Job Vacancies,* edited by Robert Ferber. New York: Columbia University Press.

Stein, Maurice. 1960. *The Eclipse of Community*. Princeton:
Princeton University Press.

Stigler, George. 1961. "The Economics of Information." *Journal
of Political Economy* 69 (June): 213–225.

—— 1962. "Information in the Labor Market." *Journal of Political
Economy* 70 (October, Part 2): 94–105.

Taira, Koji. 1970. *Economic Development and the Labor Market in
Japan*. New York: Columbia University Press.

Thompson, James D. 1962. "Organizations and Output Transactions." *American Journal of Sociology* 68 (November): 309–
324.

Törnqvist, G. 1970. *Contact Systems and Regional Development*.
Lund, Sweden: CWK Gleerup.

Travers, J. and S. Milgram. 1969. "An Experimental Study of the
'Small-World Problem'." *Sociometry* 32 (December): 425–443.

Turk, Herman. 1970. "Interorganizational Networks in Urban
Society: Initial Perspectives and Comparative Research."
American Sociological Review 35 (February): 1–19.

Udy, Stanley H., Jr. 1959. *Organization of Work: A Comparative
Analysis of Production among Non-Industrial Peoples*. New
Haven: HRAF Press.

—— 1970. *Work in Traditional and Modern Society*. Englewood
Cliffs, N.J.: Prentice-Hall.

Ullman, Joseph C. 1968. "Interfirm Differences in the Cost of
Search for Clerical Workers." *Journal of Business* 41 (April):
153–165.

Ullman, Joseph. C. 1969. "Manpower Policies and Job Market
Information." In *Public-Private Manpower Policies*, edited by
A. Weber et al. Industrial Relations Research Association.

Ullman, Joseph C., and David P. Taylor. 1965. "The Information
System in Changing Labor Markets." *Proceedings of the
Industrial Relations Research Association*: 276–289.

United States Department of Labor. 1970, 1971, 1972. *Manpower
Report of the President*. Washington, D.C.: U.S. Government
Printing Office.

United States Immigration Commission, *Reports*, vol. 2, 1911.
Washington, D.C.: Government Printing Office.

Warren, R. 1967. "The Interorganizational Field as a Focus for
Investigation." *Administrative Science Quarterly* 12 (December):
396–419.

Vogel, Ezra. 1961. "The Go-Between in a Developing Society: The
Case of the Japanese Marriage Arranger." *Human Organization*
20 (Fall): 112–120.

Warner, W. Lloyd, and J.O. Low. 1947. *The Social System of a
Modern Factory*. New Haven: Yale University Press.

White, Harrison C. 1970. *Chains of Opportunity*. Cambridge, Mass.:

Harvard University Press.

Wilcock, Richard C., and Walter H. Franke. 1963. *Unwanted Workers: Permanent Layoffs and Long-term Unemployment.* New York: The Free Press.

Yoshino, Michael. 1968. *Japan's Managerial System.* Cambridge, Mass.: Harvard University Press.

Young, Michael, and Peter Willmott. 1962. *Family and Kinship in East London.* Baltimore: Penguin.

Index

This is the original index to the 1974 edition and does not include the material added to the Second Edition such as the Afterword and Appendix D.

CPSIA information can be obtained
at www.ICGtesting.com
Printed in the USA
LVHW03s0900200918
590727LV00003B/34/P